WORLD POPULATION POLICIES

Published in cooperation with
United Nations Fund
for Population Activities

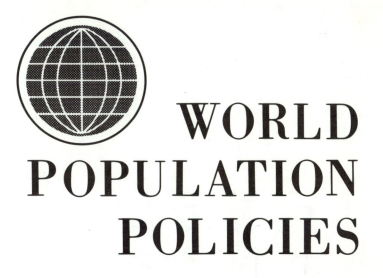

WORLD POPULATION POLICIES

edited by
Jyoti Shankar Singh

PRAEGER PUBLISHERS
Praeger Special Studies

New York • London • Sydney • Toronto

Library of Congress Cataloging in Publication Data
Main entry under title:

World population.

"Published in cooperation with United Nations Fund
for Population Activities."
 Bibliography: p.
 1. Population. 2. Population policy. I. Singh,
Jyoti Shankar, 1935–   II. United Nations Fund for
Population Activities.
HB871.W763   301.32   78-19756

PRAEGER PUBLISHERS
PRAEGER SPECIAL STUDIES
383 Madison Avenue, New York, N.Y., 10017, U.S.A.

Published in the United States of America in 1979
by Praeger Publishers
A Division of Holt, Rinehart and Winston, CBS Inc.

9 038 987654321

FOREWORD
Rafael M. Salas

This compendium of documents relating to population has been collated and published by the United Nations Fund for Population Activities (UNFPA) as a service to everyone studiously concerned with developments and trends in the population field.

The World Population Conference held at Bucharest in 1974—World Population Year—was a watershed in population policies and programs. Since Bucharest a series of regional conferences and national planning meetings has clarified the general population picture and shifted the center of gravity of concern from controversy to programs. However, the international dialogue continues, as it should.

The documents in this volume, several of which have been prepared by the United Nations Population Division, provide data and analysis that may provide a factual base for thinking, discussion, and planning on population matters.

United Nations Fund for Population Activities

ACKNOWLEDGMENTS

Three of the documents included in this collection— *Results of the Regional Consultations Subsequent to the World Population Conference, Concise Report on Monitoring of Population Trends,* and *Concise Report on Monitoring of Population Policies*—are edited versions of papers prepared by the Population Division of the Department of Economic and Social Affairs. The document on *Priorities in Future Allocation of UNFPA Resources* incorporates policy statements presented to the United Nations Development Programme/United Nations Fund for Population Activities (UNDP/UNFPA) Governing Council by the UNFPA Executive Director between June 1976 and June 1978. The chapter on recent trends in international population assistance is a revised version of a paper presented to the Bellagio Conference in 1977 by UNFPA Deputy Executive Director, Halvor Gille.

CONTENTS

LIST OF TABLES

One of the more important recommendations adopted by the Latin American Consultation was to establish "high-level councils, commissions or other equivalent units, empowered to coordinate action in the field of population."[6]

The Consultation for the African region noted that in some cases, "particularly in countries with vast natural resources," "a high rate of population growth could provide benefit for development by contributing to the supply of labour and expanding the domestic consumer market."[7] However, the possibility that rapid population growth could be an obstacle to development was also recognized. The same approach was spelled out in a resolution of the Conference of African Ministers in February 1975, which, "bearing in mind the different character of population problems in each country and region," expresses the conviction "that problems of fast population growth as well as the problem of under-population, among other things, could hamper rapid economic development in certain countries." The resolution asks governments to ensure that "family planning becomes, subject to national sovereign rights and priorities, an integral part of development, particularly where maternal and child health services, community and rural extension activities and urban development are concerned."[8]

The West Asia region did not consider rapid population growth an obstacle to its socioeconomic development. Its report emphasizes the need for collection and analysis of data on demographic variables.[9]

The European Consultation noted, in regard to Europe and North America, that "Governments were increasingly interested in the formulation of better co-ordinated and more comprehensive national population policies. Whereas formerly the majority of Governments in the region had no explicit and comprehensive policy, a considerable proportion of those Governments were now close to the announcement of a considered position and of associated policies in the field of population."[10]

The common elements in the reports of all the five regional consultations are the recognition of the interaction between demographic and socioeconomic factors; and the clear endorsement of the basic right of couples and individuals to obtain the knowledge and means to achieve responsible parenthood.

In addition to the regional consultations, the United Nations and UNFPA convened an Inter-Regional Consultative Group of Experts on WPPA in September 1975 to consider "over-all programmes, priorities, sources and coordination of assistance in relation to the implementation of the WPPA." The recommendations of the group were of a general nature, affirming once again "the importance for all countries of the adoption of national policies as integral parts of economic and social development and that such policies should take into account inter-relationships between population dynamics and socio-economic trends and, particularly in developed nations, policies on consumption and investment which relate to the issues of improving international economic equity."[11]

FOLLOW-UP BY THE UNITED NATIONS SYSTEM

The twenty-ninth session of the United Nations General Assembly, held at the end of 1974, adopted Resolution 3344 (XXIX) on the results of the WPC. It calls upon governments, as well as various UN bodies, to implement WPPA, and goes on to stress "that the implementation of the World Population Plan of Action should take full account of the Programme of Action on the Establishment of the New International Economic Order, and thus contribute to its implementation." Most UN documents, resolutions, and recommendations on population that have been issued since 1974 have indeed sought to relate population policies and programs to the emerging concepts of a New International Economic Order (NIEO). NIEO in itself, however, does not include population as a major or even a minor theme. Population was mentioned in a few speeches at the Seventh Special Session of the United Nations General Assembly (September 1–16, 1975); but the resolution on development and international cooperation adopted at the special session (Resolution 3362 [SVII]), which sought to strengthen the NIEO program of action, does not refer to WPPA or to the continuing UN program in the population field.

This may have been due to a feeling that since population had been thoroughly discussed at the Bucharest Conference there was no need to consider it again. Many of the representatives from the developing countries also felt that the focus of the NIEO negotiations was on transfer of resources from the rich to the poor countries, and that nothing should be allowed to divert them from a dialogue on this subject with the representatives of the industrialized countries.

There is perhaps yet another explanation. Population, despite the Bucharest Conference, is still regarded in some circles as a controversial or embarrassing topic. But, quite clearly, development action programs cannot avoid dealing with the economic and social problems of pressure of the growing numbers of people on the world's resources. Nor can governments ignore the increasing demand for access to family planning information and services as a matter of basic right.

Both of these points were taken up at the World Food Conference (Rome, November 1974) and the World Conference of the International

Women's Year (Mexico, June 1975). A resolution of the World Food Conference endorses the right of individuals "to determine the number and spacing of births," but makes the exercise of this right subject to "national needs."[12] The plan of action adopted by the International Women's Year Conference, however, fully supports this right, and makes the point that "the exercise of this right and the full participation of women in all aspects of national life are closely inter-related with such crucial demographic variables as age at marriage, age at birth of first child, the interval between births, age at termination of child-bearing, and total number of children born."[13]

References to WPPA are to be found in documents relating to three other UN conferences. The Report on the Conference on Human Settlements (Vancouver, June 1976) seeks to relate it to the evolution of national policies on population distribution, while the report of the Conference on Desertification (Nairobi, August 1977) mentions the relevance of population factors to programs aimed at combating the problems of desertification. Documents prepared for the Conference on Technical Cooperation Among Developing Countries (Buenos Aires, August–September 1978) link population activities to the goals set by the developing countries in the context of a New International Economic Order.[14]

All of these linkages need to be explored in detail, so that their complementarity can be translated into intersectoral development programs. Those responsible for developing the strategy for the Third International Development Decade are conscious of this need. It is fairly certain that population factors will be fully taken into account in formulating this strategy, whether or not population becomes a theme of future NIEO discussions.[15]

The main responsibility for monitoring and reviewing the implementation of WPPA lies with the Economic and Social Council, aided by one of its subsidiary bodies, the Population Commission. This Commission, at its eighteenth session in February of 1975, asked for biennial reports on action by governments relevant to the implementation of the WPPA.[16] It was in response to this request that the UN undertook in 1976 its third inquiry among governments to examine changes in population policies and programs since the Bucharest Conference.[17] Another recommendation asked the UN to develop "Guidelines on Population-Related Factors for Development Planners."[18]

In January 1977, at its nineteenth session, the UN Population Commission received two major reports, which are included in this volume: a report prepared by the Secretariat on population trends, and a report on population policies, based on the results of the third inquiry among governments.[19] The Commission also received a document comprising the guidelines mentioned above.[20] As a follow-up to these guidelines, the UN Population Division plans to produce a manual on population and development planning.

UNITED NATIONS FUND FOR POPULATION ACTIVITIES (UNFPA)

While the UN Population Division continues to monitor population trends and policies, the main responsibility for assisting governments in implementing WPPA at the national level has been undertaken by UNFPA. Several specialized agencies and other organizations in the UN system are also undertaking WPPA follow-up activities, within the scope of their own mandates.

Since Bucharest, the demand for international assistance has grown rapidly, and while UNFPA's resources increase year by year, it is expected that the demand will grow even faster. UNFPA has thus been required to establish priorities in the allocation of its resources. As the paper on "Priorities in Future Allocation of UNFPA Resources" points out, 40 developing countries out of a total of 128 have been designated as priority countries for UNFPA assistance, on the basis of the criterion of a per capita national income below $400 per annum and two or more of the following demographic threshold levels:

1. population growth rate of 2.75 percent per annum
2. gross reproduction rate of 2.75 percent
3. infant mortality rate of 176 deaths per 1000 live births
4. population density on arable land of 2.2 persons per hectare

The group of priority countries includes 17 from Africa; 14 from Asia and the Pacific; 5 from Europe, the Mediterranean, and the Middle East; and 4 from Latin America. If a 2 percent variation from the threshold levels were allowed, 14 other countries (including 8 in Africa; 2 in Asia and the Pacific; 2 in Latin America; and 1 in Europe, the Mediterranean, and the Middle East) would qualify for the priority list. A tentative ceiling of two-thirds of available program resources has been established for allocations to the priority countries, while among the nonpriority countries the 14 mentioned above are to be given special attention.

UNFPA has also defined a core program of population activities that it will assist, while encouraging governments and intergovernmental organizations to relate this core program to other aspects of developmental action. The core program comprises collection and analysis of basic population data; formulation and implementation of population policy, including family planning and population redistribution; population education and training; applied research; and communication support activities.

UNFPA has now begun to assist selected developing countries in assessing their basic needs in the population field, taking into account their own priorities. These assessments will help to determine the range and the kind of assistance that will be needed by these countries in implementing their population policies and programs.

A third element in the system of priorities is now being developed in regard to intercountry activities. These activities, which are undertaken primarily through organizations in the UN system, help to provide backstopping for country programs. Future support for such activities (including research, training, education, and communication) will continue to be provided on the basis of their relevance to promotion and strengthening of national population policies and programs.

NATIONAL POPULATION POLICIES

As WPPA states over and over again, the main responsibility for national population policies and programs lies with national authorities. Understanding of how governments' perceptions of population questions are evolving and changing is thus crucial to any analysis of current and future population programs.

Though the number of countries that have official population policies may not have increased significantly, the number of countries that consider their fertility rates "too high" has gone up from 42 in 1974 to 48 in 1976 (comprising 81 percent of the developing world's population). Of these, 18 are in Asia and the Pacific. These 18 account for the majority of the population of the region. Policies aimed at slowing the population growth rate in Asian countries by the year 2000, if they are successful, would thus have a major impact on the world population rate.

Following are some of the more significant developments in the evolution of population policies in the developing world:

1. Contraception and abortion: An increasing number of countries have reformed their laws to facilitate large-scale availability of contraceptive supplies. Several countries (for example, Hong Kong, India, Singapore, Tunisia) have also liberalized their abortion laws.

2. Raising the age of marriage: Colombia, India, Indonesia, and Iran, among others, have legally raised the minimum age of marriage for women.

3. Status of women: The International Women's Year, which followed the World Population Year, helped to focus attention on issues relating to the status and role of women. During 1975–78, several countries have undertaken measures to provide women equal civil rights, to increase educational opportunities for them, and to assist efforts to enable increasing numbers of women to undertake employment outside their homes.

4. Incentives and disincentives: Singapore was the first country in Asia to adopt a comprehensive scheme of incentives and disincentives. Several other Asian countries (India, Pakistan, the Philippines, and the Republic of Korea) are experimenting with such schemes.

Perhaps the most widely publicized are those of China.

INTERRELATIONSHIP OF POPULATION AND DEVELOPMENT

In the same way that WPPA bears a relationship to the International Development Strategy, population policies and programs have a direct relationship to overall development planning at the national level. A unified approach to main sectors of economic and social development including nutrition, health, housing, education, and employment is essential if quantitative and qualitative changes and improvements are to be brought about in people's lives. Because of the emphasis such an approach would place on the welfare of individuals, demographic factors emerge clearly as important elements in the formulation of development strategies and policies.

The guidelines prepared by the United Nations cite variables that have a direct bearing on socioeconomic development:

(a) the demands placed on the economy by rapid increase in population numbers and by population structure;
(b) the implications of demographic variables and their trends for consumption, social services, the investment potential, the external sector and over-all economic growth itself;
(c) the extent to which such trends may hamper more equitable distribution of proceeds of economic growth.[21]

The report indicates that the paucity of reliable data on population, as related to social and economic conditions, is one of the main obstacles to taking demographic factors into account in the development planning process.

Population censuses and surveys are usually designed for demographic analysis. As a rule, the data they provide on social and economic conditions are not adequate for in-depth studies of cause-

and-effect relationships between population change and social and economic development. Similarly, statistical investigations on social and economic conditions or on some specific factors of development usually do not include much information on population change. Demographic data and economic and social data are often not comparable because of differences in time reference, coverage concepts, definitions, and so on. Accordingly, there exists a need to develop a system of integrated demographic, economic, and social statistics.[22]

Many developing countries have already asked their planning departments, ministries, or commissions to integrate demographic variables fully in development planning, but this effort will take some time to succeed because these variables themselves have to be updated and more sharply defined. The information available on developments in other socioeconomic sectors is also of uneven quality. What is, however, encouraging to note is the continuing determination of most developing countries to correlate population factors with development planning. In 83 of the developing countries, the central planning bodies have been entrusted with this responsibility.[23] Several countries, particularly in Latin America, have also established national population commissions or similar authorities to initiate and coordinate all aspects of population activities.

FERTILITY

The perceptions of national governments on the rate of population growth are increasingly being translated into policies of intervention in the matter of fertility. According to the third UN inquiry, 40 developing countries (with 56 percent of world population) are pursuing policies aimed at reducing the level of fertility. Of the world's population, 31 percent live in countries (82) that do not have a policy of intervention, 10 percent in countries (20) whose governments are trying to maintain the present level, and 3 percent in countries (4) whose governments have policies aimed at raising the level.[24]

While a policy of intervention in the area of fertility may have to be formulated on the basis of the economic and social realities, governments have also to take into account "a growing demand for each individual and each family to be free to decide its own destiny."[25] Here, it is important to note that though there are only 40 developing countries with fertility limitation policies, a total of 71 developing countries (out of 97 surveyed) directly support programs aimed at providing to couples and individuals access to modern methods of birth control. Another 10 developing countries support such programs indirectly, while 25 adopt an attitude of nonintervention. In Asia and the Pacific 25 out of 30 countries provide direct support; the proportion in Latin America is 21 out of 27; in Africa 22 out of 48; in West Asia 5 out of 12; and in Europe 24 out of 39.[26] Taking into account the developed countries as well, there are only 15 countries in the world that limit access to modern contraception.

Current evidence indicates that fertility rates have begun to decline in many parts of the world. In the developed countries, fertility has fallen notably: in Austria, Belgium, the Federal Republic of Germany, the German Democratic Republic, Luxembourg, and the United Kingdom, it is below replacement level. In a number of small countries, many of them islands, such as Singapore, Fiji, the Republic of Korea, Sri Lanka, Mauritius, Barbados, Trinidad-Tobago, Costa Rica, and Chile, information researched and collected over several years points to countrywide trends toward lower fertility rates. In the case of several large Asian countries (India, China, and Indonesia), the information available indicates declining fertility, but more adequate data are needed to establish definite trends. In several Latin American countries (Colombia, Dominican Republic, Mexico) the traditional trend towards rising fertility seems to have been reversed, and what is more, a sharp downward trend may actually have been set in Mexico.[27]

Accurate worldwide assessments are somewhat difficult, especially because for many areas authentic information is not available. But the evidence available so far, from those areas where it is well documented, suggests that family planning programs and population activities are achieving increasing success, and as the United Nations cautiously puts it, "the odds favouring further fertility declines in many low-income areas in which such declines have already begun, or the near onset of substantial declines where such processes are still potential rather than realized, are no longer small."[28]

MORTALITY

In the last 25 years average life expectancy worldwide has moved up from 40–50 years about 1950 to 50–60 years in 1975. Control of epidemics and main diseases, reduction in infant mortality, and better health facilities have dramatically improved the situation in many of the developing countries. However, infant mortality still remains high in Africa (150 to 200 infant deaths per 1,000 live births) and parts of Asia and Latin America (100 to 150). Rural areas in many developing countries are still not covered by adequate health care.

As the report on monitoring of population trends notes, "the urgency of further gains in longevity remains obviously high for many parts of the world. Average expectations of life at birth in the more developed and less developed regions continue to be far apart, on average, some 20 years according to available estimates, while differences as high as 30 to 40 years can be found between many individual pairs of nations."[29]

The problem is particularly acute in Africa. Of the 48 countries in Africa, 47 consider their current levels of mortality unacceptable. In Asia and the Pacific, the proportion is 18 out of 30, in Latin America 16 out of 27, and in West Asia 6 out of 12.[30]

In the programs relating to mortality, two main trends are emerging in the developing countries, particularly those in Africa. They are intensifying their efforts to reduce excess mortality among very small children; and to raise the level of health care, particularly in rural areas. Maternal and child health programs in many of these countries are being initiated in connection with family planning programs, and in rural areas small-scale health programs emphasizing treatment are being converted into large-scale preventive programs.

MIGRATION

Migration from rural to urban areas and unplanned urbanization are of major concern to most developing countries. Of 114 developing countries, 75 have policies aimed at slowing down migration; the proportion among developed countries is 25 out of 42.[31] Interestingly, migration is the subject of official policies in only 16 of the 30 countries in Asia, whereas the proportion is 23 out of 27 in Latin America, 32 out of 48 in Africa, and 6 out of 12 in West Asia.

More governments are demographically concerned over emigration (52), than are over immigration (39).[32] Attitudes and policies in these areas remain subject to short-term economic fluctuations and political events.

SELF-RELIANCE

While international assistance has helped to launch population programs in several developing countries and supported program development and expansion in crucial sectors of population activities in many others, self-reliant action has clearly emerged as the ultimate objective of all these countries. UNFPA, in particular, has, since its inception, sought to strengthen and accelerate their progress towards this goal. Through direct funding of government projects, increasing support for recruitment and utilization of local experts, delivery of assistance with a minimum of delay, and encouragement of innovative approaches and activities, UNFPA is helping national programs to acquire a self-sustaining momentum.

The record shows that an increasing number of developing countries are investing more of their own funds and efforts in population programs. The role of international assistance remains crucial in such areas as research, training, supply of equipment, and provision of experts. But it is acknowledged that it is ultimately the national commitment, backed by allocation of national resources, that will achieve the targets and objectives set by these countries for themselves.

D. Nortman and E. Hofstatter cite the examples of several developing countries that have in recent years substantially increased their allocations to population activities.[33] These include, among others, Ghana and Mauritius in Africa; Bangladesh, Indonesia, Iran, Nepal, Pakistan, the Philippines, the Republic of Korea, Singapore, and Thailand in Asia and the Pacific; Costa Rica, El Salvador and the Dominican Republic in Latin America; and Tunisia and Turkey in the Middle East and Mediterranean region.

The most recent example is Mexico. The government of Mexico, which initiated an official population program in 1974, has increased its allocations for population programs from around $7 million in 1974 to more than $70 million in 1978. If the 1978 figure is adjusted for the devaluation of the Mexican peso in 1976, it can be seen that the 1978 expenditure in local currency is 60 percent greater than the expenditure in 1976.[34]

Another encouraging development is the gradual phasing out of international assistance for those countries that are in a position to assume complete financial responsibility for their own population programs. Two examples are Chile and Mauritius. It is hoped that by the mid-1980s several other countries will reach this stage.

INTERNATIONAL ASSISTANCE

The governmental contributions to UNFPA have increased from about $54 million in 1974 to $107 million in 1978, showing an average annual increase of 19 percent (see Table 1.1). The total volume of resources available for population assistance has, however, not grown at the same rate (the average annual increase being about 11 percent).

TABLE 1.1: Contributions to UNFPA (U.S. dollars)

Year	Contributions	Cumulative Contributions
1967/70	$ 20,426,028	$ 20,426,028
1971	28,410,238	48,836,266
1972	30,616,754	79,453,020
1973	42,514,183	121,967,203
1974	54,091,824	176,059,027
1975	63,612,019	239,671,046
1976	79,483,754	319,154,800
1977	91,714,448	410,869,248
1978 (provisional)	107,324,870	518,899,248

Source: UNFPA.

As the chapter "Recent Trends in Population Assistance" points out, it is somewhat early to assess the impact of the WPC and WPPA upon population assistance. International population assistance rose by around 34 percent over the period 1974–1977 in terms of absolute amounts. The share of population in total official development assistance has, however, remained unchanged over these four years at just over 2 percent. The remarkable growth in governmental contributions to UNFPA since 1974 has enabled the fund to double its program level by 1977, but, as pointed out earlier, the demand for UNFPA assistance continues to rise even faster.

Fertility control still seems the major objective of population assistance being provided by major donors, but many of them are now revising their policies, to bring their approach to population issues into consonance with the changing needs and requirements in developing countries.

According to indications provided to UNFPA by program personnel in various developing countries, problems of urbanization caused by the rapid growth of cities and the continuing depopulation of rural areas require increasing attention in the future. There is a widespread recognition of the need to devise and implement programs that will not only deal with the problems of crowded cities but also provide for growth of alternative "growth poles" for migrants. The problems of the aged and the young resulting from changing age-structures also need to be given special attention. Biomedical research, including contraceptive development, is another area that will require greater support in the future.

FUTURE PERSPECTIVES

It is clear that the greater awareness and understanding of population issues that was first generated by the World Population Year and the WPC have led to increasing action in several areas of population activities. Governments and international organizations, as well as nongovernmental organizations and private groups, are now beginning to look at several other areas in which vigorous efforts will be needed in the near future.

R. M. Salas, in his introduction to UNFPA's Annual Report 1977, points out that "the next phase, of consolidating these trends by assisting governments to integrate population in their basic needs programs and to respond to economic and social change foreseen as a result of changes in the demographic processes . . ., suggests that international population assistance would have to grow to a new order of magnitude if it is to match adequately the effort that developing countries will have to make to meet the challenges of the last two decades of this millenium."[35]

The WPPA called for "a comprehensive and thorough review and appraisal of progress made towards achieving the goals and recommendations of the Plan of Action . . . every five years by the United Nations System." The first such review is to take place in 1979. This should provide an extremely useful opportunity to evaluate worldwide progress toward integration of population factors into development plans, based on an accurate assessment of each country's needs, and towards provision of adequate information and services to all the couples and individuals who need them. The review should also help governments and the UN system set up goals and objectives for the 1980s, taking into account the objectives of the Third International Development Decade, and the measures related to a New International Economic Order.

NOTES

1. See GA res. 2211 (xxi), December 17, 1966; GA res. 2542 (xxiv), December 11, 1969; GA res. 2683 (xxv), December 11, 1970; GA res. 2716 (xxv), December 15, 1970; ECOSOC res. 1672 (L11), June 2, 1972.

2. UN, ESCAP, Report of the Regional Post-World Population Conference Consultation, New Delhi, E/CN. 11/1208, January 29, 1975, para. 40.

3. UN, ECLA, Segunda Reunión Latinoamericana Sobre Población, ST/CEPAL/-Conf. 54/L.9/Rev. 1, March 31, 1975, para. 160.

4. Ibid., para. 151.

5. Ibid., para. 164.

6. Ibid., para. 134.

7. UN, ECA, Report of the Regional Post World Population Conference Consultation, Lusaka, E/CN. 14/Pop/136, August 7, 1975, para. 27.

8. Resolution 273 (XII), Conference of (African) Ministers, 183d Meeting, February 28, 1975.

9. See UN, ECWA, Final Report of the UN/UNFPA Post-WPC Consultation for the ECWA Region, 1975.

10. UN, ECOSOC, Post-WPC Consultation Among Countries of the ECE Region, ESA/P/AC.5/5, August 18, 1975, para. 58.

11. Report of the Interregional Consultative Group of Experts on WPPA, UNF-PA/WPPA/20/Rev. 1, February 18, 1976, pp. 35–36.

12. United Nations, Report of the World Food Conference, E/Conf. 65/20, Resolution IX, p. 11.

13. United Nations, The World Plan of Action for the Implementation of the Objectives of the International Women's Year, E/Conf. 66/34, 1976, para. 13.

14. See UN, Report on Habitat—The UN Conference on Human Settlements, A/Conf. 70/15, 1976; UN, Report on the UN Conference on Desertification, A/Conf. 74/36, 1977; UN, Technical Cooperation among Developing Countries as a New Dimension of International Cooperation for Development, A/Conf. 79/6, July 5, 1978; UN, Report of the United Nations Conference on Technical Co-operation among Developing Countries, A/Conf. 79/13/Rev. 1, 1978; UNFPA, Population and Mutual Self-Reliance, New York, 1978.

15. The Economic and Social Council, at its sixty-second session in April 1977, asked the Secretariat to take due account of WPPA in pursuing the task of collecting data and information relevant to the formulation of a new international development strategy, and recommended to the General Assembly "that, when it considers the question of preparing a new international development strategy, the role of population and the importance of population policies and activities in their relationship to the establishment of a New International Economic Order should be given due weight, and should be duly integrated into the goals, objectives, policy measures and targets to be contained in any new strategy" (res. 2051 (LXII)).

16. UN, Report of the 18th Session of the Population Commission, July 1975.

17. A fourth inquiry was undertaken in 1978, but its results are not expected to be available until 1979.

18. UN, Report of the 18th Session of the Population Commission, July 1975, op. cit.

19. Concise Report on Monitoring of Population Trends (UN doc. E/CN. 9/323, November 8, 1976), and Concise Report on Monitoring of Population Policies (UN doc. E/CN. 9/324, November 19, 1976).

20. Guidelines on Population-Related Factors for Development Planning, UN doc. E/5780, May 10, 1976.

21. Ibid., p. 8.

22. Ibid., p. 39.

23. Concise Report on Monitoring of Population Policies, op. cit., p. 37.

24. Ibid., pp. 21–22.

25. Ibid., p. 40.

26. Ibid., p. 23.

27. UNFPA, Annual Report 1977, p. 7.

28. Concise Report on Monitoring of Population Trends, op. cit., p. 25.

29. Ibid., p. 15.

30. Ibid., p. 28.

31. Ibid., p. 32.

32. Ibid.

33. See Dorothy Nortman and E. Hofstatter, *Population and Family Planning Programs: A Fact Book* (New York: Population Council, 1978).

34. UNFPA, Annual Report 1977, op. cit., p. 14.

35. Ibid.

2 WORLD POPULATION PLAN OF ACTION

The World Population Conference, having due regard for human aspirations for a better quality of life and for rapid socio-economic development, and taking into consideration the interrelationship between population situations and socio-economic development, decides on the following World Population Plan of Action as a policy instrument within the broader context of the internationally adopted strategies for national and international progress.

BACKGROUND TO THE PLAN

1. The promotion of development and improvement of quality of life require co-ordination of action in all major socio-economic fields including that of population, which is the inexhaustible source of creativity and a determining factor of progress. At the international level a number of strategies and programmes whose explicit aim is to affect variables in fields other than population have already been formulated. These include the FAO's Provisional Indicative World Plan for Agricultural Development, the United Nations/FAO World Food Programme, the ILO's World Employment Programme, the Action Plan for the Human Environment, the United Nations World Plan of Action for the Application of Science and Technology to Development, the Programme of Concerted Action for the Advancement of Women, and, more comprehensively, the International Development Strategy for the Second United Nations Development Decade. The Declaration on

---

This is a UN Document and therefore, in accordance with UN regulations, the original numbering of the paragraphs and the English spelling have been retained.

the Establishment of a New International Economic Order, and the Programme of Action to achieve it, adopted by the sixth special session of the United Nations General Assembly (resolutions 3201 and 3202 (S-VI)) provide the most recent over-all framework for international co-operation. The explicit aim of the World Population Plan of Action is to help co-ordinate population trends and the trends of economic and social development. The basis for an effective solution of population problems is, above all, socio-economic transformation. A population policy may have a certain success if it constitutes an integral part of socio-economic development; its contribution to the solution of world development problems is hence only partial, as is the case with the other sectoral strategies. Consequently, the Plan of Action must be considered as an important component of the system of international strategies and as an instrument of the international community for the promotion of economic development, quality of life, human rights and fundamental freedoms.

2. The formulation of international strategies is a response to universal recognition of the existence of important problems in the world and the need for concerted national and international action to achieve their solution. Where trends of population growth, distribution and structure are out of balance with social, economic and environmental factors, they can, at certain stages of development, create additional difficulties for the achievement of sustained development. Policies whose aim is to affect population trends must not be considered substitutes for socio-economic development policies but as being integrated with those policies in order to facilitate the solution of certain problems facing both developing and developed countries and to promote a more balanced and rational development.

3. Throughout history the rate of growth of world population averaged only slightly above replacement levels. The recent increase in the growth rate began mainly as a result of the decline in mortality during the last few centuries, a decline that has accelerated significantly during recent decades. The inertia of social structures and the insufficiency of economic progress, especially when these exist in the absence of profound socio-cultural changes, partly explains why in the majority of developing countries the decline in mortality has not been accompanied by a parallel decline in fertility. Since about 1950, the world population growth rate has risen to 2 per cent a year. If sustained, this will result in a doubling of the world's population every 35 years. However, national rates of natural growth range widely, from a negative rate to well over 3 per cent a year.

4. The consideration of population problems cannot be reduced to the analysis of population trends only. It must also bear in mind that the present situation of the developing countries originates in the unequal processes of socio-economic development which have divided peoples since the beginning of the modern era. This inequity still exists and is intensified by lack of equity in international economic relations with consequent disparity in levels of living.

5. Although acceleration in the rate of growth of the world's population is mainly the result of very large declines in the mortality of developing countries, these declines have been unevenly distributed. Thus, at present, average expectation of life at birth is 63 years in Latin America, 57 years in Asia and only a little over 46 years in Africa, compared with more than 71 years in the developed regions. Furthermore, although on average less than one in 40 children dies before reaching the age of one year in the developed regions, one in 15 dies before reaching that age in Latin America, one in 10 in Asia and one in 7 in Africa. In fact, in some developing regions, and particularly in African countries, average expectation of life at birth is estimated to be less than 40 years and one in four children dies before the age of one year. Consequently, many developing countries consider reduction of mortality, and particularly reduction of infant mortality, to be one of the most important and urgent goals.

6. While the right of couples to have the number of children they desire is accepted in a number of international instruments, many couples in the world are unable to exercise that right effectively. In many parts of the world, poor economic conditions, social norms, inadequate knowledge of effective methods of family regulation and the unavailability of contraceptive services result in a situation in which couples have more children than they desire or feel they can properly care for. In certain countries, on the other hand, because of economic or biological factors, problems of involuntary sterility and of subfecundity exist, with the result that many couples have fewer children than they desire. Of course, the degree of urgency attached to dealing with each of these two situations depends upon the prevailing conditions within the country in question.

7. Individual reproductive behavior and the needs and aspirations of society should be reconciled. In many developing countries, and particularly in the large countries of Asia, the desire of couples to achieve large families is believed to result in excessive national population growth rates and Governments are explicitly attempting to reduce these rates by implementing specific policy measures. On the other

hand, some countries are attempting to increase desired family size, if only slightly.

8. Throughout the world, urban populations are growing in size at a considerably faster rate than rural populations. As a result, by the end of this century, and for the first time in history, the majority of the world's population will be living in urban areas. Urbanization is an element of the process of modernization. Moreover, while in certain countries this process is efficiently managed and maximum use is made of the advantages this management presents, in others urbanization takes place in an uncontrolled manner and is accompanied by over-crowding in certain districts, an increase in slums, deterioration of the environment, urban unemployment and many other social and eco-nomic problems.

9. In most of the developing countries, although the rate of urban population growth is higher than the growth rate in rural areas, the latter is still significant. The rural population of developing countries is growing at an average rate of 1.7 per cent a year, and in some instances at a faster rate than that of the urban population in devel-oped countries. Furthermore, many rural areas of heavy emigration, in both developed and developing countries, are being depleted of their younger populations and are being left with populations whose age distribution is unfavourable to economic development. Thus, in many countries, the revitalization of the countryside is a priority goal.

10. For some countries international migration may be, in certain circumstances, an instrument of population policy. At least two types of international migration are of considerable concern to many coun-tries in the world: the movement of migrant workers with limited skills, and the movement of skilled workers and professionals. Move-ments of the former often involve large numbers and raise such ques-tions as the fair and proper treatment in countries of immigration, the breaking up of families and other social and economic questions in countries both of emigration and immigration. The migration of skilled workers and professionals results in a "brain drain", often from less developed to more developed countries, which is at present of consider-able concern to many countries and to the international community as a whole. The number of instruments on these subjects and the in-creased involvement of international organizations reflects interna-tional awareness of these problems.

11. A population's age structure is greatly affected by its birthrates. For example, declining fertility is the main factor underlying the de-

clining proportion of children in a population. Thus, according to the medium projections of the United Nations, the population of less than 15 years of age in the developing countries is expected to decline from an average of more than 41 per cent of total population in 1970 to an average of about 35 per cent in 2000. However, such a *decline in the proportion* of children will be accompanied by an *increase in their numbers* at an average of 1.7 per cent a year. The demand for educational services is expected to increase considerably, in view of both the existing backlog and the continuously increasing population of children which ought to enter and remain in schools; therefore the supply of educational services must be increased. With regard to the population 15 to 29 years of age, an increase in both their proportion and number is expected in the developing countries. Consequently, unless very high rates of economic development are attained, in many of these countries, and particularly where levels of unemployment and under-employment are already high, the additional difficulties will not be overcome at least until the end of this century. Furthermore, in both developed and developing countries, the greatly changing social and economic conditions faced by youth require a better understanding of the problems involved and the formulation and implementation of policies to resolve them.

12. Declining birthrates also result in a gradual aging of the population. Because birthrates have already declined in developed countries, the average proportion of the population aged 65 years and over in these countries makes up 10 per cent of the total population, whereas it makes up only 3 per cent in developing countries. However, aging of the population in developing countries has recently begun, and is expected to accelerate. Thus, although the total population of these countries is projected to increase by an average of 2.3 per cent a year between 1970 and 2000, the population 65 years and over is expected to increase by 3.5 per cent a year. Not only are the numbers and proportions of the aged increasing rapidly, but the social and economic conditions which face them are also rapidly changing. There is an urgent need, in those countries where such programmes are lacking, for the development of social security and health programmes for the elderly.

13. Because of the relatively high proportions of children and youth in the populations of developing countries, declines in fertility levels in these countries will not be fully reflected in declines in population growth rates until some decades later. To illustrate this demographic inertia, it may be noted that, for developing countries, even if replacement levels of fertility—approximately two children per completed

family—had been achieved in 1970 and maintained thereafter, their total population would still grow from a 1970 total of 2.5 billion to about 4.4 billion before it would stabilize during the second half of the twenty-first century. In these circumstances, the population of the world as a whole would grow from 3.6 billion to 5.8 billion. This example of demographic inertia, which will lead to a growing population for many decades to come, demonstrates that whatever population policies may be formulated, socio-economic development must accelerate in order to provide for a significant increase in levels of living. Efforts made by developing countries to speed up economic growth must be viewed by the entire international community as a global endeavour to improve the quality of life for all people of the world, supported by a just utilization of the world's wealth, resources and technology in the spirit of the new international economic order. It also demonstrates that countries wishing to affect their population growth must anticipate future demographic trends and take appropriate decisions and actions in their plans for economic and social development well in advance.

PRINCIPLES AND OBJECTIVES OF THE PLAN

14. This Plan of Action is based on a number of principles which underlie its objectives and are observed in its formulation. The formulation and implementation of population policies is the sovereign right of each nation. This right is to be exercised in accordance with national objectives and needs and without external interference, taking into account universal solidarity in order to improve the quality of life of the peoples of the world. The main responsibility for national population policies and programmes lies with national authorities. However, international co-operation should play an important role in accordance with the principles of the United Nations Charter. The Plan of Action is based on the following principles:

(a) The principal aim of social, economic and cultural development, of which population goals and policies are integral parts, is to improve levels of living and the quality of life of the people. Of all things in the world, people are the most precious. Man's knowledge and ability to master himself and his environment will continue to grow. Mankind's future can be made infinitely bright;

(b) True development cannot take place in the absence of national independence and liberation. Alien and colonial domination, foreign occupation, wars of aggression, racial discrimination, apartheid and neo-colonialism in all its forms, continue to be among the greatest obstacles to the full emancipation and progress of the developing countries and all the people involved. Co-operation among nations on the basis of national sovereignty is essential for development. Development also requires recognition of the dignity of the individual, appreciation for the human person and his self-determination, as well as the elimination of discrimination in all its forms;

(c) Population and development are interrelated: population variables influence development variables and are also influenced by them; thus the formulation of a World Population Plan of Action reflects the international community's awareness of the importance of population trends for socio-economic development, and the socio-economic nature of the recommendations contained in this Plan of Action reflects its awareness of the crucial role that development plays in affecting population trends;

(d) Population policies are constituent elements of socio-economic development policies, never substitutes for them: while serving socio-economic objectives, they should be consistent with internationally and nationally recognized human rights of individual freedom, justice and the survival of national, regional and minority groups;

(e) Independently of the realization of economic and social objectives, respect for human life is basic to all human societies;

(f) All couples and individuals have the basic right to decide freely and responsibly the number and spacing of their children and to have the information, education and means to do so; the responsibility of couples and individuals in the exercise of this right takes into account the needs of their living and future children, and their responsibilities towards the community;

(g) The family is the basic unit of society and should be protected by appropriate legislation and policy;

(h) Women have the right to complete integration in the development process particularly by means of an equal access to education and equal participation in social, economic, cultural and political life. In addition, the necessary measures should be taken to facilitate this integration with family responsibilities, which should be fully shared by both partners;

(i) Recommendations in this Plan of Action regarding policies to deal with population problems must recognize the diversity of conditions within and among different countries;

(j) In the democratic formulation of national population goals and policies, consideration must be given, together with other economic and social factors, to the supplies and characteristics of natural resources and to the quality of the environment and particularly to all aspects of food supply including productivity of rural areas. The demand for vital resources increases not only with growing population but also with growing *per capita* consumption; attention must be directed to the just distribution of resources and to the minimization of wasteful aspects of their use throughout the world;

(k) The growing interdependence among nations makes international action increasingly important to the solution of development and population problems. International strategies will achieve their objective only if they ensure that the underprivileged of the world achieve, urgently, through structural, social and economic reforms, a significant improvement in their living conditions;

(l) This Plan of Action must be sufficiently flexible to take into account the consequences of rapid demographic changes, societal changes and changes in human behaviour, attitudes and values;

(m) The objectives of this Plan of Action should be consistent with the Purposes and Principles of the United Nations Charter, the Universal Declaration of Human Rights and with the objectives of the Second United Nations Development Decade; however, changes in demographic variables during the Decade are largely the result of past demographic events and changes in demographic trends sought during the Decade have social and economic repercussions up to and beyond the end of this century.

15. Guided by these principles, the primary aim of this Plan of Action is to expand and deepen the capacities of countries to deal effectively with their national and subnational population problems and to promote an appropriate international response to their needs by increasing international activity in research, the exchange of information, and the provision of assistance on request. In pursuit of this primary aim, the following general objectives are set for this Plan of Action:

(a) To advance understanding of population at global, regional, national and subnational levels, recognizing the diversity of the problems involved;

(b) To advance national and international understanding of the interrelationship of demographic and socio-economic factors in development: on the one hand, of the nature and scope of the effect of demographic factors on the attainment of goals of advancing human welfare, and on the other hand, the impact of broader social, economic and cultural factors on demographic behaviour;

(c) To promote socio-economic measures and programmes whose aim is to affect, *inter alia,* population growth, morbidity and mortality, reproduction and family formation, population distribution and internal migration, international migration, and consequently demographic structures;

(d) To advance national and international understanding of the complex relations among the problems of population, resources, environment and development, and to promote a unified analytical approach to the study of these interrelationships and to relevant policies;

(e) To promote the status of women and expansion of their roles, their full participation in the formulation and implementation of socio-economic policy including population policies, and the creation of awareness among all women of their current and potential roles in national life;

(f) To recommend guidelines for population policies consistent with national values and goals and with internationally recognized principles;

(g) To promote the development and implementation of population policies where necessary, including improvement in the communication of the purposes and goals of these policies to the public and the promotion of popular participation in their formulation and implementation;

(h) To encourage the development and good management of appropriate education, training, statistical research, information and family health services as well as statistical services in support of the above principles and objectives.

RECOMMENDATIONS FOR ACTION

Population Goals and Policies

Population Growth

16. According to the United Nations medium population projections, little change is expected to occur in average rates of population growth either in the developed or in the developing regions by 1985. According to the United Nations low variant projections, it is estimated that as

a result of social and economic development and population policies as reported by countries in the Second United Nations Inquiry on Population and Development, population growth rates in the developing countries as a whole may decline from the present level of 2.4 per cent per annum to about 2 per cent by 1985; and below 0.7 per cent per annum in the developed countries. In this case the world-wide rate of population growth would decline from 2 per cent to about 1.7 per cent.

17. Countries which consider that their present or expected rates of population growth hamper their goals of promoting human welfare are invited, if they have not yet done so, to consider adopting population policies, within the framework of socio-economic development, which are consistent with basic human rights and national goals and values.

18. Countries which aim at achieving moderate or low population growth should try to achieve it through a low level of birth and death rates. Countries wishing to increase their rate of population growth should, when mortality is high, concentrate efforts on the reduction of mortality, and where appropriate, encourage an increase in fertility and encourage immigration.

19. Recognizing that *per capita* use of world resources is much higher in the developed than in the developing countries, the developed countries are urged to adopt appropriate policies in population, consumption and investment, bearing in mind the need for fundamental improvement in international equity.

Morbidity and Mortality

20. The reduction of morbidity and mortality to the maximum feasible extent is a major goal of every human society. It should be achieved in conjunction with massive social and economic development. Where mortality and morbidity rates are very high, concentrated national and international efforts should be applied to reduce them as a matter of highest priority in the context of societal change.

21. The short-term effect of mortality reduction on population growth rates is symptomatic of the early development process and must be viewed as beneficial. Sustained reductions in fertility have generally been preceded by reductions in mortality. Although this relationship is complex, mortality reduction may be a prerequisite to a decline in fertility.

22. It is a goal of this Plan of Action to reduce mortality levels, particularly infant and maternal mortality levels, to the maximum extent possible in all regions of the world and to reduce national and subnational differentials therein. The attainment of an average expectation of life of 62 years by 1985 and 74 years by the year 2000 for the world as a whole would require by the end of the century an increase of 11 years for Latin America, 17 years for Asia and 28 years for Africa.

23. Countries with the highest mortality levels should aim by 1985 to have an expectation of life at birth of at least 50 years and an infant mortality rate of less than 120 per thousand live births.

24. It is recommended that national and international efforts to reduce general morbidity and mortality levels be accompanied by particularly vigorous efforts to achieve the following goals:

(a) Reduction of foetal, infant and early childhood mortality and related maternal morbidity and mortality;

(b) Reduction of involuntary sterility, subfecundity, defective births and illegal abortions;

(c) Reduction, or if possible elimination, of differential morbidity and mortality within countries, particularly with regard to differentials between regions, urban and rural areas, social and ethnic groups, and the sexes;

(d) Eradication, wherever possible, or control of infections and parasitic diseases, undernutrition and malnutrition; and the provision of a sufficient supply of potable water and adequate sanitation;

(e) Improvement of poor health and nutritional conditions which adversely affect working-age populations and their productivity and thus undermine development efforts;

(f) Adoption of special measures for reducing mortality from social and environmental factors and elimination of aggression as a cause of death and poor health.

25. It is recommended that health and nutrition programmes designed to reduce morbidity and mortality be integrated within a comprehensive development strategy and supplemented by a wide range of mutually supporting social policy measures; special attention should be given to improving the management of existing health, nutrition and

related social services and to the formulation of policies to widen their coverage so as to reach, in particular, rural, remote and under-privileged groups.

26. Each country has its own experience in preventing and treating diseases. Promotion of interchange of such experience will help to reduce morbidity and mortality.

Reproduction, Family Formation, and the Status of Women

27. This Plan of Action recognizes the variety of national goals with regard to fertility and does not recommend any world family-size norm.

28. This Plan of Action recognizes the necessity of ensuring that all couples are able to achieve their desired number and spacing of children and the necessity of preparing the social and economic conditions to achieve this desire.

29. Consistent with the Proclamation of the International Conference on Human Rights, the Declaration on Social Progress and Development, the relevant targets of the Second United Nations Development Decade and the other international instruments on the subject, it is recommended that all countries:

(a) Respect and ensure, regardless of their over-all demographic goals, the right of persons to determine, in a free, informed and responsible manner, the number and spacing of their children;

(b) Encourage appropriate education concerning responsible parenthood and make available to persons who so desire advice and means of achieving it;

(c) Ensure that family planning, medical and related social services aim not only at the prevention of unwanted pregnancies but also at elimination of involuntary sterility and sub-fecundity in order that all couples may be permitted to achieve their desired number of children, and that child adoption be facilitated;

(d) Seek to ensure the continued possibility of variations in family size when a low fertility level has been established or is a policy objective;

(e) Make use, wherever needed and appropriate, of adequately trained professional and auxiliary health personnel, rural extension, home economics and social workers, and non-governmental channels, to help provide family planning services and to advise users of contraceptives;

(f) Increase their health manpower and health facilities to an effective level, redistribute functions among the different levels of professionals and auxiliaries in order to overcome the shortage of qualified personnel and establish an effective system of supervision in their health and family planning services;

(g) Ensure that information about, and education in, family planning and other matters which affect fertility are based on valid and proven scientific knowledge, and include a full account of any risk that may be involved in the use or non-use of contraceptives.

30. Governments which have family planning programmes are invited to consider integrating and co-ordinating those services with health and other services designed to raise the quality of family life, including family allowances and maternity benefits, and to consider including family planning services in their official health and social insurance systems. As concerns couples themselves, family planning policy should also be directed towards promotion of the psycho-social harmony and mental and physical well-being of couples.

31. It is recommended that countries wishing to affect fertility levels give priority to implementing development programmes and educational and health strategies which, while contributing to economic growth and higher standards of living, have a decisive impact upon demographic trends, including fertility. International co-operation is called for to give priority to assisting such national efforts in order that these programmes and strategies be carried into effect.

32. While recognizing the diversity of social, cultural, political and economic conditions among countries and regions, it is nevertheless agreed that the following development goals generally have an effect on the socio-economic context of reproductive decisions that tends to moderate fertility levels:

(a) The reduction of infant and child mortality, particularly by means of improved nutrition, sanitation, maternal and child health care, and maternal education;

(b) The full integration of women into the development process, particularly by means of their greater participation in educational, social, economic and political opportunities, and especially by means of the removal of obstacles to their employment in the non-agricultural sector wherever possible. In this context, national laws and policies, as well as relevant international recommendations, should be reviewed in order to eliminate discrimination in, and remove obstacles to, the education, training, employment and career advancement opportunities for women;

(c) The promotion of social justice, social mobility, and social development particularly by means of a wide participation of the population in development and a more equitable distribution of income, land, social services and amenities;

(d) The promotion of wide educational opportunities for the young of both sexes, and the extension of public forms of pre-school education for the rising generation;

(e) The elimination of child labour and child abuse and the establishment of social security and old age benefits;

(f) The establishment of an appropriate lower limit for age at marriage.

33. It is recommended that Governments consider making provision, in both their formal and non-formal educational programmes for informing their people of the consequences of existing or alternative fertility behaviour for the well-being of the family, for educational and psychological development of children and for the general welfare of society, so that an informed and responsible attitude to marriage and reproduction will be promoted.

34. Family size may also be affected by incentive and disincentive schemes. However, if such schemes are adopted or modified it is essential that they should not violate human rights.

35. Some social welfare programmes, such as family allowances and maternity benefits, may have a positive effect on fertility and may hence be strengthened when such an effect is desired. However, such programmes should not, in principle, be curtailed if the opposite effect on fertility is desired.

36. The projections in paragraph 16 of future declines in rates of population growth, and those in paragraph 22 concerning increased expectation of life, are consistent with declines in the birth rate of the developing countries as a whole from the present level of 38 per thousand to 30 per thousand by 1985; in these projections, birth rates in the

developed countries remain in the region of 15 per thousand. To achieve by 1985 these levels of fertility would require substantial national efforts, by those countries concerned, in the field of socio-economic development and population policies, supported, upon request, by adequate international assistance. Such efforts would also be required to achieve the increase in expectation of life.

37. In the light of the principles of this Plan of Action, countries which consider their birth rates detrimental to their national purposes are invited to consider setting quantitative goals and implementing policies that may lead to the attainment of such goals by 1985. Nothing herein should interfere with the sovereignty of any Government to adopt or not to adopt such quantitative goals.

38. Countries which desire to reduce their birthrates are invited to give particular consideration to the reduction of fertility at the extremes of female reproductive ages because of the salutary effects this may have on infant and maternal welfare.

39. The family is recognized as the basic unit of society. Governments should assist families as far as possible to enable them to fulfil their role in society. It is therefore recommended that:

(a) The family be protected by appropriate legislation and policy without discrimination as to other members of society;

(b) Family ties be strengthened by giving recognition to the importance of love and mutual respect within the family unit;

(c) National legislation having direct bearing on the welfare of the family and its members, including laws concerning age at marriage, inheritance, property rights, divorce, education, employment and the rights of the child, be periodically reviewed, as feasible, and adapted to the changing social and economic conditions and with regard to the cultural setting;

(d) Marriages be entered into only with the free and full consent of the intending spouses;

(e) Measures be taken to protect the social and legal rights of spouses and children in the case of dissolution or termination of marriage by death or other reason;

40.(a) Governments should equalize the legal and social status of children born in and out of wedlock as well as children adopted;

(b) The legal responsibilities of each parent towards the care and support of all their children should be established.

41. Governments should ensure full participation of women in the educational, social, economic and political life of their countries on an equal basis with men. It is recommended that:

(a) Education for girls as well as boys should be extended and diversified to enable them to contribute more effectively in rural and urban sectors, as well as in the management of food and other household functions;

(b) Women should be actively involved both as individuals and through political and non-governmental organizations, at every stage and every level in the planning and implementation of development programmes, including population policies;

(c) The economic contribution of women in households and farming should be recognized in national economies;

(d) Governments should make a sustained effort to ensure that legislation regarding the status of women complies with the principles spelled out in the Declaration on the Elimination of Discrimination Against Women and other United Nations declarations, conventions and international instruments, to reduce the gap between law and practice through effective implementation, and to inform women at all socio-economic levels of their legal rights and responsibilities.

42. Equal status of men and women in the family and in society improves the over-all quality of life. This principle of equality should be fully realized in family planning where each spouse should consider the welfare of the other members of the family.

43. Improvement of the status of women in the family and in society can contribute, where desired, to smaller family size, and the opportunity for women to plan births also improves their individual status.

Population Distribution and Internal Migration

44. Urbanization in most countries is characterized by a number of adverse factors: drain from rural areas through migration of individuals who cannot be absorbed by productive employment in urban areas, serious disequilibrium in the growth of urban centres, contamination of the environment, inadequate housing and services and social and

psychological stress. In many developing countries, adverse consequences are due in large part to the economic structures resulting from
the dependent situation of those countries in the international economic system; the correction of these shortcomings requires as a matter of priority the establishment of equitable economic relations among
peoples.

45. Policies aimed at influencing population flows into urban areas
should be co-ordinated with policies relating to the absorptive capacity
of urban centres, as well as policies aimed at eliminating the undesir-
able consequences of excessive migration. In so far as possible, these
policies should be integrated in plans and programmes dealing with
over-all social and economic development.

46. In formulating and implementing internal migration policies, Governments are urged to consider the following guidelines, without prejudice to their own socio-economic policies:

(a) Measures should be avoided which infringe the right of freedom of movement and residence within the borders of each State as
enunciated in the Universal Declaration of Human Rights and other
international instruments;

(b) A major approach to a more rational distribution of the population is that of planned and more equitable regional development, particularly in the advancement of regions which are less favoured or
developed by comparison with the rest of the country;

(c) In planning development, and particularly in planning the location of industry and business and the distribution of social services
and amenities, Governments should take into account not only short-
term economic returns of alternative patterns but also the social and
environmental costs and benefits involved as well as equity and social
justice in the distribution of the benefits of development among all
groups and regions;

(d) Population distribution patterns should not be restricted to a
choice between metropolitan and rural life: efforts should be made to
establish and strengthen networks of small and medium-size cities to
relieve the pressure on the large towns, while still offering an alternative to rural living;

(e) Intensive programmes of economic and social improvement
should be carried out in the rural areas through balanced agricultural
development which will provide increased income to the agricultural

population, permit an effective expansion of social services and include measures to protect the environment and conserve and increase agricultural resources;

(f) Programmes should be promoted to make accessible to scattered populations the basic social services and the support necessary for increased productivity, for example by consolidating them in rural centres.

47. Internal migration policies should include the provision of information to the rural population concerning economic and social conditions in the urban areas, including information on the availability of employment opportunities.

48. In rural areas and areas accessible to rural populations, new employment opportunities, including industries and public works programmes, should be created, systems of land tenure should be improved and social services and amenities provided. It is not sufficient to consider how to bring the people to existing economic and social activities; it is also important to bring those activities to the people.

49. Considerable experience is now being gained by some countries which have implemented programmes for relieving urban pressures, revitalizing the countryside, inhabiting sparsely populated areas and settling newly reclaimed agricultural land. Countries having such experience are invited to share it with other countries. It is recommended that international organizations make available upon request coordinated technical and financial assistance to facilitate the settlement of people.

50. The problems of urban environment are a consequence not only of the concentration of inhabitants but also of their way of life which can produce harmful effects, such as wasteful and excessive consumption and activities which produce pollution. In order to avoid such effects in those countries experiencing this problem, a development pattern favouring balanced and rational consumption is recommended.

International Migration

51. It is recommended that Governments and international organizations generally facilitate voluntary international movement. However, such movements should not be based on racial considerations which are to the detriment of indigenous populations. The significance of

international migration varies widely among countries, depending upon their area, population size and growth rate, social and economic structure and environmental conditions.

52. Governments which consider international migration to be important to their countries, either in the short or the long run, are urged to conduct, when appropriate, bilateral or multilateral consultations, taking into account the principles of the Charter of the United Nations, the Universal Declaration of Human Rights, the relevant resolutions of the United Nations system and other international instruments, with a view to harmonizing those of their policies which affect these movements. It is recommended that international organizations make available upon request co-ordinated technical and financial assistance to facilitate the settlement of people in countries of immigration.

53. Problems of refugees and displaced persons arising from forced migration, including their right of return to homes and properties, should also be settled in accordance with the relevant Principles of the Charter of the United Nations, the Universal Declaration of Human Rights and other international instruments.

54. Countries that are concerned with the outflow of migrant workers and wish to encourage and assist those remaining workers or returning workers should make particular efforts to create favourable employment opportunities at the national level. More developed countries should co-operate, bilaterally or through regional organizations and the international community, with less developed countries, to achieve these goals through the increased availability of capital, technical assistance, export markets and more favourable terms of trade and choice of production technology.

55. Countries receiving migrant workers should provide proper treatment and adequate social welfare services for them and their families, and should ensure their physical safety and security, in conformity with the provisions of the relevant ILO conventions and recommendations and other international instruments.

56. Specifically, in the treatment of migrant workers, Governments should work to prevent discrimination in the labour market and in society through lower salaries or other unequal conditions, to preserve their human rights, to combat prejudice against them and to eliminate obstacles to the reunion of their families. Governments should enable permanent immigrants to preserve their cultural heritage *inter alia*

through the use of their mother tongue. Laws to limit illegal immigration should not only relate to the illegal migrants themselves but also to those inducing or facilitating their illegal action and should be promulgated in conformity with international law and basic human rights. Governments should bear in mind humanitarian considerations in the treatment of aliens who remain in a country illegally.

57. Since the outflow of qualified personnel from developing to developed countries seriously hampers the development of the former, there is an urgent need to formulate national and international policies to avoid the "brain drain" and to obviate its adverse effects, including the possibility of devising programmes for large-scale communication of appropriate technological knowledge mainly from developed countries to the extent it can be properly adjusted and appropriately absorbed.

58. Developing countries suffering from heavy emigration of skilled workers and professionals should undertake extensive educational programmes, manpower planning and investment in scientific and technical programmes. They should also undertake other programmes and measures to better match skills with employment opportunities and to increase the motivation of such personnel to contribute to the progress of their own country. Measures should be taken to encourage the return of scientists and skilled personnel to specific job vacancies.

59. Foreign investors should employ and train local personnel and use local research facilities to the greatest possible extent in conformity with the policies of the host country. Subject to their consent, the location of research facilities in host countries may aid them to a certain extent in retaining the services of highly skilled and professional research workers. Such investment should, of course, in no circumstances inhibit national economic development. International co-operation is needed to improve programmes to induce skilled personnel to return to, or remain in, their own countries.

60. Where immigration has proved to be of a long-term nature, countries are invited to explore the possibilities of extending national civil rights to immigrants.

61. The flow of skilled workers, technicians and professionals from more developed to less developed countries may be considered a form of international co-operation. Countries in a position to do so should continue and increase this flow with full respect for the sovereignty and equality of recipient countries.

62. Countries affected by significant numbers of migrant workers are urged, if they have not yet done so, to conclude bilateral or multilateral agreements which would regulate migration, protect and assist migrant workers, and protect the interests of the countries concerned. The International Labour Organisation should promote concerted action in the field of protection of migrant workers, and the United Nations Commission on Human Rights should help, as appropriate, to ensure that the fundamental rights of migrants are safeguarded.

Population Structure

63. All Governments are urged, when formulating their development policies and programmes, to take fully into account the implications of changing numbers and proportions of youth, working-age groups and the aged, particularly where such changes are rapid. Countries should study their population structures to determine the most desirable balance among age groups.

64. Specifically, developing countries are urged to consider the implications which the combination of the characteristically young age structure and moderate to high fertility have on their development. The increasing number and proportion of young persons in the populations of developing countries requires appropriate development strategies, priority being accorded to their subsistence, health, education, training and incorporation in the labour force through full employment as well as their active participation in political, cultural, social and economic life.

65. Developing countries are invited to consider the possible economic, social and demographic effects of population shifts from agriculture to non-agricultural industries. In addition to fuller utilization of labour and improvements in productivity and the levels of living, promotion of non-agricultural employment should aim at such changes in the socio-economic structure of manpower and population as would affect demographically relevant behaviour of individuals. All countries are invited to consider fully giving appropriate support and assistance to the World Employment Programme and related national employment promotion schemes.

66. Similarly, the other countries are urged to consider the contrary implications of the combination of their ageing structure with moderate to low or very low fertility. All countries should carry out, as part

of their development programmes, comprehensive, humanitarian and just programmes of social security for the elderly.

67. In undertaking settlement and resettlement schemes and urban planning, Governments are urged to give adequate attention to questions of age and sex balance and, particularly, to the welfare of the family.

Socio-economic Policies

68. This Plan of Action recognizes that economic and social development is a central factor in the solution of population problems. National efforts of developing countries to accelerate economic growth should be assisted by the entire international community. The implementation of the International Development Strategy for the Second United Nations Development Decade, and the Declaration and the Programme of Action on the New International Economic Order as adopted at the sixth special session of the General Assembly should lead to a reduction in the widening gap in levels of living between developed and developing countries and would be conducive to a reduction in population growth rates particularly in countries where such rates are high.

69. In planning measures to harmonize population trends and socio-economic change, human beings must be regarded not only as consumers but also as producers. The investment by nations in the health and education of their citizens contributes substantially to productivity. Consequently, plans for economic and social development and for international assistance for this purpose should emphasize the health and education sectors. Likewise, patterns of production and technology should be adapted to each country's endowment in human resources. Decisions on the introduction of technologies affording significant savings in employment of manpower should take into account the relative abundance of human resources. To this end it is recommended that efforts should be intensified to determine for each country the technologies and production methods best suited to its working population situation and to study the relationship between population factors and employment.

70. It is imperative that all countries, and within them all social sectors, should adapt themselves to more rational utilization of natural resources, without excess, so that some are not deprived of what others

waste. In order to increase the production and distribution of food for the growing world population it is recommended that Governments give high priority to improving methods of food production, the investigation and development of new sources of food and more effective utilization of existing sources. International co-operation is recommended with the aim of ensuring the provision of fertilizers and energy and a timely supply of foodstuffs to all countries.

Promotion of Knowledge and Policies

71. In order to achieve the population objectives of this Plan of Action and to put its policy recommendations adequately into effect, measures need to be undertaken to promote knowledge of the relationships and problems involved, to assist in the development of population policies and to elicit the co-operation and participation of all concerned in the formulation and implementation of these policies.

Data Collection and Analysis

72. Statistical data on the population collected by means of censuses, surveys or vital statistics registers, are essential for the planning of investigations and the provision of a basis for the formulation, evaluation and application of population and development policies. Countries that have not yet done so are urged to tabulate and analyse their census and other data and make them available to national policymaking bodies in order to fulfil these objectives.

73. It is up to each country to take a population census in accordance with its own needs and capabilities. However, it is recommended that a population census be taken by each country between 1975 and 1985. It is also recommended that these censuses give particular attention to data relevant to development planning and the formulation of population policies. In order to be of greatest value, it is recommended that these data be tabulated and made available as quickly as possible, together with an evaluation of the quality of the information and the degree of coverage of the census.

74. All countries that have not yet done so are encouraged to establish a continuing capability for taking household sample surveys and to establish a long-term plan for regular collection of statistics on various demographic and interrelated socio-economic variables, particularly those relating to the improvement of levels of living, well-being and level of education of individuals, factors which relate closely to prob-

lems affecting population. All countries are invited to co-operate with the World Fertility Survey.

75. In line with the objectives of the World Programme for the Improvement of Vital Statistics, countries are encouraged to establish or improve their vital registration system, as a long-term objective, and to enact laws relevant to the improvement of vital registration. Until this improvement is completed, the use of alternative methods is recommended, such as sample surveys, to provide up-to-date information on vital events.

76. Developing countries should be provided with technical co-operation, equipment and financial support to develop or improve the population and related statistical programmes mentioned above. Provision for data-gathering assistance should cover fully the need for evaluating, analysing and presenting the data in a form most appropriate to the needs of users.

77. Governments that have not yet done so are urged to establish appropriate services for the collection, analysis and dissemination of demographic and related statistical information.

Research

78. This Plan of Action gives high priority to research activities in population problems (including unemployment, starvation and poverty) and to related fields, particularly to research activities that are important for the formulation, evaluation and implementation of the population policies consistent with full respect for human rights and fundamental freedoms as recognized in international instruments of the United Nations. Although research designed to fill gaps in knowledge is very urgent and important, high priority should be given to research oriented to the specific problems of countries and regions, including methodological studies. Such research is best carried out in the countries and regions themselves and by competent persons especially acquainted with national and regional conditions. The following areas are considered to require research in order to fill existing gaps in knowledge:

(a) The social, cultural and economic determinants of population variables in different developmental and political situations, particularly at the family and micro levels;

(b) The demographic and social processes occurring within the family cycle through time and, particularly, in relation to alternative modes of development;

(c) The development of effective means for the improvement of health, and especially for the reduction of maternal, foetal, infant and early childhood mortality;

(d) The study of experiences of countries which have major programmes of internal migration with a view to developing guidelines that are helpful to policy-makers of those countries and of countries that are interested in undertaking similar programmes;

(e) Projections of demographic and related variables including the development of empirical and hypothetical models for simulating possible future trends;

(f) The formulation, implementation and evaluation of population policies including: methods for integrating population inputs and goals in development plans and programmes; means for understanding and improving the motivations of people to participate in the formulation and implementation of population programmes; study of education and communication aspects of population policy; analysis of population policies in their relationship with other socio-economic development policies, laws and institutions, including the possible influences of the economic system on the social, cultural and economic aspects of population policies; translation into action programmes of policies dealing with the socio-economic determinants of fertility, mortality, internal migration and distribution, and international migration;

(g) The collection, analysis and dissemination of information concerning human rights in relation to population matters and the preparation of studies designed to clarify, systematize and more effectively implement these human rights;

(h) The review and analysis of national and international laws which bear directly or indirectly on population factors;

(i) The assessment and improvement of existing and new methods of fertility regulation by means of research, including basic biological and applied research; the evaluation of the impact, both in short-term and long-term effects, of different methods of fertility regulation on ethical and cultural values and on mental and physical health; and the assessment and study of policies for creating social and economic conditions so that couples can freely decide on the size of their families;

(j) The evaluation of the impact of different methods of family planning on the health conditions of women and members of their families;

(k) The interrelationships among patterns of family formation, nutrition and health, reproductive biology, and the incidence, causes and treatment of sterility;

(l) Methods for improving the management, delivery and utilization of all social services associated with population, including family welfare and, when appropriate, family planning;

(m) Methods for the development of systems of social, demographic and related economic statistics in which various sets of data are inter-linked, with a view to improving insight into the interrelationships of variables in these fields;

(n) The interrelations of population trends and conditions and other social and economic variables, in particular the availability of human resources, food and natural resources, the quality of the environment, the need for health, education, employment, welfare, housing and other social services and amenities, promotion of human rights, the enhancement of the status of women, the need for social security, political stability, discrimination and political freedom;

(o) The impact of a shift from one family size pattern to another on biological and demographic characteristics of the population;

(p) The changing structure, functions and dynamics of the family as an institution, including the changing roles of men and women, attitudes towards and opportunities for women's education and employment; the implications of current and future population trends for the status of women; biomedical research on male and female fertility, and the economic, social and demographic benefits to be derived from the integration of women in the development process;

(q) Social indicators, to reflect the quality of life as well as the interrelations between socio-economic and demographic phenomena, should be encouraged. Emphasis should also be given to the development of socio-economic and demographic models.

79. National research requirements and needs must be determined by Governments and national institutions. However, high priority should be given, wherever possible, to research that has wide relevance and international applicability.

80. National and regional research institutions dealing with population and related questions should be assisted and expanded as appropriate. Special efforts should be made to co-ordinate the research of these institutions by facilitating the exchange of their research findings and the exchange of information on their planned and ongoing research projects.

Management, Training, Education, and Information

81. There is a particular need for the development of management in all fields related to population, with national and international attention and appropriate support given to programmes dealing with its promotion.

82. A dual approach to training is recommended: an international programme for training in population matters concomitant with national and regional training programmes adapted and made particularly relevant to conditions in the countries and regions of the trainees. While recognizing the complementarity of these two approaches, national and regional training should be given the higher priority.

83. Training in population dynamics and policies, whether national, regional or international, should, in so far as possible, be interdisciplinary in nature. The training of population specialists should always be accompanied by relevant career development for the trainees in their fields of specialization. Training should deal not only with population variables but also with the interrelationships of these variables with economic, social and political variables.

84. Training in the various aspects of population activities, including the management of population programmes should not be restricted to the higher levels of specialization but should also be extended to personnel at other levels, and, where needed, to medical, paramedical and traditional health personnel, and population programme administrators. Such training should impart an adequate knowledge of human rights in accordance with international standards and an awareness of the human rights aspect of population problems.

85. Training in population matters should be extended to labour, community and other social leaders, and to senior government officials, with a view to enabling them better to identify the population problems

of their countries and communities and to help in the formulation of policies relating to them.

86. Owing to the role of education in individual's and society's progress and the impact of education on demographic behaviour, all countries are urged to further develop their formal and informal educational programmes; efforts should be made to eradicate illiteracy, to promote education among the youth and abolish factors discriminating against women.

87. Educational institutions in all countries should be encouraged to expand their curricula to include a study of population dynamics and policies, including, where appropriate, family life, responsible parenthood and the relation of population dynamics to socio-economic development and to international relations. Governments are urged to co-operate in developing a world-wide system of international, regional and national institutions to meet the need for trained manpower. Assistance to the less developed countries should include, as appropriate, the improvement of the educational infrastructure such as library facilities and computer services.

88. Governments are invited to use all available means for disseminating population information.

89. Governments are invited to consider the distribution of population information to enlighten both rural and urban populations, through the assistance of governmental agencies.

90. Voluntary organizations should be encouraged, within the framework of national laws, policies and regulations, to play an important role in disseminating population information and ensuring wider participation in population programmes, and to share experiences regarding the implementation of population measures and programmes.

91. International organizations, both governmental and non-governmental, should strengthen their efforts to distribute information on population and related matters, particularly through periodic publications on the world population situation, prospects and policies, the utilization of audio-visual and other aids to communication, the publication of nontechnical digests and reports, and the production and wide distribution of newsletters on population activities. Consideration should also be given to strengthening the publication of international professional journals and reviews in the field of population.

92. In order to achieve the widest possible dissemination of research results, translation activities should be encouraged at both the national and international levels. In this respect, the revision of the *United Nations Multilingual Demographic Dictionary* and its publication in additional languages is strongly recommended.

93. The information and experience resulting from the World Population Conference and the World Population Year relating to the scientific study of population and the elaboration of population policies should be synthesized and disseminated by the United Nations.

Development and Evaluation of Population Policies

94. Where population policies or programmes have been adopted, systematic and periodic evaluations of their effectiveness should be made with a view to their improvement.

95. Population measures and programmes should be integrated into comprehensive social and economic plans and programmes and this integration should be reflected in the goals, instrumentalities and organizations for planning within the countries. In general, it is suggested that a unit dealing with population aspects be created and placed at a high level of the national administrative structure and that such a unit be staffed with qualified persons from the relevant disciplines.

RECOMMENDATIONS FOR IMPLEMENTATION

Role of National Governments

96. The success of this Plan of Action will largely depend on the actions undertaken by national Governments. To take action, Governments are urged to utilize fully the support of intergovernmental and nongovernmental organizations.

97. This Plan of Action recognizes the responsibility of each Government to decide on its own policies and devise its own programmes of action for dealing with the problems of population and economic and social progress. Recommendations, in so far as they relate to national Governments, are made with due regard to the need for variety and flexibility in the hope that they may be responsive to major needs in the population field as perceived and interpreted by national Governments. However, national policies should be formulated and imple-

mented without violating, and with due promotion of, universally accepted standards of human rights.

98. An important role of Governments with regard to this Plan of Action is to determine and assess the population problems and needs of their countries in the light of their political, social, cultural, religious and economic conditions; such an undertaking should be carried out systematically and periodically so as to promote informed, rational and dynamic decision-making in matters of population and development.

99. The effect of national action or inaction in the fields of population, may, in certain circumstances, extend beyond national boundaries; such international implications are particularly evident with regard to aspects of morbidity, population concentration and international migration, but may also apply to other aspects of population concern.

Role of International Cooperation

100. International co-operation, based on the peaceful co-existence of States having different social systems, should play a supportive role in achieving the goals of the Plan of Action. This supportive role could take the form of direct assistance, technical or financial, in response to national and regional requests and be additional to economic development assistance, or the form of other activities, such as monitoring progress, undertaking comparative research in the area of population, resources and consumption, and furthering the exchange among countries of information and policy experiences in the field of population and consumption. Assistance should be provided on the basis of respect for sovereignty of the recipient country and its national policy.

101. The General Assembly of the United Nations, the Economic and Social Council, the Governing Council of UNDP/UNFPA and other competent legislative and policy-making bodies of the specialized agencies and the various intergovernmental organizations are urged to give careful consideration to this Plan of Action and to ensure an appropriate response to it.

102. Countries sharing similar population conditions and problems are invited to consider jointly this Plan of Action, exchange experience in relevant fields and elaborate those aspects of the Plan that are of particular relevance to them. The United Nations regional economic commissions and other regional bodies of the United Nations system should play an important role towards this end.

103. There is a special need for training in the field of population. The United Nations system, Governments and, as appropriate, non-governmental organizations are urged to give recognition to this need and priority to the measures necessary to meet it, including information, education and services for family planning.

104. Developed countries, and other countries able to assist, are urged to increase their assistance to developing countries in accordance with the goals of the Second United Nations Development Decade and, together with international organizations, make this assistance available in accordance with the national priorities of receiving countries. In this respect, it is recognized, in view of the magnitude of the problems and the consequent national requirements for funds, that considerable expansion of international assistance in the population field is required for the proper implementation of this Plan of Action.

105. It is suggested that the expanding, but still insufficient, international assistance in population and development matters requires increased co-operation; UNFPA is urged, in co-operation with all organizations responsible for international population assistance, to produce a guide for international assistance in population matters which would be made available to recipient countries and institutions and be revised periodically.

106. International non-governmental organizations are urged to respond to the goals and policies of this Plan of Action by co-ordinating their activities with those of other non-governmental organizations, and with those of relevant bilateral and multilateral organizations, by expanding their support for national institutions and organizations dealing with population questions, and by co-operating in the promotion of widespread knowledge of the goals and policies of the Plan of Action, and, when requested, by supporting national and private institutions and organizations dealing with population questions.

Monitoring, Review, and Appraisal

107. It is recommended that monitoring of population trends and policies discussed in this Plan of Action should be undertaken continuously as a specialized activity of the United Nations and reviewed biennially by the appropriate bodies of the United Nations system, beginning in 1977. Because of the shortness of the intervals, such monitoring would necessarily have to be selective with regard to its informational content

and should focus mainly on new and emerging population trends and policies.

108. A comprehensive and thorough review and appraisal of progress made towards achieving the goals and recommendations of this Plan of Action should be undertaken every five years by the United Nations system. For this purpose the Secretary-General is invited to make appropriate arrangements taking account of the existing structure and resources of the United Nations system, and in co-operation with Governments. It is suggested that the first such review be made in 1979 and be repeated each five years thereafter. The findings of such systematic evaluations should be considered by the Economic and Social Council with the object of making, whenever necessary, appropriate modifications of the goals and recommendations of this Plan.

109. It is urged that both the monitoring and the review and appraisal activities of this Plan of Action be closely co-ordinated with those of the International Development Strategy for the Second United Nations Development Decade and any new international development strategy that might be formulated.

3 RESULTS OF THE REGIONAL CONSULTATIONS SUBSEQUENT TO THE WORLD POPULATION CONFERENCE

INTRODUCTION

Background Information

The principle of intergovernmental consultation at the regional level had been applied as part of the preparatory work for the World Population Conference in the series of meetings held under the auspices of the regional commissions[1] in the period April–May 1974.[2] The World Population Plan of Action[3] adopted at Bucharest endorsed the principle as one of the means of ensuring an appropriate response to the Plan. Subsequently, the General Assembly, in its resolution 3344 (XXIX) of 17 December 1974 called, *inter alia,* upon the Population Commission, the United Nations Fund for Population Activities (UNFPA) and the regional commissions, to consider how best they could assist in the implementation of the Plan of Action. Further, in the consultations prepatory to the Conference, proposals had been made to convene post-Conference meetings early in 1975.

The post-Conference consultations[4] organized by the United Nations, through the Population Division of the Department of Economic and Social Affairs, and by UNFPA, in collaboration with the regional commissions, were held as follows:

(a) For the region of the Economic and Social Commission for Asia and the Pacific (ESCAP), at Bangkok, Thailand, from 14 to 20 January 1975;

(b) For the region of the Economic Commission for Latin America (ECLA), with the Centro Latinoamericano de Demografía (CELADE) collaborating, at Mexico City, from 3 to 7 March 1975;

(c) For the region of the Economic Commission for Africa (ECA), at Lusaka, Zambia, from 16 to 22 April 1975;

(d) For the region of the Economic Commission for Western Asia (ECWA), at Doha, Qatar, 24 and 25 March 1975; and at Beirut, Lebanon, 1 and 2 May 1975;

(e) Among the countries of the region of the Economic Commission for Europe (ECE), at Geneva, from 7 to 11 July 1975.[5]

Consequently, during the period from April 1974 to July 1975, Governments in all five regions consulted twice on the World Population Plan of Action, in addition to participation in the World Population Conference at Bucharest.

Participation

The post-Conference consultations were attended by representatives of Governments of States members and associate members of the regional commissions, and by a limited number of observers from non-member Governments which requested invitations. The level of representation varied from the ministerial level of the ECLA region to middle-level government functionaries in some regions or countries therein.

The United Nations bodies working in the field of population were represented in terms of the relationship agreements between the United Nations and the agencies. A number of non-governmental organizations in consultative status with the Economic and Social Council and of intergovernmental organizations were invited to send observers, in response to requests.

Purpose of the Consultations

It was hoped that the consultations would yield information on specific government policies and action programmes recommended in the World Population Plan of Action, to guide the United Nations and UNFPA on the types and levels of substantive, human and financial support required to respond to national, regional and global needs, with an indication of priorities attached to the various fields referred to in the Plan.

What has emerged from the consultations mainly takes the form of recommendations at the regional level on the rationale of population policies; the areas to be addressed by policies; the inputs for formulating, implementing and evaluating them; and the need for international co-operation. Again, the meeting in Europe was exceptional: something in the nature of an examination of conscience on recent demographic trends and implications of possible continuation of fertility decline, which gave pause for thought but not for definite policy conclusions.

Relationship to the Pre-Conference Consultations

At the pre-Conference consultations, each region gave its reactions to the draft of the World Population Plan of Action and offered proposals for changes, many of which were incorporated in one way or another in the final version. Although the consensus at Bucharest was reaffirmed, application has required further consideration by countries and sometimes by regional bodies of different levels of responsibility. The process was related to the evolution of ideas from the pre-Conference period and to the conceptual problems in the post-Conference period on the means of integration of population policies in development planning:

(a) The countries of the ECE region have avoided anything resembling recommendations on population policies; nevertheless, the post-Conference consultation was informed by a sense of common understanding, recognition of some common problems, current and potential; and a foreshadowing by a number of Governments of announcements of considered positions as a result of the adoption of the Plan of Action;

(b) In the ESCAP region, a defined position on population control was established before the Conference; and some concessions were made at Bucharest in the interests of international solidarity, with a subsequent reaffirmation of the pre-Conference position with a modification of its rationale in the development context;

(c) In the ECLA, ECA and ECWA regions, there was essential continuity of positions throughout, with more elaboration, especially in the ECLA region, as a result of the Conference. In the ECLA and ECA regions, the emphasis on the problems of development and the international aspects thereof reflects the importance attached to the New International Economic Order in the post-Conference consultations.

In the case of the ESCAP region, the New Delhi Declaration (resolution 154 (XXXI) of March 1975), though subsequent to the post-World Population Conference consultation, elaborates an authoritative regional reaction to the New International Economic Order in which rapid rates of population growth are seen as one of the problems causing or aggravating difficulties in the achievement of development objectives.

In the case of the ECA region, the resolution on "Integrated programmes on population" (E/CN.14/Res/273 (XII)) adopted by the

Third Conference of African Ministers in February 1975 must be taken into account as another authoritative statement bearing directly on issues discussed in the consultation; and, in effect, endorsing action to reduce population growth by those countries which consider the current rate too high and endorsing the right to responsible parenthood.

Presentation of the Recommendations of the Post-Conference Consultations

The findings of the post-Conference consultations are presented by region and in the order followed in the Plan of Action. Where possible, objectives and measures are distinguished, with an attempt to reflect the reasoning behind the positions adopted.

However, for some topics and for the European meeting, the presentation could not conveniently be standardized in this way. At the consultation in Europe, interactions among demographic variables and also multiple reactions among these and socio-economic variables were so stressed that it was not easy to isolate particular demographic variables. In the other regions, the problem was incidental to internal procedures in the meetings and to variations in the detail of the reports which made it difficult to do equal justice to the underlying arguments. The ECLA report is a comprehensive progression from normative considerations, to juridical and institutional instruments for population policies, to objectives and goals and thence to recommendations for action. The ESCAP and ECWA reports are concise statements of areas addressed and recommendations for action. In the case of the ECA meeting, the report must be read in conjunction with the background paper "Proposals for a population programme of action for Africa following from the recommendations of the 1974 World Population Conference" (E/CN.14/POP/135), the former being essentially an elaboration and clarification of the latter, together presenting both recommendations for action and the arguments underlying them.

RECOMMENDATIONS FOR ACTION BY GOVERNMENTS

Population Goals and Policies

Population Growth

At the consultation among countries of the ECE region, it was observed that for a number of reasons most countries in the region had not regarded their declining rates of population growth as alarming and that they had, *de jure* or *de facto,* permitted growing freedom in respect of control of fertility. Yet, the consultation recognized the implications (highlighted by the lower projection in the ECE paper on post-war demographic trends (ESA/P/AC.5/2)) of a possible decline in absolute numbers from around the turn of the century. A few countries had already modified their positions on population growth, and the consultation raised the question whether in the future Governments might see a need to take pro-natalist action, perhaps in ways not reconcilable with their customary support of individual freedom of action in this domain.

The socio-economic consequences of recent demographic trends were serious issues, and questions were raised regarding oscillations which could occur in the course of demographic change, and which could require successive adjustments in such areas as school-building programmes, housing, urbanization and migration, levels of living and employment.[6]

Though the implications of growth of world population were not discussed in any detail, reference was made to the seriousness of the long-term problem of food supply in relation to the growth of population and of the short-term danger of intermittent periods of acute shortage.

In the ESCAP Region.[7] As had been recommended at the pre-Conference consultation in the ESCAP region, the post-Conference consultation reaffirmed its support of quantified and dated targets for the reduction of population growth "in the interests of all nations and the common good". Those targets went beyond the regional level, recommending that the goals should be the reduction of population growth rates by 1985 to an average of 1.7 per cent for the world, an average of 0.6 per cent for the developed countries and an average of 2.0 per cent in the developing countries. It may be recalled that the World Population Plan of Action used those same rates not as targets but as levels to which population growth might decline in 1985.[8]

In the discussions, representatives of Bangladesh, India, Indonesia, Iran, Malaysia, Pakistan, the Republic of Korea, the Republic of South Viet-Nam, Singapore and Thailand reported targets for reduction of population growth (in a few cases, they expressed them in terms of reduction of fertility) adopted on the grounds that population growth was hampering goals of promoting human welfare. The World Population Conference, however, had reinforced a growing opinion in many of the countries that success in achieving demographic objectives required broad action in the socio-economic field and that opinion was reflected in recommendations on socio-economic policies made by the consultation.

In the ECLA Region. The consultation in the ECLA region emphasized the distinction between an equal need for action in respect of critical situations arising from the interaction of socio-economic, political and demographic structures and critical situations deriving from the demand for services generated by population dynamics, with particular emphasis on demand for education, health services, housing and other facilities clearly related to the trends of population growth, distribution and structure.[9]

Although it was recognized that the high density and rapid population growth had created critical situations in some countries where rates of economic growth had not kept pace with population growth,[10] it was also noted that most of the instruments of action adopted by Governments in the region were "primarily aimed at achieving social and economic objectives while also affecting the population variables"; others had been devised "mainly to influence population dynamics and supplement the former".[11]

In the ECA Region.[12] In the ECA region, it was recognized that in some cases, particularly in countries with vast natural resources, "a high rate of population growth could provide added benefit for development through a large supply of labour and an expanded domestic consumer market".[13] This approach reflected the emphasis placed upon questions of national development, international equity and economic co-operation. However, the possibility that rapid population growth could be an obstacle to development was also recognized, and resolution 273 (XII) of the Conference of Ministers in 1975 spelled out the right of countries to take action to reduce population growth if it was believed to be such as to hamper development.

In the ECWA Region.[14] In the view of the consultation in the ECWA region, "rapid population growth in the area does not constitute an obstacle in the way of the socio-economic development. In essence, the question of growth is a question of development and optimum utilization of available and potential resources and capacity which can absorb population growth in the region".[15] It was also indicated that the development process might overcome the implications of the continued rise in reproduction rates and the natural increase of population.

Morbidity and Mortality

Among Countries of the ECE Region. The increasing proportion of the aged in the ECE region had tended to halt or even reverse the decline in the crude death rate, and levels of mortality among infants and children were nearing the limit of improvement. There was an implicit recognition that the changing age structure would require measures for the attainment of uniformly high levels of life expectancy and of differentiated care for the diseases and general welfare of the aged.

Note was taken of the fact that in four countries there were no legal grounds for abortion.[16] In the other countries, the grounds for abortion varied greatly, but the tendency had been towards greater freedom; and, in three countries, there had been a reintroduction of restrictions.[17]

In the ESCAP Region.[18] In the ESCAP region, targets were set as follows: countries with the highest mortality levels should have as their objective, by 1985, an expectation of life at birth of 62 years, a maternal mortality rate of not more than 210 per 100,000 live births and an infant mortality rate of less than 120 per 1,000 live births.

The World Population Plan of Action,[19] although proposing the same target for infant mortality, set a target of "at least 50 years" for the expectation of life for countries (in all regions) with the highest mortality and made no reference to targets for maternal mortality.

Priorities for reduction of morbidity and mortality were: environmental sanitation and mass immunization campaigns; health services, including maternal and child health, for all parts of the country; nutritional programmes; health insurance programmes; reduction of health risks associated with illegal abortion; and giving of consideration to liberalization of abortion legislation so as to lower morbidity and mortality caused by illegal abortion.

In the ECLA Region. In the context of the principle that "independently of the realization of economic and social objectives, respect for human life is basic to all human societies",[20] the consultation in the ECLA region reiterated that every person had the right to access to such health services as technological development made possible and to adequate food and health at home and at work.[21]

It was recommended[22] that countries should consider some minimum objectives: reduction of general morbidity and mortality, particularly infant, peri-natal and maternal morbidity and mortality, with consideration of the goals laid down in the Ten-Year Health Plan of the Americas; the achievement of the goals should be based mainly on the reduction, or, if possible, the elimination of the discrepancies between various sectors of the population, as advocated in the Plan of Action; reduction of malnutrition with the establishment of specific objectives: (a) food education campaigns; (b) improvements in food production to meet current and anticipated needs; (c) supplementary nutritional programmes to meet minimum requirements, especially of infants, pregnant women and nursing mothers.

The direct measures[23] to eliminate social differentials include: the development of preventive medicine; extension of health services to rural areas; community organization programmes to provide education in health, nutrition, and environmental hygiene and to promote community participation therein; nutritional policies, such as enrichment of food of low nutritive value; and programmes for potable water and human waste disposal.[24]

In the ECA Region.[25]   Targets specified in the background paper for the ECA region proposed achievement of an expectation of life of not less that 65 years by 2000, and an infant mortality rate of fewer than 80 per 1,000 live births by 2000 (or at least a gain of 20 years in life expectancy at birth by 2000). These goals were regarded by some participants in the consultation "as rather arbitrary and unrealistic due to a weak data base," but no alternatives were proposed. There was consensus that countries should have as their objective a rapid reduction in morbidity and mortality, and the international community was urged to offer "maximum assistance possible" in this regard.

Measures proposed or implicit included action programmes in the field of health, especially in rural areas; emphasis on preventive rather than curative medicine; need for comprehensive maternal and child health services; reduction of cost of medical services to individuals; raising the levels of nutrition, with emphasis on local foods; transnational co-operative programmes for the control of specific diseases; health measures to control involuntary sterility and sub-fecundity; abortion, though possibly contrary to African ideals and values, was given qualified approval on the grounds of health and where the survival of either mother or child, or both was threatened (in this case, facilitating legislation should be enacted).

In the ECWA Region.[26]   At the consultation for the ECWA region, note was taken of the continued high mortality rates and relatively low expectation of life at birth; and of the persistence of endemic diseases, especially among infants and children, in some parts of the region.

Priority action was suggested to reduce mortality, particularly among infants and children.

The measures suggested included accelerated efforts to promote and extend the services of mother and child health centres; more rapid implementation of health security; development of medical and health centres to eradicate contagious and endemic diseases; comprehensive planning of health services at local level; and use of paramedics.

Reproduction, Family Formation, and the Status of Women

It was observed that responsible parenthood played two distinct roles, appearing:

(a) *As a fundamental human right.* All regions endorsed the principle, but it was not made explicit in the ESCAP region. There was agreement: (i) in seeing its application as a means to ensure the health and welfare of the mother and children or of the family in general; (ii) in favouring the implementation of measures, such as education, information and availability of means to enable couples to exercise the right; (iii) in urging Governments and the international organizations to provide the requisite assistance;

(b) *As an instrument of population policy.* The outstanding position was that of the ESCAP region, where the reduction of fertility and/or of population growth was viewed as a major objective of population policy and family planning as a major means of attaining the objective.

In the other regions, no such emphasis was evident on the reduction of fertility through the exercise of responsible parenthood. The proposals neither excluded nor promoted official action for fertility reduction, and naturally so, because official attitudes differ from country to country. In Europe and in the ECLA consultation, it was stated that the rights of couples in respect of fertility should not be restricted in any way to satisfy an objective of demographic policy.[27]

All regions acknowledged the interrelations between reproduction, family formation and the status and roles of women, the most complex formulation being in Europe, where low fertility levels and manpower shortages in some countries were compensated by international migration of workers and/or by increasing participation of women in the labour force.

Among Countries of the ECE Region. Changes in age structure, in age at marriage and in nuptiality in general had been responsible for short-term fluctuations in crude birth rates in the post-war period, but the dominating feature was seen to be the downward trend in completed family size. Rising educational levels of women and their greater participation in economic activities, together with the new concept of women's role in society, were important; but the motivation of most couples to restrict their number of children to one or two, or at most three, was still inadequately known. The evidence appeared to indicate that economic, social, cultural and psychological factors were more decisive than contraceptive methods in influencing fertility. However, divergent opinions were expressed about the likely effects under modern conditions of shorter term or longer term economic fluctuations upon fertility. It was acknowledged that this relationship was highly complex, depending upon a number of sociological and psychological factors, the effects of which were difficult to foresee.[28]

In the ESCAP Region.[29]   In the ESCAP region, the objective was to promote family welfare as well as to lower fertility.

The recommended measures included: (a) improvement of management of family planning programmes in respect of supply and distribution of contraceptives, especially to rural areas; establishment of family planning clinics in public places; and integration of all available field extension personnel, all suitable private organizations, local committees and service units in industry; (b) direct incentives to keep the family size small; (c) reduction of sterility and sub-fecundity; (d) establishment of legal minimum age at marriage, taking into account economic and social conditions and cultural values.

In this connexion, the ESCAP consultation reaffirmed its pre-Conference recommendation specifying the following goal: "that all countries ensure availability, to all persons who so desire, the necessary information and education about family planning and the means to practice it effectively and in accordance with their cultural values and religious beliefs, if possible by the end of the Second United Nations Development Decade, but not later than 1985".[30] It also reinvited countries with very high birth rates to reduce them by 10 per 1,000 before 1985 and to try to reach replacement levels of fertility in two or three decades or as soon as possible; the goal of developed countries should be to attain replacement levels of fertility by 1985 and near-stationary population growth as soon as practicable.

In the ECLA Region.   The objectives in the ECLA region were protection of the family as the basic unit of society by appropriate legislation and policy; preparation of the social and economic conditions for the exercise of the right to responsible parenthood and to achievement of desired family size, irrespective of demographic goals; and complete integration of women in the development process.[31]

In respect of measures to be implemented, attention was drawn to the possible impact on fertility of the attainment of a fundamental development objective, such as the full-scale incorporation of women in economic, social and political activity; and, consequently, to the juridical measures and the programmes and actions that were conducive to that end.[32]

Stress was also placed on the effect on fertility of higher levels of living, especially improved education. More specifically, attention was drawn to the following forms of action: development of maternal and child health services and family planning services; measures designed to raise fertility levels, such as special marriage and birth grants; specialized medical services which would help to eliminate the causes of sub-fertility and sterility and to reduce general and infant mortality.[33]

Educational programmes should be expanded so as to reduce or eliminate real and functional illiteracy and to ensure that better use was made of the human and natural resources of the countries of the region.

In the ECA Region.[34]   The objectives in the ECA region were to raise and sustain the quality of family life; to safeguard African cultural values and practices in regard to marriage and the roles and status of family members; and to secure that couples attain the size of the family appropriate to the achievement of a high level of living.

The consultation recommended measures to include: (a) family planning services in maternal and child health services; (b) integration of health and nutrition programmes and implementation of such programmes through practical social and economic measures; (c) promotion of the status of women and their participation in educational, social, economic and political activities; (d) greater efforts to secure paid employment of women in both urban and rural areas; (e) action to ensure free choice of couples in marriage; (f) establishment of minimum ages at marriage for men and women for socio-economic and health reasons; (g) definition and guarantee of rights of widows, widowers, divorcees and of their children, as well as of illegitimate children; (h) evolution and strengthening of social development policies; (i) protection of the young and elimination of child labour; and (j) strengthening of ongoing population programmes in some countries of the region.

In the ECWA Region.[35]   In the ECWA region the objectives were to obtain more adequate understanding, through data collection and research, of the interrelations between reproduction and the socio-economic and cultural levels of the family and individuals in order to formulate policies and programmes; to secure the exercise of the right to responsible parenthood; to promote the role and status of women and their full participation in economic and social life.

The measures recommended were: (a) inclusion of family planning services in integrated health programmes; (b) co-operation between countries in the region supported by international organizations, especially to extend family planning services through maternal and child health services; (c) promotion of the education of women, as well as of males; and (d) increase in women's participation in economic activities.

Population Distribution and Internal Migration

Among Countries of the ECE Region. The consultation among the countries of the ECE region did not consider this question as a separate issue, but it did take note of some aspects related to it. For example, in some instances, high (over-all) densities were a factor in moderating any objections Governments might have had to declining fertility and population growth, and higher rural fertility had until recently compensated for lower urban fertility. In the latter instance, there was no certainty that such a compensatory effect would operate in the future.[36]

In the ESCAP Region.[37] In many countries of the ESCAP region, rural-urban migration and maldistribution of population had become urgent national problems. Though people should be able to move freely within national boundaries, the following measures should be considered: (a) relocation of existing industries and location of new industries in rural areas; (b) resettlement of urban squatters; (c) decongestion of primary cities through rural development and the establishment of regional urban growth centres; (d) identification, development and opening up of public lands for resettlement; (e) land reforms to improve life in rural areas; (f) provision of information, incentives, avenues of productive employment and income for people in rural areas which might induce them to remain and to participate in the socio-economic development of those areas; and (g) settlement of nomadic populations.

In the ECLA Region.[38] In the ECLA region, the minimum objective was to influence the scatter of the population, migratory movements, population spread and excessive urban concentration by means of comprehensive agrarian, regional and urban development programmes, in line with the countries' interests and within the context of their overall economic and social development strategies.

In order to attain those general objectives, the following specific objectives were recommended: (a) to promote the grouping of the geographically scattered population through the establishment of communities equipped with the basic services necessary for their over-all development; (b) to adapt population spread to the possibilities and requirements of regional development, on the basis of special human settlement programmes; (c) to take action to establish and further develop groups of small and medium-sized towns in order to bring urban trends into balance and to improve the planning of urban and rural population centres so as to ensure the efficient provision of public services; (d) to reorient migration movements from the countryside to the towns by eliminating their causes and respecting at all times the right of freedom of movement and residence within the territory of each State; (e) to encourage people to remain in their place of origin by means of economic and social incentives conducive to its over-all development; and (f) to harmonize internal migratory movements with the requirements of the regional development of each country.

It was pointed out that some countries of the region had adopted some policies and measures to reduce and orient rural-urban migration, to stimulate the growth of medium-sized cities and to occupy territorial space:

(a) Regional development policies: administrative regionalization and demarcation of economic zones; promotion of development centres; regional industrialization policy; priority development of the services infrastructure in the less developed zones.

(b) Rural development and agrarian reform policies: transformation of land tenure structures; transfer of economic resources to the agricultural sector and promotion of agro-industry; financial and technical support of small-scale and medium-scale industry situated in rural areas; programmes aimed at concentrating the scattered rural population so as to facilitate its access to services and raise its level of living; specialized training programmes for improving the skills of the agricultural labour force.

(c) Land settlement programmes, including the bringing of new land under cultivation.

In the ECA Region.[39]   In the ECA region, the objectives set forth were to promote uniform economic development and to protect the rights of resettled persons and of migrant workers and their families.

The measures specified included: (a) establishment of economic growth centres with adequate facilities for education, sanitation and other social services; and (b) formulation and implementation of rural development programmes with attention to diversified agricultural development, conservation of agricultural resources, land reform and organization of production and marketing, the decentralization of appropriate industries to provide employment opportunities and provision of housing, education and other services designed specifically for rural development needs.

In the ECWA Region.[40] The objectives stated at the consultation for the ECWA region were to narrow the gap between rural and urban areas in all fields in order to offset the negative effects of internal migration, and to collect data and conduct research on the interrelationship between development and geographical distribution of population.

The measures recommended were: (a) to build up, wherever possible, the population in underpopulated areas to provide better work opportunities; (b) to establish and develop smaller and medium-sized towns in the framework of balanced development; and (c) to conduct a comprehensive survey on the economic and demographic characteristics of the bedouin, with a view to improving their conditions and making better use of their capacities.

International Migration

Among Countries of the ECE Region. At the consultation among countries of the ECE region, several participants took note of the important influence of international migration on the attitudes of Governments towards levels and trends of population growth, in that immigration or emigration had tended to compensate for deficits or surpluses within the indigenous labour force. Moreover, as, in some countries, levels of immigration were very low where female participation in the labour force was very high, consideration should be given to the questions of labour productivity, female participation and age at retirement. There appeared to be a quantitative threshold of immigration above which socio-political tensions required intervention; and some doubts were expressed whether the benefits of international migration had not, in fact, been outweighed by their costs.

Several participants pointed to a problem of reconciling economic, social, demographic and humanitarian requirements affecting migrant workers. A number of Governments of countries that had accepted a considerable inflow of migrant workers to supplement their labour force had limited further immigration, with the exception of families joining established immigrants. That measure had been taken either because of the probable social and psychological strain upon the immigrant, or because of the strain upon the host communities if the number of immigrants were to have increased further. In that respect, the recommendations of the World Population Plan of Action affecting protection of migrant workers were supported by the participants, though they recognized that very sensitive adjustments would be involved in seeking an equilibrium among the various factors involved.

In the ESCAP Region.[41]   In the ESCAP region, international migration was not regarded as a very important means of alleviating national population pressures in the region, but the "brain drain" caused serious concern because it hampered development efforts.

The objectives of policy were to stop the "brain drain" and to protect the rights of migrants and the interests of the countries concerned.

The following measures were recommended: (a) to discourage the "brain drain", suitable employment opportunities should be provided in the home countries; (b) international firms operating in developing countries should employ and train more local people and should provide them with suitable amenities, opportunities and facilities in order to retain highly skilled personnel in those countries; (c) the more developed countries should do all within their power, consistent with human rights, to discourage the inflow of highly qualified personnel from less developed countries and to encourage their return; (d) to protect and assist migrant workers and to protect the interests of the countries concerned, there should be a standardization of the skills of these workers.

In the ECLA Region.[42]   The minimum objective in the ECLA region was the reduction of the emigration of professionals and skilled technicians.

The measures relating to international migration in general included: (a) comprehensive planning of education and human resources; (b) investment in scientific and technical programmes; (c) adoption of other measures to adapt the training of professionals and technicians to development needs and to facilitate their incorporation in this process; and (d) establishment of international agreements to protect the interests of the less developed countries affected by the exodus of technicians and professionals.

With regard to migration between neighbouring countries, which had increased in recent years, reference was made to the following measures: (a) administrative action designed to regularize the legal status of immigrants; and (b) action designed to provide access for immigrants to social security systems.

In order to slow or reverse the "brain drain", mention was made of: (a) the drafting of legal provisions to facilitate the return of migrants to their country of origin or the admission of highly skilled aliens by granting importing facilities and installation credits; creation of opportunities for stable employment at adequate levels of remuneration; programmes of advanced training and professional specialization inside the country.

In the ECA Region.[43]   At the consultation in the ECA region, international migration gave rise to intensive discussion: movement across borders was frequent, often because the borders divided homogeneous ethnic groups; and the "brain drain" also was causing serious concern.

The objectives set forth were: (a) to accord first importance to the principle of national sovereignty; (b) to encourage agreements, bilateral or multilateral which would facilitate international movement, including movement of migrant workers where the latter was significant to the national economies involved; to avoid racial considerations; (c) to protect the civil and socio-economic status of migrants in terms of internationally agreed instrument; to facilitate the settlement and rehabilitation of refugees; and (d) to discourage the "brain drain."

Such measures as the following should be adopted: (a) countries concerned with the outflow of migrant workers should promote national employment opportunities and more developed countries should assist through provision of capital, technical assistance, export markets and production technology; (b) countries receiving migrant workers should provide social welfare and other necessary services to protect them and their families; (c) those provisions should be in terms of international instruments for the protection of human rights and the elimination of discriminatory treatment; (d) laws to limit illegal migration should relate also to those inducing or facilitating such migration; (e) international co-operation on various levels should be directed to solution of problems affecting refugees, displaced persons and the outflow of skilled persons; and (f) the Governments of countries in Africa, in order to retain skilled workers and professionals, should undertake programmes to effect a better match between skills and employment opportunities, and foreign investors should employ and train local personnel and use local research facilities where possible.

In the ECWA Region.[44]   The consultation in the ECWA region distinguished intraregional from international migration, the former being considered "a positive phenomenon" as the region was seen as an entity for development purposes—one labour market serving a group of culturally homogeneous states.

The objectives set forth were to relate international migration to over-all development policies, to develop population policies connected with the labour force, to stop the brain drain and to protect the rights of migration workers and their families.

The measures to be adopted were: (a) to proceed with planning of human resources from local to regional level; (b) to facilitate the movement of individuals and technical and scientific skills within the region; (c) to formulate a regional plan for advancing scientific skills within the framework of balanced development; and (d) to draft an integrated plan at the Arab level for surveying Arab skills, studying the brain drain and proposing solutions.

A category of forced migration was considered by the consultation, which appealed for international efforts for its cessation.

Population Structure

Among Countries of the ECE Region.[45]   At the consultation among countries of the ECE region, it was mentioned that if the assumptions in prospect II of the ECE paper (ESA/P/AC.5/2) were fulfilled, spectacular changes in the age distribution would occur. While the consultation considered the projection to be merely illustrative of possibilities, it highlighted the potentially serious economic and social consequences. New socio-economic approaches and provisions affecting the greatly increased proportions of aged persons would be required; the emergence of youth as a social force meant that their interests, too, would require reconsideration.

In the ESCAP Region.[46]   In view of the rapid increase in the already large proportion of young people in the population of most countries of the ESCAP region, the consultation strongly endorsed development strategies affording priority to the needs of children and youth. Emphasis was placed on measures to: (a) expand basic educational facilities and discourage child labour; (b) deal with school drop-outs; (c) prevent juvenile delinquency; and (d) provide more employment opportunities for young persons, including highly educated youth.

In the ECA, ECLA and ECWA Regions.   Measures such as those mentioned above were implicit rather than explicit in the ECA, ECLA and ECWA regions; and the discussions reflected many matters related to the structure of the population by age, sex, urban/rural distribution and industry, with special reference to agricultural and non-agricultural activities.

Socio-economic Policies

All regions reaffirmed the concept of population policy as an integral part of development policy; and it is evident in the preceding sections that in all regions, socio-economic measures of various types were in operation or were proposed as conducive to improved quality of life, irrespective of the demographic impact of the measures. However, as was made clear at the consultation among countries of the ECE region in particular, the demographic impact was not to be ignored even when it could not be foreseen with any degree of reliability. Again, the consultations, recognizing also the interrelations among demographic, economic and social change, were conscious of the impact that demographic change might have on development, which, as in the reverse case, could not be foreseen with any certainty.

The socio-economic measures most emphasized by the developing countries were related to health; food and nutrition programmes, education, employment, information and services related to responsible parenthood; regional planning and rural development. At the same time, those measures supported directly and/or indirectly the attainment of various demographic objectives. The protection of the environment and the practice of economy in the use of natural resources were related issues recognized but not dealt with in any detail. It was only in the ESCAP region that the socio-economic objectives and measures were separately enumerated: a more equitable distribution of opportunity and income; and full employment for both males and females.[47] Appropriate levels of social security might be achieved by the following means: (a) implementation of subnational development measures; (b) use of labour-intensive techniques of production; (c) mobilization of rural manpower through small-scale and medium-scale industries; (d) promotion and strengthening of farmers' associations and rural co-operatives; (e) provision and strengthening of social welfare measures, especially for the poor and the aged; (f) protection of adopted children and rehabilitation of underprivileged children; and (g) provision of day-care centres to enable women to enter the labour force.

In terms of the consensus reached at the World Population Conference and in the light of other international strategies, such as the New International Economic Order, achievement of development aims should be based both on national sovereignty and on international solidarity in an increasingly interdependent world. It was in the ECLA[48] and ECA[49] regions that questions of interdependence were given most intense consideration, and it was there that the need for international economic co-operation to secure justice for all and equality as between developed and developing countries was most keenly felt. A corollary of that view was that national Governments, in formulating policies in the economic and social field, including population policies, should take into account possible repercussions at the international level.

Promotion of Knowledge and Policies

Data Collection and Analysis

Among Countries of the ECE Region.   At the consultation among countries of the ECE region, there were no formal references to the needs for data nor to the methods of collecting them; however, it was clear from the many references to research, dealt with in the next section, that modifications of the data base or in the utilization of existing data were necessary if the research recommendations were to be fulfilled.

In the ESCAP Region.[50]   In the ESCAP region, priority was accorded to: (a) censuses in those countries which had not carried out a first or a recent census; (b) supporting analysis and publication of census data; (c) provision of support to sample surveys; (d) support to continuous study of multipurpose household surveys; (e) support to vital registration projects; (f) improvement of medical data in vital registration; (g) provision and improvement of computer facilities for analysis of demographic data; (h) development of administrative records as data sources; (i) organization of national and subregional seminars and workshops to increase awareness and utilization of population data; (j) provision of appropriate incentives to retain computer-trained personnel in the public sector; (k) participation in the World Fertility Survey; and (l) collection of data on income distribution in relation to family size.

Population data collection and analyses should give particular attention to data essential to development planning and to formulation of population policies.

In the ECLA Region.[51]   The consultation for the ECLA region found that there was a clear need to improve the quantity, quality, coverage, periodicity and timeliness of the requisite data to be furnished systematically and as judged appropriate by Governments, especially as a basis for population policies.

The consultation considered that, to meet that need, efforts should be made: (a) to ensure greater continuity in the work of preparing, taking and publishing censuses; (b) to test new methods for carrying out census operations; (c) to review existing machinery for the formulation of international recommendations in the carrying-out of censuses, account being taken of differing national circumstances and of the need for the data necessary for formulating, implementing and evaluating population policies which would, at the same time, permit comparative intercountry analyses to be made; (d) to establish regular channels, as agreed upon by the Governments, for consultation between producers and users to ensure that the information provided should be suited to the needs of the latter; and (e) to promote the exchange of experiences in that field between countries.

It was recommended that, in addition to continuing their efforts to improve their vital and other current statistics, countries should give particular attention to obtaining such data from population sample surveys.

In the ECA Region.[52]   In the ECA region, the needs for data were regarded as fundamental to deriving indicators of the state of the economy and as basic to formulation, implementation and evaluation of policies and programmes.

The first priority was a population census between 1975 and 1985, taking advantage of the services of the African census programme, and with at least a decennial periodicity in the future.

Governments should develop national capabilities for household surveys of various demographic and other related socio-economic variables of relevance to the improvement of levels of living and the general welfare of the community. The survey programmes, which should be planned on a long-term and regular basis, should also focus on fertility, mortality and migration as important elements of the dynamics of population change.

Countries were urged to establish or improve their vital registration systems as a long-term objective beginning with sample registration areas.

The view was expressed that the scope of data collection should not be limited to data that were essentially demographic in character. It was, for example essential to have data that could facilitate the measurement of the effects of social policies pursued by Governments on the population, especially in the rural areas.

Countries were urged to utilize to the fullest extent existing collaborative arrangements and assistance offered by both national and international donor agencies and organizations.

In the ECWA Region.[53]   The objectives set forth at the consultation for the ECWA region were: (a) to devote special attention to methods of demographic data collection, classification and publication; (b) to pay attention to the organization of civil registration, improve the registration of vital events and enact appropriate laws to facilitate this work; (c) to draw up a regional programme of data collection, including the necessary arrangements for organizing and conducting comprehensive censuses, sample surveys and specialized surveys, and for evaluating and analysing the results, on the basis of standardized concepts, questionnaires and tabulations; (d) to utilize and develop demographic analysis techniques for extracting population indicators and direct special attention to benefiting from defective data and to use direct and indirect methods for that purpose; (e) to conduct periodic censuses, at least once every 10 years, and create a permanent government body in each country to supervise census operations; and (f) to strengthen and support central statistical systems and establish and develop statistical units in various government agencies.

Research

It cannot be doubted that the World Population Plan of Action has had a profound effect on the focus of thinking in the area of research: in every region, the consultation gave emphasis to the priority attached to research as a basis for formulation, implementation and evaluation of policies affecting demographic behaviour, whether direct or indirect in their operation, and research on the integration of population programmes in development planning. It is worth noting that the countries of the ECE region, relatively advanced as they are in the demographic transition and in their levels of development, were explicit in their concern for greater knowledge of multiple relations as well as of the interaction of particular demographic and socio-economic factors as a basis for action, particularly in view of possible reversals of or fluctuations in trends. Indeed, in every region, recognition of the reciprocal effects of population and socio-economic variables underlay the emphasis on investigation of interrelationships between factors.

All regions supported the principle of promotion of national research activities and the sharing of research findings; strong support was also given to research at the regional level. Further, as concerns Europe, an expanding role for the Economic Commission for Europe was recommended in the resolution adopted by the consultation. In the case of ECLA, proposals for research by ECLA and CELADE on the demographic areas discussed in the World Population Plan of Action included also a number of specific suggestions for studies and research related to the integration of population policies into regional development strategies and policies.[54]

It may be mentioned in this connexion that the recommendations for implementation of the World Population Plan of Action regarding monitoring of population trends and policies and review and appraisal of the Plan[55] require more extensive research into the demographic variables and into national policy formulation and implementation.

Among Countries of the ECE Region. Several major research themes pervaded the discussions in the consultation among countries of the ECE region: (a) the interrelations between the various factors determining the trend towards declining fertility, and the possibilities of changing patterns of family building and of oscillations in fertility levels; (b) the elucidation of differentials in morbidity and mortality within countries with regard to sex, socio-economic and ethnic groups, regions, urban and rural areas and environmental factors; and (c) the relationships between availability of manpower, rates of population growth, benefits and costs of permitting a compensatory immigration, potential compensation of greater participation of women in the labour force, and the demographic, social and economic implications of a dual role for women, as mothers and workers. Continuing research was recommended on the interrelations between population, the environment and natural resources, and between population and international migration.

In the ECLA Region.[56] At the consultation for the ECLA region, in considering research requirements for the formulation and evaluation of population policies, recommendations were made for the conduct of:

(a) Biomedical research to develop means of improving health conditions, and especially of reducing maternal mortality, peri-natal mortality and mortality among children aged 0–4 years; to evaluate existing contraceptive methods and to develop better methods and to improve procedures for the diagnostics and treatment of sterility; supported by operational research to evaluate the efficiency of various ways and means of providing health services for the population, especially in respect of maternal and child health;

(b) Social research in which priority should be given to research directed to establishing the interrelationships between population and development in specific historical contexts, particularly where that would make it possible to identify the effects produced and to anticipate probable future effects of different modes or patterns of development on population dynamics. Research relevant to the formulation and evaluation of population policies in the relatively less developed countries should be encouraged.

In the ESCAP Region.[57]   In the ESCAP region, priority was given to research into the implementation and evaluation of family planning programmes and the interrelationships between population and socio-economic variables. Specific areas to be investigated were: (a) factors inhibiting acceptance of family planning; (b) interrelations between fertility and development; (c) social and psychological determinants of family size; (d) feasibility of incentive schemes to encourage reduction in family size; (e) studies on unwed mothers and illegitimate children; (f) development of methods for population model-building; (g) determinants and consequences of internal migration; (h) reliability and safety of alternative contraceptives; (i) various aspects of mortality; (j) alternatives to basic food staples; (k) social consequences of contraceptive practice; (l) methods for integrating population inputs and goals in development plans and programmes; (m) review and analysis of laws that bear on population factors; and (n) methods of fertility regulation and of correcting sterility.

In the ECA Region.[58]   The consultation for the ECA region stated that research in the field of population should be intensified if population policies, as an integral part of development policies, were to have the desired impact on the development process in the continent. Among the areas requiring special attention were: (a) patterns, trends and differentials in morbidity, mortality, fertility, population distribution and migration; (b) attitudes towards family size, family planning and factors affecting its operation of success; (c) interrelationships between population variables and socio-economic development; and (d) population policies and factors influencing their formulation and implementation. Traditional medicine was an additional area proposed, and the consultation expressed the view that research should, in so far as possible, be oriented to African development problems, with special emphasis on rural development.

In the ECWA Region.[59]   The deficiency in the field of collection and analysis of demographic data in the ECWA region had limited the fields of research undertaken. Despite some of the initiatives in that domain, research work had not yet dealt with many problems except casually, for example, the relationship between demographic variables and other socio-economic variables, or the determinants of fertility or mortality levels, or research on the Arab brain drain and other matters. It was therefore recommended that research should be undertaken on the levels and trends of demographic variables and their interaction from the standpoint of their effect on the level and nature of economic development and the effect of development on them; and on integration of population policies in economic and social development strategies.

Management, Training, Education and Information

Management. The need for strengthening the infrastructure for management of population programmes was the subject of direct reference only at the ESCAP consultation, where note was taken of the need for specialized training of family planning administrators. However, the importance of management was implicit in the many references to implementation of policy decisions and especially in the functions attributed to the high-level national units to formulate and administer population policies proposed by the ECLA consultation.[60]

Training. Except in the consultation among countries of the ECE region, training was specified as an essential need, intensified by the losses of qualified personnel to other countries. Recommendations from the four developing regions covered or implied recognition of basic requirements for trained personnel for interdisciplinary, policy-oriented approaches to development planning:

(a) For design and conduct of field operations for the collection of demographic and other data;

(b) For development of other activities related to data collection and compilation;

(c) For publication, evaluation and analysis of data;

(d) For population projections and the study of their socio-economic implications;

(e) For research on the factors affecting demographic levels and trends and the interrelations among factors;

(f) For methodological studies on integration of population policies in development;

(g) For design, conduct, management and evaluation of population programmes designed directly to influence population variables such as the family planning programmes in the ESCAP region, or the programmes to reduce morbidity or mortality from specific causes (in Africa and elsewhere); and also for personnel involved in socio-economic programmes affecting population indirectly. The latter are too numerous to count, but health, food and nutrition, education, employment and rural development programmes were strongly emphasized.

It was considered, particularly in Africa, that the aim should be to provide training at the national level; indeed, the consultation for the ECA region recommended that each country, where the need existed, should train one demographer per year for the subsequent five years so that their own nationals could take an active part in the 1980 round of national censuses. The work of the United Nations-sponsored training centres in the regions and of various other training facilities was helping substantially to fill the gap in country requirements, but extra facilities were needed in some fields.

Levels of training was another issue. For example, in the ESCAP region, the consultation saw the need for continuing efforts to provide advanced population training abroad, and the ECLA consultation recommended that the regional agencies should intensify their action to meet, *inter alia,* the shortage of high-level planners and senior-level professionals. However, the consultations did not examine systematically the whole range of levels of skills needed, Africa, in particular, being understandably concerned with acute shortages mainly, but by no means exclusively, at the middle level.

Education and Information.   Education in matters of population was recommended as a component of formal curricula and as part of out-of-school instruction. Some reservations were expressed about the scope of sex education as such, but there was agreement, in principle, on the need for instruction in family life, health, nutrition and environmental hygiene.

In schools and universities, there should be instruction also in the role of population in development, and training programmes should be provided for those working in social and health services.

Those measures should be supplemented by information activities to cover the entire population by ways and means suited to local circumstances and cultural values. The mass media were of obvious utility, but recourse would be needed also to folk media and person-to-person communication. The objectives of those information programmes were to create awareness of matters related to population, and, in the context of endorsement of the fundamental right to responsible parenthood, to provide the information necessary to the exercise of that right. The contribution of the non-governmental organizations was considered especially helpful in that area of activity.

There were already active communications systems at the regional levels in Africa, Asia and Latin America which ensured a circulation of technical and other information to and from countries.

Development and Evaluation of Population Policies

As previously mentioned, all five regions supported the integration of population policies in development within the framework of the

World Population Plan of Action and implicitly or explicitly endorsed the allocation of responsibility to a defined entity of the Government. The ECLA consultation firmly endorsed the idea of a high-level unit of the Government with a functional relationship to policy-making bodies and with responsibilities covering formulation, implementation, evaluation and co-ordination of population activities.

INTERNATIONAL ACTION TO IMPLEMENT THE WORLD POPULATION PLAN OF ACTION

Lessons Learned from the Consultations

It may be asked how one can assess the results of the consultations from the viewpoint of guidance given to the United Nations and UNFPA on the types and levels of substantive, human and financial support required to help countries implement the World Population Plan of Action, and on the order of national priorities. The answer is that, although the consultations did not yield information on which to estimate with any precision levels of and priorities for support needed by countries, they did yield extensive information on the types of support needed.

In retrospect, one can perceive the difficulties confronting Governments in the context of policy formulation and implementation responsive to the World Population Plan of Action: decisions on the nature and scope of population policies are dependent upon decisions about the nature of over-all national development policy and also upon consideration of the technique of integrating population policy into development planning, so that population policies along with other sectoral strategies[61] may make their contribution to development.

The difficulty is the more acute in that approaches to development are themselves the subject of major national concern and international consultation, and the problems to be solved are both conceptual and technical. It is, therefore, worthy of note that in the consultation among the countries of the ECE region, despite the relatively advanced levels of development obtaining there, the integration of population policies in national social and economic planning was considered one of the most important conclusions drawn from the recommendations of the World Population Plan of Action, and the form of integration would "obviously vary according to the institutional structure associated with national planning in each country."[62] A further observation was that, irrespective of the formality or otherwise of the arrangements for integration, important decisions had continuously to be made with regard to changes in factors and to their feedback effects on other factors.[63] The recommendations of the ECLA consultation also revealed recognition of these problems,[64] as did the reports of the other regional consultations, though to a lesser extent.

A significant result of the consultations is the clear emergence of a theme that has some regional variations, but is essentially common to both developed and developing countries:

(a) Population policies and programmes are an integral part of national development planning;

(b) Although development factors influence demographic behavior, the latter also affects the former;

(c) The interrelations between population and development factors are imperfectly understood, and, consequently, the effects of indirect action in the field of population (through socio-economic measures) and of direct action (through programmes directed towards affecting specific population variables) cannot be foreseen with any precision;

(d) Research on the interrelationships must be undertaken or intensified to ensure that Governments shall have a better base for: (i) formulating policies, implementing them, evaluating them; (ii) for integrating them in planning for development.

International co-operation is needed to supplement the resources of countries in need, and assistance should be provided in areas supportive to population policy and to its integration in the development context. These areas include data collection, research, management, training, education and information, each of which requires recognition of the interdisciplinary nature of the broader concept of population policy endorsed in the World Population Plan of Action.

Population Activities in the United Nations System

The regional consultations were not an isolated series of meetings but one of a number of developments since the World Population Conference at Bucharest, directed towards implementation of the Plan of Action. In particular, the work programmes of the Department of Economic and Social Affairs, of the regional commissions and of the United Nations agencies include many of the elements recommended by the consultations, seen from the point of view of global or regional or sectoral activities intended to serve the needs of Member States. Complementarity of the work programmes is ensured through the Administrative Committee on Co-ordination Sub-Committee on Population and at the working level by established channels of consultation. Revisions in the programme of the Department of Economic and Social Affairs, effected in response to General Assembly resolution 3344 (XXIX) of 17 December 1974, give further emphasis and extension to such areas as population and development and population policies, especially in respect of intercountry comparative studies, and, in this connexion, provide for intensified research on the interrelationships among the factors affecting demographic behaviour.

A case in point is the monitoring of population trends and policies.[65] It is, of course, essential that national Governments themselves evaluate their population policies and programmes, and the global exercise in monitoring is by no means a substitute for this; rather, it is an extended example of intercountry comparisons in respect of demographic behaviour and of formulation and implementation of national population policies.

In accordance with resolutions and decisions of the Economic and Social Council at its fifty-eighth session, arrangements are in hand for the first round of monitoring. As agreed at the eleventh session of the Administrative Committee on Co-ordination Sub-Committee on Population, the regional commissions and agencies have received requests for inputs to the monitoring of population trends specific to their areas of competence. Also according to the agreement in the Sub-Committee, a questionnaire on national population policies drafted in the United Nations Population Division has been sent to the regional commissions and the agencies for comment; after revision, the questionnaire was sent to Governments in late 1975. A report on monitoring, covering both population trends and population policies, will be submitted to the Economic and Social Council, through the Population Commission, in spring 1977. There is every reason to believe that the results will greatly clarify problems at the country, regional and global levels in formulating and implementing population policies.

In accordance with the provision of Economic and Social Council decision 87 (LVIII) of 6 May 1975, that the Population Commission contribute advice on review and appraisal of the Plan of Action and report its findings to the Council, preparatory work is being undertaken with consideration being given, *inter alia,* to the relation between the biennial monitoring of population trends and policies and the quinquennial review and appraisal of the Plan of Action.

Assistance in the Population Field

This article is not intended to deal with population assistance as such, a review of which is available elsewhere, but merely to refer to some points which follow from the regional consultations:

(a) Where feasible, developing countries should endeavour to assist one another and developed countries should assist the developing countries to the extent possible;

(b) Multilateral and bilateral channelling of assistance should be increased, as should assistance form non-governmental organizations; the consultations endorsed the efforts of UNFPA in increasing the assistance available to Governments;

(c) The United Nations, its regional commissions and the specialized agencies and other bodies should assist to the maximum extent possible in their fields of competence.

Whether in terms of substantive support, or support relating to human and financial resources, there is little doubt that considerable effort will be needed for some years to come to provide the total level of assistance required by countries to achieve the objectives of the World Population Plan of Action. The framework that emerged from the regional consultations should prove useful as a guide to the international community.

NOTES

1. Owing to the nature of the mandate of the Economic Commission for Europe in the field of population, the consultation among countries of that region was convened by the United Nations in co-operation with the Executive Secretary of ECE.

2. See "Reports of the regional consultations preparatory to the Conference" (E/-CONF.60/CPB/34).

3. *Report of the United Nations World Population Conference, 1974,* Bucharest, 19–30 August 1974 (United Nations publication, Sales No. E.75.XIII.3), chap. I, para. 107.

4. The reports of the consultations are as follows: for the Economic and Social Commission for Asia and the Pacific, E/CN.11/1208; for the Economic Commission for Latin America, ST/ECLA/CONF.54/L.9/Rev.1; for the Economic Commission for Africa, E/CN.14/POP/136; for the Economic Commission for Western Asia, E/ECWA/POP/-CONF.2/11; for the Economic Commission for Europe, ESA/P/AC.5/5 and Corr.1.

5. This consultation, like the pre-Conference consultation, was convened by the United Nations, in co-operation with the Executive Secretary of the Economic Commission for Europe.

6. ESA/P/AC.5/5 and Corr. 1, para. 45.

7. E/CN.11/1208, paras. 20, 23 and 24.

8. *Report of the United Nations World Population Conference, 1974,* chap. I, para. 16.

9. ST/ECLA/CONF.54/L.9/Rev.1, paras. 153–56.

10. Ibid., para. 157.

11. Ibid., para. 160.

12. E/CN.14/POP/135, paras. 9–12 and E/CN.14/POP/136, paras. 27–29.

13. E/CN.14/POP/135, para. 10.

14. E/ECWA/POP/CONF.2/11, paras. 16 and 18.

15. Ibid., para. 16.

16. Though it would appear more suitable to treat abortion as an aspect of reproductive behaviour, it is included here to correspond with the placement in the World Population Plan of Action, para. 24(b), which fits better the positions of the developing than the developed countries.

17. See Dirk J. van de Kaa, "Population policies in Europe and North America" (ESA/P/AC.5/4), paras. 60–62.

18. E/CN.11/1208, paras. 25–26.

19. *Report of the United Nations World Population Conference, 1974,* chap. I, para. 23.

20. Ibid., chap. I, para. 14(e).

21. ST/ECLA/CONF.54/L.9/Rev.1, paras. 124–125.

22. Ibid., para. 151.

23. Ibid., para. 162.

24. See also reference to sub-fertility and sterility in the section below on "Reproduction, family formation and the status of women."

25. E/CN.14/POP/135, paras. 17–23; and E/CN.14/POP/136, paras. 33–40.

26. E/ECWA/POP/CONF.2/11, para. 17.

27. ESA/P/AC.5/5 and Corr.1, para. 52; and ST/ECLA/CONF.54/L.9/Rev.1, para. 127.

28. ESA/P/AC.5/5 and Corr.1, para. 56. See also the reference to abortion in the preceding section on "Morbidity and Mortality."

29. E/CN.11/1208, paras. 20 and 27–35.

30. Ibid., para. 27.

31. ST/ECLA/CONF.54/L.9/Rev.1, para. 126.

32. Ibid., para. 163.

33. Ibid., para. 164.

34. E/CN.14/POP/135, paras. 24–31; and E/CN.14/POP/136, paras. 41–54.

35. E/ECWA/POP/CONF.2/11, paras. 18 and 19.

36. ESA/P/AC.5/5 and Corr.1, para. 55.

37. E/CN.11/1208, para. 36.

38. ST/ECLA/CONF.54/L.9/Rev.1, para. 151, subparas. 5–6 and para. 61.

39. E/CN.14/POP/135, paras. 32–36, and E/CN.14/POP/136, paras. 55–61.

40. E/ECWA/POP/CONF.2/11, para. 20.

41. E/CN.11/1208, paras. 37–38.

42. ST/ECLA/CONF.54/L.9/Rev.1, para. 151, subparas. 7–8 and paras. 165–166.

43. E/CN.14/POP/135, paras. 32–36, and E/CN.14/POP/136, paras. 62–66.

44. E/ECWA/POP/CONF.2/11, paras. 21–22.

45. ESA/P/AC.5/5 and Corr.1, paras. 36–40.

46. E/CN.11/1208, para. 39.

47. E/CN.11/1208, para. 40.

48. ST/ECLA/CONF.54/L.9/Rev.1, paras. 120–123.

49. E/CN.14/POP/136, paras. 25–28.

50. E/CN.11/1208, paras. 41–42.

51. ST/ECLA/CONF.54/L.9/Rev.1, paras. 136–138.

52. E/CN.14/POP/135, paras. 49–55, and E/CN.14/POP/136, paras. 67–70.

53. E/ECWA/POP/CONF.2/11, para. 23, subparas. 1–8.

54. ST/ECLA/CONF.54/L.9/Rev.1, para. 167.

55. *Report of the United Nations World Population Conference, 1974,* chap. I, paras. 107–108.

56. ST/ECLA/CONF.54/L.9/Rev.1, para. 139.

57. E/CN.11/1208, para. 43.

58. E/CN.14/POP/135, paras. 56–59, and E/CN.14/POP/136, paras. 72–77.

59. E/ECWA/POP/CONF.2/11, para. 24.

60. ST/ECLA/CONF.54/L.9/Rev.1, para. 134 and subparas. 1–6.

61. *Report of the United Nations World Population Conference, 1974,* chap. I, para. 1.

62. ESA/P/AC.5/5 and Corr.1, para. 66.

63. Ibid., para. 73.

64. ST/ECLA/CONF.54/L.9/Rev.1, paras. 167–169.

65. *Report of the United Nations World Population Conference, 1974,* chap. I, "World Population Plan of Action," para. 107.

4 CONCISE REPORT ON MONITORING OF POPULATION TRENDS

PREVIEW OF HIGHLIGHTS

World and regional population trends during 1950–1975 have been marked by extraordinary dynamism and momentous breaks with the past. Global growth rates, which for much of the period have hovered about a 2 per cent mark, give few clear signs of abating from levels extending far beyond those of any earlier era. Imbedded within the recent global rates have been enormous regional disparities, almost surely no less unique in history.

In the more developed regions (used here synonymously with "industrialized," "high-income," "low-fertility" or "low-mortality" regions), as in many of their national parts, rates of natural increase have slowed to a point where near-equality of births and deaths could soon be in sight if recent downtrends continue only a little longer. The current tendency towards near stagnation of natural increase in these regions differs from all previous ones. It has occurred despite the near elimination of mortality as a factor affecting replacement, since mortality under age 50 is already so low that even its full disappearance would have slight influence on either actual growth or long-run potentials for increase. National fertility levels, the current dominant cause by far of growth potentials among industrialized populations, are typically close to or at the lowest magnitudes ever reached in history, except possibly in periods of acute depression or war. Unless the recent fertility downtrends reverse themselves or at least cease, today's high-income regions of the world could be facing a negative balance between

82

births and deaths, if not outright population decline after net migration, not long after the end of this century.

These patterns and prospects are in remarkable contrast with the situation in the less developed (also "newly developing," "low-income," "high-fertility," or "high-mortality") regions, probably to a greater extent than at any period in at least several centuries. Growth in these regions as a whole appears to have averaged well above 2 per cent annually over the last quarter century and is today not far below 2.5 per cent. Both rates go well beyond the highest ever estimated before 1950 for any sizable combination of national populations within or between major regional areas.

Although a mounting number of developing nations, including some of the largest ones, give recent signs of decelerating growth, the reliability of the available indications is often subject to question, while other such populations may well be accelerating. As yet, therefore, one can be much more confident that the growth rate of the developing regions in aggregate is at an unprecedented order of magnitude than about either its precise amount or the possibility that it has started to turn downward. There is reason to believe that fertility has not fallen far below traditional levels on average among such regions, but also that it has begun to decline from centuries-old patterns in a no longer small number of individual nations.

If the facts were known, the present over-all difference of more than 1.5 percentage points between the less and more developed regions might well be found to exceed the largest disparities at any period in human history among comparably large geographic groupings of populations. Similarly, current levels of fertility in the less developed regions appear to be some 2.5 times higher over-all than those in the developed regions. If this ratio is approximately accurate, it would almost surely be an historic peak compared to earlier international ranges of fertility behaviour.

As striking as these comparative patterns themselves, has been the speed with which they have emerged. In the case of fertility, the essential dynamic elements recently have been precipitous declines in large parts of the industrialized regions within a period of a few years, often following sharp increases after the Second World War. In the case of growth rates, the prime mover has been mortality in the less developed regions. Dozens of low-income, high-mortality countries with reliable data have experienced rates of mortality declines without precedent anywhere in the modern era. For dozens more, highly pronounced downtrends can be inferred from indirect but persuasive indications. As a result of this "mortality revolution," most of the populations of Latin America and Asia, along with a possibly not small part of Africa, have suddenly moved well within the twentieth century range of mortality levels in the industrialized regions, after traditionally lagging behind the latter by a century or more. Probably in no other realm of major socio-economic importance has there been so massive and ramified a convergence between richer and poorer nations as in the case of life expectancy.

A second, only relatively less dramatic, process of converging longevity has taken place within the more developed regions. As a result of a strongly inverse relation between life expectancy about 1950 and subsequent amounts of change to 1975, practically all nations in these regions have life expectancies today which are close to or above 70 years. The convergence itself, which continues, and the associated fact that the nations with highest longevity have registered only minimal gains over the past decade, suggest an important interpretive conclusion: for the first time in the modern era, a technological ceiling on length of life is being approached throughout today's developed regions. Intraregional differences in social system, economic structure and levels of living in these regions are likely to have only secondary influence on future longevity gains unless or until major medical breakthroughs take place against the diseases of old age. In the case of males, some tendencies towards rising adult mortality in a number of low-mortality countries could conceivably lead to a decline in longevity if sustained. Whether or not this tendency proves transitory, it constitutes the first potential threat to long-run downtrends within low-mortality populations in a century or longer.

Until recently, declining mortality rates in the infant, childhood and young adult years have been the overwhelmingly important determinants of gains in expectation of life at birth for either sex. This has been true of all regions, both more and less developed. Today, for the first time in history, a major portion of the world's population has reached a stage at which further large uptrends in longevity would have to depend predominantly on mortality in the advanced years of life. Indeed, so far has the convergence of mortality at the younger ages progressed within the more developed regions that male-female differences of life expectancy within nations have typically come to be far higher than the differences between nations for either sex.

Innovative patterns of change, of kinds and magnitudes often not known in the modern era, have also been characteristic of international migration movements over the 1950–1975 period. Three major shift points in this respect have been the changing direction of the main movements within Europe, the sudden turn-around of that continent from being a net sender to being an apparently net receiver relative to other continents, and the sharp recent acceleration of the numbers migrating from the less developed to the more developed regions.

Recent decades have witnessed unprecedented change and drastic transitions in the scale and growth of world urbanization. Although urban aggregates are often amalgams of geographical, administrative and demographic criteria, applied in variable fashion over time and space, some major orders of magnitude seem clearly enough indicated. In broad terms, the global urban population more than doubled between 1950 and 1975, implying a greater increase than in all previous history. Although meaningful historical series of urban trends by region are lacking, it is obvious that the current 4 per cent annual rate of urban increase in the less developed regions could not have been long sustained in the past, if indeed it has ever been reached before. About 1975, a new world demographic milestone was reached when the urban size of the less developed regions became equal to that of the more developed regions. It seems safe to say that, measured by population aggregates, urbanization in today's agrarian regions is likely not to be exceeded again for centuries, if ever, by urban size in the world's currently most industrialized areas. Yet as recently as 1950, urban population of the developed regions outnumbered the urban number in less developed areas by something like a two-to-one margin.

The contrasts between population trends in the rural parts of the more and less developed regions have been no less outstanding, though differently structured, than in their urban areas. Starting about mid-century, the developed regions as a group began to lose rural population and the rate of decline has apparently been mounting ever since. This cross-over from rising to falling non-urban numbers has been the result of a massive process of social evolution, one which first became important among a few of the earliest developing nations in the nineteenth century and has since extended to every industrialized population today. In the less developed regions, on the other hand, despite high rates of out-migration to urban areas, rural population has continued to grow at elevated rates. As a result, the ratio of rural numbers in the less to the more developed regions has accelerated in probably unparalleled fashion, from over three-to-one in 1950 to a six-to-one margin in 1975.

The uniquely expanded dimensions of global population change during the postwar decades have had necessarily novel impacts in social and economic spheres. This can be seen directly with respect to labour force educational trends, labour-force dependency patterns and food supply, the areas to be singled out for special attention in this report.

SIZE AND GROWTH

Some Key Parameters of Global and Regional Change

World population rose to 4 billion as the third quarter of the century came to a close. The 60 per cent increase represented by this size over the 1950 level of about 2.5 billion was equivalent to an average annual growth rate of nearly 2 per cent, was well over double the rate during the first half of this century and three to four times the 1800–1900 rate, and almost certainly ranks as the sharpest longer-run uptrend by far in world history. Currently, one billion persons are being added within 15 years and the doubling time of population is well under 40 years. If current growth conditions were continued until not much beyond the end of this century, the time needed for additions of one billion would be halved; it would average no more than a decade in length over the next 40-year period as a whole.

Both size and growth of world population have been concentrated in recent decades in regions with relatively elevated vital rates. Such regions consist essentially of the less developed nations, including as defined here all of Africa, Asia less Japan, Latin America less a temperate zone consisting of Argentina, Chile and Uruguay, and Melanesia, Micronesia and Polynesia in Oceania. In combination, these areas account for about 2.8 billion persons or 70 per cent of the world's current total, and for roughly 1.2 billion or 80 per cent of the rise in global numbers since 1950.

Because of major gaps in data, involving a possibly 5 to 10 per cent margin of error in estimated population size, the growth characteristics of the less developed regions are best described by orders of magnitude rather than by seemingly precise measures. In broad terms, it appears that their 1950–1975 annual rates of increase have been substantially above 2.0 per cent, their annual rise in numbers currently approximates 2.5 per cent or 65 to 70 million, and their doubling time is about 30 years. Whether their aggregate growth rate has started to recede in recent years cannot be ascertained, owing to indirect and often conflicting indications on this score, but some deceleration of trend seems more probable than does an acceleration. The next decade or two should be crucial for resolving this question, which is perhaps the most central uncertainty of all concerning world population prospects.

The remaining or "more developed" regions, comprising all of Europe, the Union of Soviet Socialist Republics, Northern America (Canada and the United States of America), Japan, the above-cited temperate zone of South America, and the large countries of Oceania

(Australia and New Zealand), provide essentially correct and complete data on their main population facts. Hence it can be accurately reported that the aggregate population of these regions rose from about 850 million to 1.125 billion between 1950 and 1975, amounting to about 20 per cent of the estimated increase globally. The much slower growth rates in these regions compared to the less developed areas averaged about 1.1 per cent annually for the entire 1950–1975 period and were falling during its second half. As a result, their share of world population declined from above 34 per cent to below 30 per cent, an enormous change of relative position for so short a time span.

It is a measure of the demographic times today that an annual growth rate of 1 per cent, now relatively low by global and interregional standards, would match the rate prevailing in today's developed regions during the half century of their maximum expansion, or 1850 to 1900, and is well above any earlier half-century global rate on record.

Sources of Change

The prime element in the 1850–1900 expansion of the more developed regions had been declining death-rates. Since then, changing birth-rates have become the dominating determinants of population growth rates in these areas, and such dominance has been steadily increasing. Thus, their accelerated growth shortly after the Second World War was almost wholly the result of a rise in birth-rates, the first upswing of consequence after at least a century of predominantly downward trends. Similarly, their decelerating growth rates between the early 1950s and 1970s have been essentially attributable to a resumption of fertility downtrends. Today, fertility in the more developed regions as a whole, as well as in many of their national parts, has reached its lowest point of the modern era and probably of all history. In round terms, the deceleration in their average growth rate by nearly 0.5 percentage points or one third over this 20-year period was the net product of a growth-enhancing decline of the death-rate by 0.1 points and a growth-depressing decline of the birth-rate by 0.6 points (with net migration making a relatively minor contribution).

Since the social forces making for continued low, if not even lower, levels of fertility in the more developed regions appear likely to persist, a downward-drifting tendency to a 0.5 per cent annual growth rate over the last 25 years of this century seems more probable than a return to the 1.0-plus level of the quarter century just ended. This tendency is likely to be reinforced by slowing mortality decline and older age composition, which in combination have begun to raise crude death-rates in a number of countries since the 1960s and may well continue to do so in the decades ahead.

In the less developed regions, as might be expected from their contrasting demographic and social situation, the relative influence of changing birth- and death-rates on recent growth rates have been the opposite of the ones just discussed. Their great acceleration of numbers over the 25-year period just ended has clearly been the result of declining death-rates in the main. Birth-rates, so far as can be judged from uncomfortably uncertain bases for judgement, have more probably moved downward than upward over the period as a whole, but in any event by much smaller amounts than was true of the shift in death-rates.

As to the future, there are gathering indications, both statistical and circumstantial, that recent tendencies towards declining fertility in a number of high-fertility areas will persist and may well extend to other such areas. In addition, it seems unlikely that the pace of the 1950–1975 downtrends in death-rates can be sustained, even with allowance for latecomers to the post-war mortality transformations among low-income countries. The net implication of these assessments, one too surrounded by risks of error to be more than highly contingent, is that the less developed regions as a whole face a period of decelerating growth. At least, this seems more likely than accelerated or unchanging rates of increase. Should birth-rates become the primary determinant of growth in these regions, compared to death-rates, the changing vital balance would become analogous in this respect to an historical sequence which was first observed in the more developed regions about three quarters of a century earlier and has endured there ever since.

Variations within Broad Regions

Since both the less and more developed regions consist of very large groupings of populations, their demographic similarities and differences internally have significance no less than do their tendencies in the aggregate. Here again, for purposes of both description and interpretation, the contrasts between the two sets of regions provide an excellent basis for general conclusions.

In the more developed regions, population trends of the past 25 years have led to rapid and massive convergence of growth rates, fertility and mortality. As of about 1950, annual growth rates in Northern America and the USSR were more than double that of Europe, while within the latter continent its eastern, southern and western regions all had rates over twice those obtaining among its northern populations. By the early 1970s, in contrast, the corresponding differences between growth rates had narrowed drastically, to about half their earlier magnitudes. In effect, all of these regions experienced decelerating trends but in degrees generally inverse to initial levels. Although the Oceanic populations of Australia and New Zealand continued to occupy an "outlier" position throughout the period compared to other parts of the more developed areas, with comparatively high growth rates owing to high net immigration, these too saw their rates of change fall by an appreciable margin. Japan, despite some temporary current perturbations which represent "echo effects" of changing vital rates during the early post-war period, has occupied a relatively centrist position with respect to pace of increase during most of the last quarter century and is likely to continue to do so in the foreseeable future.

Fertility and mortality differentials among the more developed regions also declined by substantial margins. Declining variability of birth-rates contributed directly to the compression of growth rates just cited, as birth-rates in the four regions of Europe, the USSR, Japan and Northern America evolved from a range of 16 to 25 per 1,000 in 1950–1955 to one of only 15 to 19 per 1,000 in 1970–1975. Although the inclusion of Temperate South America and Oceania, where the rates were initially high and declined only moderately, would enlarge the high-low range among all regions, weighting the regional measures by population size would again lead to a two thirds decline in the range, such as was found for Europe, the USSR, Japan and Northern America alone. Along with birth-rates, gross reproduction rates showed analogous patterns of convergence; while these are theoretically more reliable indicators of fertility proper than are birth-rates, the two measures tend to move in a broadly similar manner. In the case of mortality, the convergence of regional experiences was even more marked. Differentials in expectation of life at birth fell by well over half between the early 1950s and 1970s, from a range of about seven person-years around an average of 65 years for the developed regions as a whole to one of less than three years centering about 72. Although the variability of crude death-rates rose somewhat, this was a result of the increasing tendency of these measures to distort comparisons among low-mortality populations. Specifically, the range of regional death-rates moved from the narrow interval of 9 to 11 per 1,000 in 1950–1955 to one extending between 7 and 11 per 1,000 in 1970–1975. Much of this widening is explained by the especially low values currently found in Japan, the USSR and Australia plus New Zealand in Oceania.

In contrast to these strongly converging tendencies of vital patterns among the industrialized populations, divergence appears to have been the norm within the less developed regions. While regional growth rates apparently rose everywhere, their range also increased somewhat beyond the approximately 1.5 to 3.0 per cent interval of annual rates encountered in the early 1950s. A rising, rather than declining, range of growth rates is likely to endure for several decades, since high-low differences between these regions appear resistant to decline, at least foreseeably. Thus, the highest rates throughout the past quarter century have been those of Middle America and Tropical South America, while the pace of growth in Africa, which has been increasing since about 1950, is not likely to abate for some time to come. On the low side have been China throughout the post-war period and Other East Asia (defined as East Asia less Japan and China), the last after very large but temporary perturbations around the Korean War period.

Further, a rising spread among fertility levels in the less developed regions is suggested by the juxtaposition of a seeming—or at least so far undiscoverable—absence of large changes in Africa and major parts of South Asia, on the one hand, and the apparently substantial declines that have been taking place in practically all of East Asia as well as in parts of the Caribbean and other Latin American regions, on the other hand. To rough orders of magnitude, gross reproduction rates currently range from about 2.0 among most East Asian populations to approximately 3.0 in all regions of Africa and South Asia, and in Middle America and Melanesia, with the Carribbean, Tropical South American and Micronesian-Polynesian populations at intermediate levels.

A number of individual nations have pierced the 2.0 level in the last decade or so, while probably many more have remained or gone beyond the 3.0 level. Foreseeably, a 1.5 level of gross reproduction rates will be a more indicative separation point between national populations in the less and more developed regions than will the 2.0 level which has prevailed during most of the post-war period.

Mortality in the low-income continents is more difficult to judge with respect to past and prospective variability, since highly dynamic trends have been operative in all of these regions. It is not unreasonable to suppose, however, that many nations in which expectation of life at birth is today beyond 60 years, as in much of Latin America, East Asia and Micronesia-Polynesia, are much further from the populations at the 40-to-45 year levels estimated for Eastern, Middle and Western Africa than was true a quarter century ago. The remaining regions in the less developed areas, or Northern and Southern Africa, Melanesia and Eastern, Middle and Western South Asia, are all estimated to be at approximately 50-to-55 year levels, or roughly midway between the extremes.

Growth rates in the less developed areas might well diverge, rather than begin to converge, over the first part of the quarter century ahead, if death-rate differentials between some regions began to trend downwards. Thus, crude death-rates throughout Africa appear to be between 15 and 25 per 1,000 in broad terms, while the rate for Other East Asia is below 10 per 1,000. Rapid declines in the former region from these higher to lower orders of magnitude would not be uncommon in the light of the international experience of recent decades, and could add between one half to a full percentage point to the present divergence between its growth rate and the Other East Asian rate. Although further mortality declines in both regions could offset each other to an extent, they are not likely to do so completely, given the probably limited scope for further declines of the death-rate below 10 per 1,000.

Fertility, too, is likely to make for increasingly divergent growth rates within the less developed areas. Two of the regions with relatively low fertility at present, Latin America and Other East Asia, are also the ones in which recent declines have been most prominent and where further decreases appear most probable in the near future.

To sum up, powerfully dynamic vital trends everywhere in the more developed regions over the past quarter century have led to low growth and the prospect of continued deceleration, along with increasing similarity in the mortality and fertility patterns underlying growth. In the less developed regions, on the other hand, the trends have fostered increasing diversity of both growth and underlying vital patterns, a condition which may endure for several decades to come.

A widening of regional growth-rate differentials in the less developed areas, if it were to happen, could be simultaneous with either a reduction or increase of their over-all growth rate. Since this last is a population-weighted average of component national rates, its trend is determined by both weights and rates and it appears that the populations with decelerating growth in the developing regions will outnumber those with non-accelerating tendencies. Moreover, the average growth rate for these regions might well fall, whether both the high and low parts of the range diminished simultaneously or even if the high-low difference increased. All things considered, therefore, an over-all decrease in their pace of growth appears more likely than an increase over the long run. If this proves to be the case, the growth rate of the newly developing nations of Africa, Asia and Latin America may well have reached an historic peak within the past quarter century, one which cannot be expected to recur in the foreseeable future over comparably long periods. In turn, this would almost surely imply that world population growth as well would subside from its recent record heights, perhaps never to reach such levels again.

A population grouping within the newly developing regions which is of special current interest consists of the nations commonly classified as "least developed". Numbering 29 in all, these contain about 250 million persons at present, are among the fastest growing in the world today and are likely to remain so for the rest of this century. Reliable data for these nations are especially scarce, but available estimates suggest elevated birth-rates of between 45 and 50 per 1,000. Mortality is estimated to be between 40 and 45 years as measured by expectation of life at birth and between 20 and 25 per 1,000 as measured by the crude death-rate. Growth could be beyond 2.5 per cent and is currently accelerating, with the result that total population can be expected to double within the next 25 years.

A point meriting special emphasis in this and related connexions is the need for disaggregating regional measures by individual countries for many purposes of interpretation. Thus, on the one hand, the considerable number of less developed nations which have experienced large declines in their growth rates over the past two decades have included, in conspicuous degree, small or island populations. On the other hand, no less than six of the eight less developed countries with populations over 50 million (India, Indonesia, Bangladesh, Pakistan, Nigeria and Mexico) experienced substantial increases in growth rates between the early 1950s and early 1970s, one (China) may have had a mild uptrend, and the single case with an apparent decline (Brazil) has involved a fall from somewhat over 3 per cent to a rate only somewhat below this elevated level.

As a further illustration of the same general point, it is clear that the Arab populations in the Western South Asia region should be clearly distinguished from other parts of that geographic grouping in terms of demographic structure, characteristics and prospects.

MORTALITY

Levels and Trends

World life expectancy took an astounding leap forward during the quarter century just past, rising from approximately midway between 40 and 50 years at the start of the period, to about midway between 50 and 60 at the end. The sheer size of the increase, some 20 per cent, makes it evident that few, if any, comparable upsurges could have happened before, whether under relatively stable mortality circumstances or even reactively after major catastrophes, such as the Black Plague.

With respect to the geographical prevalence of the recent increases in longevity, substantial gains appear to have occurred among most populations in all regions, or in effect nearly everywhere. This can be inferred from the essentially accurate and complete data available for the more developed regions, from reliable enough evidence for at least several dozen nations in the less developed regions, and from estimates whose accuracy can be described as probably adequate in broad terms for many dozens more in the latter regions.

Strongly suggested by the real, probable and apparent trend measures at hand for 1950–1975 is that average longevity in the less developed regions rose by significantly more than the six-year average increase found in the world's industrialized areas. A large fraction of the populations of Asia and Latin America, plus a substantial number of areas in Africa, may well have registered mortality gains since the Second World War which the populations of the more developed regions needed several generations, or even half centuries, to accomplish. As of 1950, practically all nations in Africa, Asia and Latin America were at a stage in their mortality history corresponding to an 1850 or earlier stage in many of today's low-mortality nations. By 1975 such lags in life expectancy had often become so drastically reduced that dozens of higher-mortality populations were no more than a few decades behind average longevity in the low-mortality regions. Further, a number of individual populations have moved well into the 65–70 interval of experience. On the other hand, longevity gains in more developed nations, once they have reached the level of 70 years or so, have tended to decelerate markedly.

The massive international convergence of survival prospects implied by those comparisons—"massive" in the sense of the numbers of both persons and nations involved—matches or exceeds the degree of convergence to be found in any major sphere of social behaviour during the twentieth century. Its long-run implications, though still far from being well understood, will surely be enormously profound and ramified, reaching deeply into such individual and societal realms as fertility, life-cycle planning by households and Governments, labourforce size and productivity, widowhood, consumption and savings patterns, educational needs and housing patterns, among others.

Future Prospects

To date there have been no signs of longer-run relapse or upturns of trend within the higher-mortality regions. Contrary instances seem in every case to have involved special circumstances during brief periods, so far as can be established with any confidence. Apparently, no higher-mortality population which has experienced major mortality declines over the post-war period has been confronted with the threat of an enduring reversal in trend and no instance of a rising trend in mortality under reasonably normal circumstances can be documented anywhere in the less developed regions. However, this statement may in good part be a function of what is unknown, in addition to what is known. In particular, the short-run and longer-run situations alike in Africa since 1970 remain distressingly unclear.

In any event, the urgency of further gains in longevity remains obviously high for many parts of the world. Average expectations of life at birth in the more developed and less developed regions continue to be far apart on average, some 20 years according to available estimates, while differences as high as 30 to 40 years can be found between many individual pairs of nations. Furthermore, the gaps between areas and regions may become less amenable to reductions in future than they have been in the past few decades. It remains to be seen how well or quickly the world's highest-mortality nations, now concentrated in Africa and the Middle East, can emulate the post-war trends in large parts of Latin America and Asia, particularly in view of the special climatic and other adverse natural conditions prevailing in major portions of those nations.

Also unclear is the extent to which further gains are probable among the higher-mortality nations in which substantial downtrends have already occurred. In most or all of these cases, the predominant causal elements have been controls over mass infectious diseases, since present-day medical, public health and sanitary technologies are such as to permit populations to leapfrog over generations of over-all socioeconomic development in the process of effecting major mortality declines. Once such controls have been initially exploited, however, the typically slower forces of development tend to become increasingly strategic for achieving large additional gains. As further declines in death-rates from communicable causes become less important relatively and other causes more significant, the newer causal changes needed—improved nutrition, housing, individual medical care and hospital facilities, among others—tend to be much more difficult to achieve and apply than the previous main controlling elements. Evidence that this is in fact the case is suggested by the apparent slowdown of longevity gains after 1960–1965 in many less developed areas which had experienced large gains during the preceding decade or two.

An obvious factor conditioning interpretation of future interregional mortality differences is whether the more developed regions will provide moving and progressive targets, or stationary ones. Viewed in this light, the pronounced tendency towards decelerating mortality trends in these regions as between the first and second halves of the past 25 years has significance for comparative purposes, in addition to having intrinsic importance of its own. Starting in the early 1950s, by which time any major mortality effects of the initial post-war period had been essentially eliminated in both the belligerent and non-belligerent parts of the developed regions, their average expectation of life at birth increased by nearly five years in the decade following. In contrast, between the early 1960s and 1970s, the corresponding increase was two thirds lower, or well under two years. Moreover, since there was very substantial convergence of mortality levels among individual regions and nations, the lowest-mortality populations tended to register much smaller gains than did those with relatively higher mortality. In combination, these aspects of the recent trends suggest strongly that powerful and pervasive "ceiling effects" have come into play. Simply put, the possible mortality benefits to be reaped from existing medical technology appear to have reached a saturation or near-saturation level practically everywhere in the world's industrially most advanced regions. Such benefits were closely associated historically with declines in deaths resulting from infectious diseases and were largely concentrated in infancy, childhood and the earlier adult years of life. Today, infectious causes have come to have secondary or tertiary significance compared to new leading causes, while their maximum possible further impact on mortality, both over-all and within individual age groups, has become severely constrained.

As a simple example of these points, it is enough to consider the effects on expectation of life at birth in the more developed regions if their mortality under age 50 were to be eliminated fully. Although the effects would obviously vary to an extent, both between individual nations and by sex, they would also be remarkably limited relative to previous actual trends. Among female populations, national expectation of life at birth (obtained as the sum of actual life expectancy at age 50 in a recent period plus 50) would rise by amounts of only three to five years; for males, because of higher mortality under 50, the corresponding range of effects would be between about four to eight years. For either sex, despite the extreme nature of the assumption, the gain would be well below the actual gain registered in many countries since as recently as 1950 and in nearly all others since about 1940. It follows that the longevity gains of even relatively short recent periods, much less longer-run ones, cannot possibly be matched within the developed regions in future, unless a wholly new pattern of age-specific mortality decreases were to emerge. These would have to involve revolutionary magnitudes of decline at the older ages, beginning roughly at 50 or 60. In turn, this would require a quantum move forward of scientific and technological capabilities for coping with human aging processes and their associated main causes of death. Conversely, barring such progress (and abstracting from the possibility of large upward and downward fluctuations of death-rates), a long lull in mortality trends would have to be anticipated for the low-mortality populations of the world, during which life expectancy moved by only minor or secondary amounts over lengthy periods of time.

If, under these circumstances, longevity gains in the less developed regions merely kept pace with those in the more developed regions, or reduced existing gaps only somewhat, many of the hopes raised in the international health field for further world-wide progress would in effect suffer a substantial setback. Such tendencies would imply a large loss of momentum in raising life chances among the world's higher-mortality populations, not only as compared to their own recent trends, but also relative to the historic trends among the low-mortality nations as well.

The Changing Usefulness of Crude Death-rates

An important further implication of recent international mortality trends has been the sharply diminished relevance of the crude death-rate as an indicator of comparative mortality conditions over space and time. The distortions often implicit in the use of such rates, owing to their sensitivity to age or other compositional variables, has long been well recognized, but until about 1950 they were still generally adequate for identifying at least the upper and lower subranges of international mortality distributions. In particular, they were adequate for distinguishing between mortality levels in the less developed and more developed regions, as well as between either Eastern or Southern Europe and Northern or Western Europe. Since crude death-rates tend to be more available and timely than more refined measures of mortality, and since such rates also afford a direct linkage between mortality changes and the growth rate, they were put to considerable use. Today, however, many previously justifiable comparisons of death-rate levels and trends can no longer be updated usefully.

One reason has been the pronounced diminution of differences in death-rates between numerous populations of the less developed regions and all parts of the more developed regions. In numerous instances for which the available data are reliable enough to judge, the current death-rate for a higher-mortality nation is found to be below the rate for many low-mortality countries, thereby reversing the comparisons indicated by life expectancy or other more reliable measures of mortality proper.

Similarly, within the more developed regions themselves, the great post-war convergence of mortality has led to often inverse relations between crude and refined measures. Until some years after 1950, differences in age composition between the higher-mortality countries in these regions, essentially in Eastern and Southern Europe, and their lower-mortality national areas, were still dominated by mortality differences proper in their effects on cross-national comparisons. This is no longer the case. Furthermore, national trends within the low-mortality regions have also changed rather abruptly. During the 1950s, shifts in age composition were tending to raise the death-rate almost everywhere but were not yet sufficient in most instances to overcome the effects of declining age-specific mortality. As a result, crude death-rates typically declined, especially among the higher-mortality populations of Eastern and Southern Europe. However, the end of the 1950s appears to have been a watershed period, in that compositional effects attained the ascendent influence. Specifically, such effects have not only acted to raise death-rates, as they have throughout the post-war decades, but also have come to dominate the effects of mortality changes proper. In nations in which age-specific death-rates were declining, the crude death-rate nevertheless tended to rise. In nations in which age-specific rates were rising, the death-rate rose for both compositional and mortality reasons, but typically more because of the former than the latter.

The recent slowdown in mortality declines within the more developed regions, the prospect of a continued slackening in the downtrend, and the upward-biasing tendencies to be expected from shifts in age composition—taken in combination, these factors suggest that death-rates will tend to rise in the foreseeable future for these regions as a whole and for most of their national parts. Any developing tendencies to rising age-specific mortality, such as began to appear in some countries during the 1960s, would add to this expectation.

Rising crude death-rates in turn would imply a negative impact of mortality trends on population growth. The appearance of such impacts as a normal, longer-run tendency would signify the end of a prolonged historical era of opposite or growth-enhancing impacts. These have been registered, essentially without interruption, in Northern and Western Europe plus the non-European parts of today's more developed regions for well over a century, while in Eastern and Southern Europe the same has been true since the beginning of vital records about a century ago.

The preceding discussion concerning the declining usefulness of the crude death-rate need not apply to the many parts of the less developed regions for which reliable refined measures of mortality are lacking at present. Since many of these areas have much higher mortality than do the reliably documented parts of the world, estimated death-rates which provide at least broadly correct ordinal rankings and magnitudes are likely to be valuable additions to knowledge. Unfortunately, even this contingent use of death-rates will depend upon advances in mortality-measuring systems which seem far distant for a large number of high-mortality nations.

However, crude death-rates for the less developed regions can be usefully applied in a wholly different direction, even if more by analogy and extrapolation than through the direct availability of data. On average, it would appear that future declines in death-rates in the less developed regions could raise their growth rates by amounts on the order of 5 per 1,000 or 0.5 per cent annually starting from the present level of some 15 per 1,000. This would not appear to be an excessive expectation of average effects for the coming 10 to 25 years, although it could of course require considerable adjustment for specific national or regional circumstances. Some main factors which would appear to support this expectation include the rapid mortality declines found achievable in many low-income areas with present disease-control technology, the broad possibilities apparently still at hand for achieving future declines in numerous such areas, and the downward-tending effects on the death-rate of young age composition. In all of these respects, the contrasts today with the more developed regions should continue to be operative.

The possibilities for increased growth rates through future reductions in mortality appear especially great for the 29 least developed nations, where the death-rate may still often be as high as 25 per 1,000 and expectation of life at birth as low as 40 years.

An important but as yet unresolved question is whether the direct numerical relation holding between changes in growth and crude death-rates should be modified in any substantial way for possible indirect effects of mortality changes on fertility. Since improved health and longer life can tend to raise fertility as well as lower it, given the complex of biological, social and attitudinal elements potentially involved, even the direction of possible indirect impacts is far from clear. Conceivably, the balance could lean in one direction for some high-fertility areas, such as Africa, but in an opposite direction elsewhere, such as large parts of Asia and Latin America. Conceivably, too, the net effects could change direction over time, as the micro-level and social consequences of mortality declines became more pronounced, probable or enduring. Unfortunately, despite the mounting need for investigating these relations, their inherent complexity has so far eluded reasonably definitive conclusions.

Age-specific Patterns and Differentials by Sex

An important, and as yet only potentially ominous, development of recent years has been the appearance of rising age-specific death-rates among a number of adult male populations in low-mortality regions. Such increases have become especially manifest since about the middle of the 1950–1975 period in Eastern and Western Europe. In the latter region, for example, age-specific mortality rose on a region-wide basis between 1960 and 1970 for males in most ages beyond 15. Whether these increases represent only short-lived reversals of trends or the initial stage of an enduring turn-around cannot be foretold as yet. Current patterns have been too variable, within countries over time and between ages within countries, to warrant general characterization, although available data going beyond 1970 suggest that some of the recent increases have been too durable to be accidental. This seems particularly indicated—perhaps surprisingly so—in the 15–25 range of ages. At the upper adult ages, to which more public attention has been drawn, age-specific mortality since 1970 has often moved downward following increases in the late 1960s.

For females, despite the occasional appearance of a rise in the post-1960 years, either sustained declines or resumptions of declines have been the predominant patterns.

The tendency for male mortality during the 1950s to decline less rapidly than female mortality, and since 1960 either to continue such a pattern of lag or to edge upwards while the rates for females eased downwards, has sustained a striking related trend in the more developed regions, one whose origins go back to the early decades of this century. Since about 1920, with remarkable persistence over time and space alike, the world's industrialized nations have experienced rising differences between female and male life expectancy. Such increases have continued to climb both during the rapid longevity uptrends for both sexes in the 1950s and again during the decelerating changes of the 1960s. Today, differentials in life expectancy by sex in all parts of the more developed regions are at the highest points ever recorded except during periods of major wars. Not only is this the case for expectation of life at birth, but also at later ages—for example, for the years beyond 30 and again beyond 65.

Unfortunately, neither the volume nor the quality of the data for less developed regions permits generalized description of age-sex patterns. With respect to age, perhaps the most useful general point to make is that recent changes of mortality and survival rates (both in absolute and percentage terms) have approximated the same types of functions by age as those encountered in the low-mortality regions during their own earlier periods of downtrends from high mortality. Hence, the effects of such changes on age composition have also been roughly similar to what they have been in the past—that is, limited in magnitude and tending to reduce rather than raise average age of population (as discussed below). With respect to sex differentials, the less developed regions continue to provide the only cases on record during the past quarter century of apparently higher male expectation of life at birth. Interestingly, the instance involving probably the highest accuracy of estimation in this regard, for Sri Lanka, indicates a change from an initially higher male to a subsequently higher female measure. It may well be that national female longevity levels in the high-mortality regions, even if typically higher than male levels, are considerably less removed from the latter than has been typical of the more developed regions in recent decades.

Infant Mortality

It seems safe to assume that a leading causal element affecting mortality-childbearing interrelations is the risk of death in the early ages of life. If this is so, then not only is infant mortality a major indicator of environmental influences affecting death-rates, but its levels, trends and differentials among social or spatial sectors can be safely assumed to have prime importance for fertility behaviour as well. Regarding infant mortality from mortality and fertility viewpoints simultaneously, therefore, gives added significance to the sharp international differences found currently among the less developed nations and regions. Available estimates suggest an upper-range interval of about 150 to 200 infant deaths per 1,000 live births or higher in Africa's regions, a medium range of 70 to 100 in Latin America and East Asia, and one of about 100 to 150 in most other parts of Asia, plus the larger high-mortality populations of Oceania. Unfortunately, the few cases of well measured rates available for any of these regions provide little or no basis for making geographic extrapolations or other deductions of interest, other than that they are practically all far higher than nearly all published national rates for the more developed regions. Since the better documented parts of the less developed areas tend to have lower rates than do the undocumented ones, the comparisons that can be made between the two sets of regions are undoubtedly biased downward relative to typical national differences or average regional ones.

It is also likely that the estimated and published infant mortality rates for less developed areas tend to be understatements of the actual rates for the documented areas themselves. A special difficulty in this connexion involves deaths occurring very shortly after birth. Often in such instances, both births and deaths tend to be excluded from the calculated rates, and since the mortality rate for this excluded group equals unity by definition, its omission imparts a downward bias to the rate based upon the included births only. The larger the relative number of excluded birth-and-death cases, the larger becomes the bias. Moreover, a changing bias over time could affect an apparent trend in ways that are even more difficult to allow for than the bias for a single period. Similar difficulties arise, analogously, in dealing with differentials over space.

Nevertheless, it seems safe to infer from the available sources that the gap between infant mortality in many less developed areas and the more developed regions as a whole has fallen greatly since 1950. In a number of apparently contrary instances, involving low percentage declines for some higher-mortality populations between 1950 and 1975, the explanations are essentially consistent with the same conclusion, since they involve slowdowns following extremely rapid declines very shortly before 1950 or demographically atypical circumstances. Moreover, absolute differences between infant rates in the less and more developed regions could well decline even with larger percentage declines in the latter areas. This arithmetic-type effect has become especially prominent in dealing with many low-mortality regions since the war, since even small absolute changes in these areas can imply large percentage shifts relative to low initial or base-period values.

In nearly all countries belonging to these regions, including those with relatively elevated levels about 1950, infant death-rates have fallen to less than half their initial height during the past 25 years. Not infrequently, the decline has been by as much as two thirds of the original measures. Barring future upward fluctuations or reversals of trend, therefore, the declines of the past quarter century in infant mortality can never again be duplicated in the more developed regions, not only on average but also in nearly all of their component national areas as well.

This is not to deny that some substantial internal variations within the low-mortality regions still exist. Thus, for parts of Eastern and Southern Europe to reach the average or lowest national levels now encountered in other such regions would entail further declines of about one half to two thirds.

Data on the time structure and causes of infant mortality, which in usable form exist essentially for more developed regions only, show especially large post-1950 decreases in post-neonatal (second through twelfth month) mortality rates and associated causes of death. Lesser declines are found in neonatal (under one month) mortality. As a result, with the exception of parts of Eastern and Southern Europe, first-month mortality currently accounts for well over half of all first-year deaths in low-mortality areas. At the same time, considerable recent progress has been registered in reducing late foetal and early post-natal mortality, as evidenced by often pronounced declines in the rates of neonatal and perinatal (between seven months gestation and seven days after birth) deaths. Although congenital malformations have tended to remain relatively resistant to change, substantial declines have been registered in deaths from other late pre-natal and early post-natal causes.

Many of the attributes of international mortality patterns for the first year of life carry over to the childhood ages one to five. Mortality risks in the first half of this four-year interval are far higher in all regions than in the second half, death-rates are highly differential between the less and more developed regions with respect to deaths caused by infectious diseases, and the rates within countries tend to vary with socio-economic status, ethnic factors and residential life styles. With respect to the last, the tendency to lower urban than rural childhood mortality today in much of Europe and parts of Asia merits emphasis for a number of reasons, not least because it contrasts with the opposite nineteenth century tendency in today's low-mortality regions. Almost surely, such cross-overs in urban-rural differentials bring out the enhanced strategic role of medical and sanitary control factors during this century.

Maternal Mortality

Maternal mortality has fallen rapidly during the post-war period in all parts of the more developed regions and in the few upper-mortality areas for which published records exist. Something like a three fourths reduction can be calculated for both of these groups of population, though only the first group has region-wide significance. Wherever measured, the declines in deaths from childbearing causes stand out relative to several bases: number of births, number of women and deaths from all causes. While the declines have been substantial at all ages, maternal mortality continues to be a sharply upward-sloping function of age beyond 20, much as it has been traditionally.

Social and Urban-Rural Differentials

Mortality differentials among socio-economic categories of population tend to be less often available for analysis than are fertility differentials. Hence, few general conclusions can be safely made on this score, even within the more developed regions or their best recorded parts. Such as it is, however, the informational base at hand suggests a typically positive correlation between socio-economic status and survival chances, or equivalently, an inverse one between status and mortality. In particular, occupational and educational classifications of status suggest clear and even pronounced tendencies along these lines. Marital status is occasionally documented as another source of differentiation between mortality risks which is worth noting. Thus, both married males and females about age 50 in a number of countries show lower death-rates than do their single, widowed or divorced counterparts. On the other hand, while the highest rates for females are most often found among single persons, those for males are among the divorced. Rates for the widowed are typically at an intermediate level for both sexes.

It is worth stressing that both occupational and marital-status differentials in mortality pose numerous problems of interpretation. For example, current occupation at time of death may differ from main lifetime occupation, while marital status may be an effect as well as a cause of differential health and mortality risks.

With respect to urban-rural residence, neither levels nor trends have been uniformly higher or lower by type of area in the more developed regions. The available national data show differences in both directions, sometimes varying by sex, as well as variable amounts of differences between countries. In less developed areas, for which statistical documentation is very sparse, the available indications point strongly to lower mortality in urban areas. As noted earlier with respect to infant mortality, the contrast in this regard with historical experience during the nineteenth century is strongly suggestive of a changed mix of main causal factors. These would appear to involve the increased relative importance of applied disease-control technology in the world's low-income areas during recent decades, compared to the state of the technology that could be applied in the more developed regions about a century ago.

FERTILITY

Levels and Trends

Several general features stand out among the mass of details concerning regional and national trends in fertility during the last quarter century. First, the gap between the more and less developed regions continues to be very large, with fertility in low-income areas averaging between two and three times the level found in higher-income areas. Since the gap between the two sets of areas has seemingly not narrowed, indeed has more probably increased, the current ratio may well be the highest in centuries, perhaps even the highest in millenia.

Second, the past 25 years has been the only long-run period on record since at least 1800 to witness a major reversal of trend among any substantial number of populations in today's more developed regions. Although the reversals, which were especially prominent in most of Western Europe, Northern Europe and Northern America, were relatively short-lived, their re-occurrence can no longer be ruled out as too improbable to be considered in making projections for the future. A third general aspect, which may at least currently throw doubt on this observation, is that the large majority of nations in the more developed regions have experienced very rapid declines in fertility in recent years. The countries in these regions which began the period after the Second World War with an upsurge of fertility, as in Northern America and Western Europe, have all reversed course again, either since the 1950s or 1960s. Meanwhile, the countries of Eastern and Southern Europe have tended to follow a more or less steady downpath throughout the entire period since 1950. Fourth, as a result of very rapid changes since about 1965 within both of these groups of countries, fertility in the more developed regions is often close to or below replacement. Gross reproduction rates (which very nearly equal the corresponding net rates) are currently within about 10 per cent on either side of unity in well over half the national populations of these regions; several others further from this level are on the low side. Moreover, the momentum of past downtrends appears far from exhausted in many individual areas. Only about a half-dozen countries out of the more than 30 involved would appear to be safely above replacement level for the foreseeable near future, judging from various trend measures for 1970–1975.

Fifth, a noteworthy aspect of the recent trends in the more developed regions has been the degree to which their relative fertility patterns have become altered. In particular, large parts of Eastern and Southern Europe have reached levels falling well below those holding for major parts of Northern Europe, Western Europe and Northern America, thereby reversing the rankings in existence about 1950. Should recent movements persist for only a short while into the future, the areas with highest fertility could soon be Australia and New Zealand, along with the perennial case of Ireland, in place of such countries as Poland, Romania, Yugoslavia, Spain and Portugal, which were leaders before 1950. Sixth, no less striking is the extent to which near-homogenization of fertility levels within the more developed regions looms as an oncoming prospect. Given the directions and magnitudes of recent changes, the next quarter century could well become witness to a massive convergence of fertility in these regions by the year 2000, analogous in its way to the great convergence of their mortality rates during the past quarter century.

In sharp contrast to the more developed regions, the higher-fertility areas of the world appear subject to trends which would lead to a significant widening of national differentials. While fertility promises to come down substantially from prior or traditional levels in many instances, in others it may well remain unchanged or even rise. Thus a seventh aspect of recent demographic history, one which could prove as momentous as any for future world population size and growth, has been the fact that fertility has begun to decline by significant amounts in a growing number of countries which had high fertility levels before 1950. It is true that such declines have often occurred under special geographic or cultural circumstances—for example, among small or island populations—or must be estimated under a cloud of uncomfortably large margins of error. It is also true that neither the level nor, even more, the trend of fertility can be reliably measured for a single one of the seven largest nations in the less developed regions, comprising fully two thirds of the total population of the developing regions and half the world's population. Nevertheless, the odds favouring further fertility decline in many low-income areas in which such declines have already begun, or the near onset of substantial declines where such processes are still potential rather than realized, are no longer small. A forecast that widespread, large and rapidly diffusing fertility transformations will soon occur in such areas may still be more hypothesis than fact, but it is no longer mere speculation about the future based on minimal probabilities. Nor can one exclude the possibility that future fertility downtrends in today's high-fertility areas will often be more rapid than earlier downtrends in other areas, much as has been the case with mortality.

Simultaneously, however, an eighth generalization of recent international patterns is that fertility continues to be not far from traditional or long-run elevated levels among many or most of the individual populations of Africa, Asia and Latin America. A similar conclusion could well hold for the combined populations of these regions if considered as a group. In Africa, according to the highly uncertain estimates available up to now, a number of national fertility levels may well have risen in recent years and some might continue to do so, while many might at least not fall, for an indefinite period. However, the true situation in this area, as it stands now or in the near future, may never be known accurately, just as little is known even now about the apparent fertility increases suggested for not a few Latin American countries during the 1950s.

Differentials

Differential fertility patterns within countries, often a useful harbinger of national trends to come, have shown mixed tendencies over the past 25 years, both as between the more and less developed regions and within the latter group of populations alone. Unfortunately, many of the comparative patterns seeming to hold between or within regions may be statistical artifacts, given the many variations to be found in the contents, availability, time reference and quality of the data at hand. For reasons of convenience and feasibility, attention is focused only in differentials by urban-rural residence and by education, though even here it is occasionally necessary to take account of variable classifications.

So far as the scarce data available for Africa, Asia and Latin America indicate, fertility is more likely to decline than to rise or to remain constant with urban residence and increasing education. However, intervening variables such as health, marital status and differential quality of reporting may be significant partial determinants of the observed urban-rural variations in these regions, in addition to fertility propensities proper. In the case of education, deterrent effects on fertility may first become pronounced beyond a relatively high threshold, such as completion of primary school, rather than in a continuous manner with numbers of years of schooling. Even with these qualifications, there are exceptions or apparent exceptions to the rule in each of the three high-fertility continents. Possibly because of more abundant data, Latin America appears to provide more uniformly encountered patterns of urban and educational impacts on fertility than do Africa or Asia; possibly, however, this differentiation among the three regions reflects correctly the many major socio-economic, cultural and historical forces distinguishing each of these areas from the others.

It is also worth noting that pronounced urban-rural or education differentials, ranging from more than one child to several children in orders of magnitude, are to be found in each of the same three regions. If this is representative of the facts on a broad geographic scale, then a rapid spread of the lower-fertility patterns already found in the more modernized sectors of all of the world's high-fertility continents could lead to the early onset of sharp aggregate downtrends. Such could be the case whether the differentials themselves widened for an interim period, as has often been the case historically in regions experiencing demographic evolutions to lower vital rates, or tended to contract more or less steadily from their current levels.

Among the more developed regions, subnational differentials by both urban-rural residence and education have become almost necessarily low in absolute size, given their pronounced average levels of fertility as of 1975. Although higher rural than urban levels are still widely prevalent in these regions, as has apparently been the case throughout the modern era, the recent evidence on trends points universally to a more or less sustained narrowing of differences. A number of Eastern European countries and the Soviet Union gave evidence of widening tendencies during an earlier part of the 1950–1975 period, but this has been reversed. As a result, the excess of rural over urban lifetime fertility levels had become greatly diminished or essentially eliminated nearly everywhere in the low-fertility regions by 1975.

Educational differentials, similarly, have shown a clear modal tendency to contract during recent decades in these regions. In 1975, as in 1950, education and fertility continued to be in predominantly inverse relation with each other, but the scale of variation had undergone substantial decline. The occasional appearance of an upturn in relative fertility among the highest educational categories is also worthy of note.

In sum, the pronounced tendencies found towards homogenization of fertility behaviour within the developed regions since 1950 have been along two dimensions: internationally among countries and domestically among major subsectors of national populations.

Attitudinal Aspects

Data problems at least as severe as those confronting the study of international fertility levels or trends arise in dealing with their attitudinal correlates. Not least among such problems is the relative newness of the subject. Statistical attempts at documenting "ideal", "expected" or "desired" numbers of children have first begun to emerge within a period of less than two decades, and to attain a satisfactory degree of international comparability in concepts and measures within several decades would be a considerable achievement. All "finely tuned" comparisons suggested by the data up to now should be weighed in the light of these reservations. And conversely, the greater the confidence which can be justifiably placed on an available international or interregional comparison of recent fertility attitudes, the more general or unrefined is likely to be the substantive content of the comparison.

Thus, the main comparative conclusion which seems clearly substantiated by the data is also the least surprising, though the accumulation of specific numerical aspects over the past 10 to 15 years marks a major step forward in needed knowledge. That is the sharp distinction—approximating three children on average—between the numbers of children considered ideal or desired among population groups surveyed in the less developed regions and the lower corresponding numbers in more developed areas. To a rough order of magnitude, one can now estimate that something like a three-child differential represents the motivational transformation needed if the world's high-fertility populations are to become satisfied with the childbearing patterns characteristic of low-fertility populations.

A second and much more tentative interpretation of the data concerns the possible fertility changes that might occur in the less developed regions even if national or social values affecting childbearing remained essentially constant. Data consulted for high-fertility areas on expected numbers of children, although involving only two countries, are at least consistent in showing that these exceed ideal or desired numbers. Furthermore, several other such areas show ideal numbers of children to be above desired numbers. The first of these findings can at least arguably be interpreted as a proxy for discrepancies between individual fertility behaviour and individual goals, while the second suggests discrepant tendencies between traditional social prescriptions and current individual choice. Either or both interpretations, if valid, could imply a developing potential for reduced fertility, even if individual or social value structures proved resistant to change. These speculations, though vague and essentially unsubstantiated, can no longer be prudently excluded from the prominent possibilities to be considered in anticipating fertility trends in many parts of the less developed regions over the next several decades.

Within the lower-fertility and more developed regions, in contrast, the near equality found between ideal and expected numbers of children (practically no data being available on desired numbers), suggests close correspondence between motivation and performance. Hence, the statistics at hand as such give little basis for anticipating fertility uptrends or downtrends. They are, further, much too dated typically to have current relevance, given the pace of the actual fertility movements that have occurred since many of them were compiled.

Nuptiality

Another class of explanatory factors related to fertility, as well as one which has significance in its own right from social viewpoints, concerns nuptiality levels and trends. Here again, unfortunately, summary and analysis are often beset by large data gaps, problems of inaccuracy and definitional incomparabilities. In addition, cross-sectional ("stock-type") measures of nuptial patterns, such as distributions by marital status according to censuses, may obscure or even misstate intertemporal ("flow-type") characteristics. For example, the percentage of divorced persons according to successive censuses may change little even while annual divorce rates are rising rapidly, provided re-marriages have also been increasing at a high rate.

In Africa, for which nothing of a region-wide nature can be deduced from the statistical information available, perhaps the main finding of interest has involved Mauritius, where sharply declining fertility has accompanied a pronounced rise in the proportion of single females under age 25 between the early 1950s and 1960s. Analogous associations have occurred over the past 25-year period in the few cases in Asia, all involving small or island populations, for which trends in marital status have been documented. On the other hand, Latin America since 1950 appears to show constant and even decreasing fractions single at ages under 25 among some countries which have experienced fertility declines. The interpretative significance of this apparent deviation from nuptiality-fertility correlations elsewhere is not clear. Since statistical biases in this region are so interlaced with fact, owing to the prevalence of consensual unions, interpretation of the data on behavioural trends may simply be precluded.

An interesting modal tendency in all three of these continents has been for the fractions of women eventually married to remain fairly stable or to rise, as indexed by the proportions between the ages of 40 and 50 who are reported as ever married. At these ages also, differences between the proportions ever married and currently married has tended to narrow substantially, perhaps mainly as a result of declining mortality. It seems probable that declining widowhood among women in the late reproductive ages has become a widespread phenomenon in most parts of the less developed regions, given what is known about their mortality trends. But this is the only major general inference about their nuptiality trends that can be made with confidence. Even if major trends or differentials were evolving in much of Latin America, Africa and Asia, they would not be discoverable from the current store of factual knowledge.

In the more developed regions, the relatively abundant data at hand—though far from being complete or adequately current—give a clear picture of great changes within recent decades. Following reactive-type recoveries of marriage rates during the early postwar years in most of Europe, North America, and the developed countries in Oceania, the trends typically turned downward during the 1950s, were succeeded by upturns in the 1960s, and have shown variable directions of movement thereafter. Post-1970 rates have been below those of the 1960s in a number of countries but higher in others, the disparate trends being partly related to variable "echo" effects of the early postwar changes in fertility on some age distributions.

In part, however, the recent divergent trends have been a reflection of changing nuptiality proper. There are not a few indications that highly dynamic and possibly even revolutionary developments in the marriage patterns of most industrially advanced populations could occur in the near future, should recent trends persist. Rates of marital dissolution for non-mortality reasons, whether measured in flow terms by annual divorce rates or in stock terms by changing census values of the proportion divorced, have risen almost everywhere. Moreover, either of these sources would tend to understate the facts, since the divorce-rate series ignore dissolutions of alliances between non-married partners, while the census series are always net of remarriages and often fail to allow for separations among married couples.

Especially insightful interpretations on this score are provided by cumulative rates of marital dissolution among female marriage cohorts. Information available for approximately a dozen countries in Northern America and Northern, Eastern and Western Europe reveals pronounced uptrends of the rates in most instances when successive cohorts are compared at given durations of marriage. Although these rates may be somewhat biased, they appear to suggest clearly that lifetime divorce rates among current first marriages are in excess of 15 to 20 per cent in numerous areas and go well beyond 25 per cent in a number of others. To this should be added allowances for the widening prevalence of informal and consensual types of living arrangements in a growing number of industrialized areas. Should these trends continue and become magnified, as seems currently indicated in several countries, the long-standing predominant pattern of marriage to a single lifetime partner could soon be challenged by new prototypical arrangements. In this event, the next quarter century could usher in a new era in nuptiality patterns, one going far to replace a system which has endured for centuries.

What such a development, if it came to pass, might imply for fertility is difficult to envisage, given its novelty. Some leading clues may begin to emerge as the linkages between recent or current marital and childbearing movements in industrialized societies become more fully explored. It also remains to be seen whether some recent tendencies to converging nuptial patterns in the more developed regions, such as the narrowed variability of marriage rates, will continue or will be reversed. Assuming such tendencies continue, another major dimension would have been added to the many thrusts towards homogenization of vital rate characteristics which have been observed in these regions during the post-war decades.

Programmes to Influence Fertility

Socially organized attempts to achieve large declines in fertility have been among the most distinctive features of the past quarter century's demographic record. The scale and spread of such attempts, based upon programmes of persuasion and technical aid, identify them as being clearly unique in history. Certainly, no precedents can even begin to approach the present programmes with respect to any one of numerous criteria for identifying their scope: number of nations with programmes, size of populations involved, degree and rapidity of the behavioural transformations being sought, amounts of resources invested, or extent of governmental—and international—commitments to announced programme goals. Originating from diverse sources— demographic, developmental, political or socio-economic—programmes having national, subnational and regional birth-affecting objectives can be found today in all less developed regions.

Opinions concerning accomplishments of the programmes to date have been variable, not only as between countries but often within the same area. Inherent difficulties of evaluation, the newness of many programmes, scarcity of performance data and inexperience in analysing such data as do exist—all of these have contributed to the current indecision and debates. In addition, programme activities have varied widely in objectives, main implementing mechanisms and performance, the last either assessed by scale of inputs (services delivered) or by outputs in the form of effects on fertility. Clearly, therefore, another decade or more will be needed before substantial evidence and an informed consensus can develop concerning realism of targets and adequacy of achievements. Part of the obstacle to an early verdict is that so little is known about the "fine structure" of beginning phases of long-run fertility declines. Descriptions of past declines and so-called "fertility transitions" have typically condensed decades or generations of experience, with little elucidation of specific starting points, main initiator groups or dominant causal factors. Little, if anything, can be inferred about how today's low-fertility areas would have responded to rapidly introduced social pressures favouring large declines in the birth-rate. Indeed, viewed from this perspective, evaluation of family planning programmes in the less developed regions of tomorrow may help cast new light on earlier patterns of evolution to low fertility.

So far as the present main indications go, perhaps the outstanding unambiguous fact emerging from the programmes to date concerns the large numbers of persons in higher-fertility areas who have been found willing to adopt, or at least experiment with, birth-limiting behaviour patterns. Reproductive propensities in many high-fertility areas, far from being the monolithic or tradition-dominated entities presupposed by conventional theory and simplified description, have been found on closer examination to show considerable flexibility, extensive variability among groups and individuals, and high latent potential for rapid change. Even with a large allowance for misinterpretation or incorrect estimation of the facts, or for recidivism in behaviour by temporary programme participants, it seems clear that many millions residing in numerous parts of the high-fertility regions have been willing to adopt family-limiting methods on both permanent and temporary bases. It follows that neither fertility values alone, nor the mere availability of birth-control methods (including programmes of persuasion), need have decisive causal influence on the reproductive decisions of today's high-fertility populations. Rather, the two would often seem to be in a potentially shifting ends-means relation to each other, with considerable substitution possible between family size and other goals. For example, a rise in socially sanctioned efforts to reduce fertility could in time achieve that result even if preferences for children and other preferences remained essentially constant at the micro- or family level. Since such preferences form an extended set of values, changing the ease or difficulty of achieving alternative goals could alter actual choices, both of number of children and other objectives. Moreover, increasing rather than declining substitution among goals is to be expected as post-war trends to ever-widening communications continue on what appear to be irreversible paths. Some apparently supportive statistical indications on these scores—all subject to wide margins of error, however—are the high rates of increase of "acceptors" (i.e., new users of government programme services) which have been reported since 1970 for numerous areas; the fact that some instances of small increases or even decreases in the number of acceptors have involved countries with already well-established declines in fertility or relatively successful programmes, and hence, presumably with relatively limited numbers of "eligible acceptors" left; and the declining average age of acceptors reported according to a number of series. Given these indications, the frequently encountered opinions that family planning programmes have fallen far short of success, and that no programme has been known to initiate a major fertility downtrend in a large rural population, may be premature. Certainly the failure of nearly all programmes to reach targets initially proclaimed by administrators or proponents (at home and, often, abroad) is neither a realistic nor as yet an adequately seasoned basis for assessing prospects.

INTERNATIONAL MIGRATION

Like other vital trends over the past quarter century, international migration movements have been characterized by frequent breakaway tendencies when viewed by pre-war standards. Following the enormous war-related dislocations and resettlements of population which took place during the 1940s, mainly in Europe and Asia, the new migration patterns developed gradually. During the 1950s the main sending region continued to be Europe, while the main receiving areas were those of Northern America and Oceania, as had been the case since the nineteenth century. Also in keeping with long-term traditional patterns, Europe's international net movements, which after 1950 had become mainly voluntary except in the case of special circumstances, continued to be more overseas than continental in nature. Little is known about movements among the less developed nations, but they were probably small relative to both sending and receiving populations in nearly all instances. Those between the less and more developed regions were similarly limited except for a few small countries. Both of these latter tendencies were also in line with precedent. Since about 1955–1960, however, international migration has undergone major alterations in structure. One structural shift has been the enormous expansion in Europe of south-to-north movements, in particular from Italy, Spain, Greece, Yugoslavia and Portugal, among the main areas of origin, to France, the Federal Republic of Germany, Switzerland, Belgium and the Netherlands, among the primary destinations. These have largely replaced the predominantly east-to-west continental movements which had long been characteristic of Europe during the period between the First and Second World Wars and in previous periods. A second shift has been the apparent end of Europe's long-standing status as a major net sender of population to other continents. Net movements between Europe and overseas appear to have fallen drastically between the 1950s and 1960s, possibly almost to zero, and to have reversed direction since about 1970 and become positive. A prominent factor in both of these change-overs from the high negative balances during previous decades has been a large-scale redirection of net movements out of Southern Europe, away from overseas areas of destination and towards northern areas within the continent.

For a number of reasons, including the decline of permanent east-west migration, the growing ease of crossing national borders for employment reasons, and the passage in Western Europe of legislation restricting movements during times of labour surplus, international flows of population within Europe appear also to have become increasingly responsive to short-term economic conditions. Should these tendencies persist, the proportions of such flows as are temporary rather than relatively permanent could rise sharply in the decades ahead, a possibility that appears well borne out by the migration experience of many European countries during recent recession periods. An analogous expectation over the long run would be for the distribution of emigrants coming from various sending countries to shift greatly, as relative levels of living and employment opportunities become transformed in major areas of origin and destination. This, too, has been suggested factually by recent experience.

A third significant transformation of international migration patterns during recent decades has involved the accelerating numbers moving from less to more developed regions. Among the most important of such developments have been the flows from Latin America and parts of Asia to Northern America, from Commonwealth areas in the Caribbean region, South Asia and Africa to the United Kingdom during the 1950s and 1960s, from Northern Africa to France and from Turkey to Western Europe. In all of these cases, political factors have been important determinants of the observed behaviour patterns. Thus, permissive legislation passed during the 1960s in the United States of America helps explain the first of these migration streams, while passage of restrictive legislation has greatly curtailed the last three over the past decade.

For the past 25 years as a whole, the main individual receiving areas in terms of absolute numbers, each with an estimated net intake of over one million migrants, have been the United States of America, the Federal Republic of Germany, France, Canada, Australia and Israel. Corresponding main sending areas have included the German Democratic Republic, Italy, Portugal, Spain, Yugoslavia and Turkey. In terms of rates relative to population, the largest net losers of population have included Cuba, Cyprus, the German Democratic Republic, Ireland, Malta, Portugal, Trinidad and Tobago, Puerto Rico and Surinam, while the largest net gainers have included the Federal Republic of Germany, France, Switzerland, Canada, Australia, New Zealand and Israel. Available data for other parts of the world, though less reliable, suggest that there has been substantial emigration from such countries as Algeria, Lebanon and Paraguay, and considerable immigration into Argentina, Venezuela, Hong Kong, the Libyan Arab Republic, Kuwait and a number of other oil-producing states in the Middle East. South Africa is an important net importer of labour and there are indications, though no precise quantitative measures, that a number of other countries of that region are subject to immigration or emigration on a significant scale.

The high ratios of foreign to total labour force in several parts of the world indicate that at least cumulative net migration, if not its current rate, can have major social and economic significance under specific circumstances in all regions, both developed and developing. Although current and even cumulative magnitudes of net out-movements from the less developed to more developed regions have been minor fractions of the aggregate population size of either group of areas, a newly emerging possibility may be worth noting in looking ahead, even if the likelihood of its occurrence is still small. Should the recent downtrends in rates of natural increase persist within the more developed regions, while recent accelerations of net movements into these regions continued, net migration could conceivably become a prominent part of their total population change. Conceivably, too, though more difficult to foresee at present, such migration could offset negative natural increase, if not on a fully region-wide basis then at least for major parts of the low-growth regions. The recent experience along these lines in the German Democratic Republic and the Federal Republic of Germany could prove to be an early harbinger of analogous developments that may occur elsewhere among the industrialized nations before the close of this century.

URBAN-RURAL DISTRIBUTION AND REDISTRIBUTION

A far-reaching aspect of the world's population trends since 1950 has been the tendency for natural increase to concentrate populations in the relatively rural nations on an international scale of observation, even while internal migration has been relocating them towards urban settings within nations. Neither tendency is new, but both have reached new levels of intensity during the past 25 years. Differences in natural increase between agrarian and industrialized regions have attained historic heights during the past several decades, as noted earlier, while the scale of internal migration to urban areas has also accelerated enormously, for the world as a whole and especially in its less industrialized parts.

Global data, though based upon often uncertain and variably defined national measures of urban and rural population, suggest that the world's urban population has expanded by about 3 per cent annually between 1950 and 1975. Since this has been well above even the record growth rate holding for total population during this period, the urban fraction has risen phenomenally, from about 25 to 40 per cent. In the more developed regions, the rapid rise in this fraction, from about 50 to 70 per cent, has been brought about in part by a decline in the absolute size of rural population. In the less developed regions, on the other hand, the proportion of urban population has doubled, from about 15 to 30 per cent, despite rapid rural expansion. The expansion rate of urban numbers in these regions, about 4 per cent annually on average, has been well above the corresponding rate in the more developed regions. As a result, the urban populations in the two groups of regions are currently about equal in size, if not for the first time in recorded history then surely in several centuries at least. Involving about 750–800 million in each group, the current equality contrasts sharply with the corresponding numbers of 500 million in the more developed regions and 250 million in the less developed areas in 1950, very nearly a 2:1 ratio. Given the differing trends which underlie this contrast, it appears obvious that the current situation of approximate equality will soon be superseded by rapidly growing inequalities.

It is worth stressing, however, that these estimates require considerable modification from the viewpoint of socio-functional interpretation. In the more developed regions, far more than the two thirds to three fourths of the population now counted as urban are in fact urbanized, given the increasingly integrated communications, labour-force and transportation networks connecting their farm and non-farm areas. The opposite is almost surely the case in the less developed regions, where urbanization has been so rapid as to outstrip social change and economic development in other respects. An important indication of this point is that urban labour force as measured in the less developed areas has a substantially higher proportion engaged in agriculture than is the case in the more developed economies.

Some qualifications, too, are called for by the substantial variations in urban-rural composition found within both groups of regions. In the case of the industrially advanced areas, the proportions of urban population range currently from about three fifths in the USSR to five sixths in Australia plus New Zealand. For individual countries within Europe alone, the proportions extend from about one half in a number of southern and eastern areas to over three fourths in large parts of the continent's northern and western regions. The range of variation is even higher in the newly developing regions, from about one fifth in Africa and South Asia to nearly three fifths in Latin America. This last proportion, which comprises an extraordinary high-low range of nearly 50 percentage points between individual countries, stands out further by its marked deviation from average urbanization-development relationships in the past. South Asia, about one fifth of whose population is urban, has an even greater spread among the urban proportions of its individual national areas.

Despite the great differences in urban patterns between the agrarian and industrial regions, both appear to have been remarkably similar in the relative contributions made to urban growth by natural increase and net migration. As a rule, in both groups of regions migration appears to have contributed to between 40 and 50 per cent of the urban growth, with such contributions ranging from about one third to three fifths in most individual regions. The situation has been very different, however, in the rural sectors. In the more developed regions, rural natural increase has generally been outweighed by net out-migration, while in the less developed regions it has been greatly in excess of transfer movements.

Age selectivity of rural-to-urban migration has tended to be similar in all parts of the world, thereby leading to higher proportions of young and middle adults, along with lower childhood proportions, in urban sectors. Selectivity by sex, in contrast, has tended to vary by individual areas, within both the more and less developed regions. In particular, female selectivity of such migration in Latin America has been in contrast with the marked tendency to male selectivity holding for much of Africa and Asia.

Just as recent growth of total population, when rapid, has implied the early emergence of enormous nations in various parts of the world, so has the urban growth of the past two decades often laid the basis for new massive urban agglomerations. The main incidence by far of such agglomerations, as indexed by numbers of cities of one million and over, has been in the less developed regions, where the number of such cities has quadrupled during the past 25 years. This compares with an approximate doubling of the corresponding number in the more developed areas.

DEMOGRAPHIC STRUCTURE AND CHARACTERISTICS

Age Composition

Since fertility has far greater effect than does mortality on the distribution of population by age, most broad comparisons of the latter over space or time are closely related to levels or trends of childbearing. Mortality being linked to age structure by percentage changes in age-specific survival rates (and not by either absolute or percentage changes in age-specific mortality rates), its effects tend to be limited except for changes between extreme high-mortality and low-mortality situations. Moreover, the effective factors are even more limited than survival-rate percentage variations as such: what really counts are the differences between relatively high and low percentage variations at different ages, rather than the size of the variations as such at any one age. Most past percentage variations over time have involved relatively large values for persons under age 5 and lower changes beyond that age, with occasionally high relative variations at the upper ages of life, say beyond 50 or 60. Since most percentage changes in age-specific survival rates are limited to begin with, while the age-to-age differences between such changes are even smaller, their impacts on age structure tend to be restricted or even negligible. Barring extreme comparisons, such as between pre-modern and today's high survival rates, it can be said that past mortality movements have tended to increase only somewhat the proportions of population under 15, mildly reduce the proportion 15 to 50 or 60, occasionally raise the proportion of older persons, and to lower average age. Analogous effects have held for variations in survival rates over space.

In the more developed regions, where survival rates throughout the younger years of life are close to a maximum value of unity, future effects on age distribution of mortality declines below age 50 are likely to be even more limited than they have been in the past. It follows that upper-age percentage variations in survivorship could begin to have a rising relative impact on age composition, as compared to young-age variations. If this proves to be the case, future mortality declines could tend to raise average age rather than decrease it. Whether they would do so by significant amounts would depend upon whether the upper-age variations attained substantially higher orders of magnitude than have been usual until now. Conceivably, for the first time in modern demographic history, such variations could lead to rapid increases in the proportion of aged persons because of mortality alone.

In the less developed regions, increases in age-specific survival rates over the coming several decades are likely to resemble the classic patterns encountered in the more developed regions over the past century. As a rule, therefore, they can be expected to raise the proportions of young persons, reduce the fraction in the main ages of reproduction and labour-force activity, and lower the average age of population. Not infrequently, though with less probability, they could raise the fraction over 50. In the case of Africa and other areas with unusually low life expectancy, a very rapid uptrend of longevity could have an atypically large effect in these directions.

Since the effects of mortality and fertility variations on age are similar for either sex, their linkages to the age distribution of total populations are essentially independent of the relative number of males and females. The same is true of international migration, since this too is similarly age-selective for either sex. Essentially, therefore, recent age distributions among major regions and subregions have been the product of their fertility histories.

Viewed in this light, the enormous differences in average age found currently between the more and less developed regions further attest to their vastly disparate childbearing patterns. Median age is close to 30 among the world's low-fertility countries and below 20 among its high-fertility populations. Furthermore, it has risen perceptibly since 1950 in the former areas and appears to have remained unchanged in the latter, a reflection of their dissimilar fertility trends over the past 25 years. Among individual regions, the lowest median ages tend to be found in Africa, where fertility is highest, while the oldest such ages are encountered in Europe, where national fertility levels are typically lowest.

For analogous reasons, projections assuming moderate declines in regional fertility levels everywhere (the United Nations medium variant) would lead to something like a 10 per cent rise in average age of both sets of regions by the year 2000.

Turning to some main characteristics of recent age distributions by region, the "40/40" rule that birth-rates of about 40 per 1,000 tend to be associated with 40 per cent or higher fractions of the population under 15, is applicable to the less developed regions as a whole, to all of Africa and South Asia, and to most of Latin America. East Asia represents an intermediate position, reflecting low fractions, about 20 to 25 per cent. Only the Caribbean areas fail to accord with the expected pattern, their atypically high fraction under 15 being associated with only intermediate-level birth-rates owing to large-scale out-migration of young adults.

Regional proportions of population over 65 are in effect mirror images of these patterns. The more developed regions show fractions averaging some two to three times the average for less developed regions, the estimated values being about 10 and 4 per cent, respectively, for the two combined groupings of areas. Among individual regions, the highest fractions are at present in Europe and the lowest in Africa, while the remaining regional measures range downward from those in North America and the USSR, to the atypically low value for a more developed region found in Australia plus New Zealand, to the atypically high value among less developed regions in the Caribbean, and then to East Asia, the rest of Latin America and South Asia. Both atypical cases reflect unusually heavy migration effects.

Since international differences between population proportions under 15 tend to be much larger numerically than over-65 differences, it follows that the less developed regions consistently show far smaller fractions of population aged 15 to 65 than do the more developed regions. The average fractions for the two groups of areas, about 55 and 65 per cent, respectively, imply total (young-age plus old-age) population dependence ratios approximating 80 and 55 per cent, a nearly 50 per cent differential.

This last differential has been enhanced by the above-average rate of growth estimated for the 15–25 age group in the less developed regions over the past decade, both as compared to other age groups in these regions and all age groups in the more developed areas. Other recent "age-specific" rates of growth having special interest have been the 1965–1970 declines of the under-5 age group in Europe and Northern America, a rapid rate of decline of the 15–25 group in the latter region, and large rates of increase in the 65-plus population in both the more and less developed regions. Since 1950 the world's older population has risen by roughly two thirds. By far the largest share of such increase is in the more developed regions, where the proportion of older population has risen markedly everywhere in direct reflection of recent declines of fertility. In the less developed regions, despite an equally rapid average rate of growth in the older population, the proportion over 65 has changed very little, an indication that their small changes in fertility on an over-all basis have dominated their often spectacular declines in mortality with respect to age structure.

Both the young-age and upper-age growth patterns just indicated for the industrially advanced regions imply clearly major social and economic adjustments in the decades ahead. The declines or sharp decelerations of the under-15 population taking place in these areas have already had significant impact on educational needs. Analogous impacts on family formation, labour force and size of future birth cohorts are sure to emerge once the age cohorts now in the childhood years begin to move into adulthood. Similarly, the current and clearly foreseeable rise in these regions of older population, both in absolute and relative terms, augurs a major rise in social preoccupation with the economic security, medical care, housing, employment opportunities and psychic needs of the aged. To a lesser but no longer minor extent, rising concern with such problems will also loom large in the less developed regions if, as expected, high growth rates of their over-65 populations continue into the future. Although the micro- and macro- (in particular, familial and governmental) contexts of such concerns will often differ greatly from those of the higher-income nations, many aspects are likely to become increasingly similar as economic development proceeds on a global scale.

Social concerns related closely to recent demographic trends also involve the especially rapid growth of the 15–25 age group in the less developed regions and the imminent sharp decline of this age group in the more developed regions. The former tendency will inevitably bring with it added problems of labour-force absorption and new dimensions of urban-rural redistribution, while the latter is sure to imply novel productive adjustments because of declining numbers of labour-force entrants and almost certain rapid changes in family and household formation.

Sex Ratios

Unlike age distribution by sex, regional or national sex distributions by age are unaffected by fertility, since variations in fertility over time and space, however large, are neutralized by the near invariance of the sex ratio at birth. Since the last rarely lies outside the narrow range of about 105 male per 100 female births plus or minus 1 per cent, the dominant determinant as a rule of the sex ratio at later individual ages or for all ages combined is mortality. More specifically, variations in the ratio of males to females at any age depend on their comparative survival rates since birth, except to the extent that significant modifications result from relatively large and sex-selective net migration.

Global estimates suggest a current sex ratio which is close to unity, with both male and female populations numbering some two billion.

The approximately 5 per cent drop between the sex ratio at birth and this all-age ratio reflects the fact that on a global scale, female survival chances between birth and later ages tend to be higher than those for males. So pronounced and consistent has this tendency been in the more developed regions that their sex ratios form a steadily declining function of age. In less developed regions, the absence of a sustained fall of the average sex ratio before about age 60 implies fluctuating comparative levels of male and female survival rates to various ages, with an approximately equal rate for the 0–60 span as a whole. Not until the upper adult years do the sex ratios in these regions begin an uninterrupted decline, such as would occur with steadily higher female age-specific survival rates at the latter ages of life. There is no way, however, of judging the extent to which these under-60 and 60-plus patterns may be linked to uncertain estimates.

A relatively clear-cut conclusion suggested by the estimates is that the surviving members of male and female birth cohorts in the more developed regions become equalized at a considerably earlier age, at approximately age 35, than they do in the less developed areas where equalization occurs at age 60 or so. Such a difference would be consistent with the fact that survival-rate differentials favouring females have historically been higher or more uniformly encountered, or both, in European-type populations than has been true in most parts of Africa, Asia or Latin America.

The often rapidly changing role of women during the post-war decades—in the labour force, in education and within the family itself—is sure to have major cause and effect interrelations with childbearing and nuptiality patterns over large parts of the world. As yet too new to be clearly specified, such interrelations will pose numerous challenges to social and demographic research, along with a host of major issues for policy, in the decades ahead. A second set of interrelations, centered on the diminishing ratios of male to female numbers in the upper ages of life, is likely to command similar analytic and policy attention, as problems of human resources from both productive and welfare viewpoints come increasingly to the fore.

Labour Force

Between 1950 and 1975, the world's economically active population rose from 1 billion to 1.5-plus billion, according to available estimates, a rise of about 50 per cent. Its lower rate of increase as compared to the 60 per cent growth of total population implies a 5 to 10 per cent decline in the global crude (all-age) rate of labour force participation, a trend almost wholly attributable to declining participation rates among younger and older males. Age composition, another factor potentially capable of causing a shift in the aggregate participation rate, was comparatively unimportant. It changed relatively little in the less developed regions, for reasons already discussed, and its main shifts in the more developed regions were compensating ones at ages under 15 and over 65, which have little significance for average participation probabilities. Although changes in age composition between 15 and 65 may have been of some importance in a number of individual industrially advanced nations, their effects have been secondary from a global viewpoint.

The rate of participation for males aged 10-plus over the world as a whole appears to have fallen sharply since 1950, from about 60 per cent to below 55 per cent. Downtrending tendencies of age-specific male rates by age, which have been marked at the ages under 25 and over 55 and mildly so between these two central years of labour-force activity, have been in contrast with the more variable corresponding trends for women. Over-all, the crude female participation rate rose in both the less and more developed regions, owing to sharp increases in the 25–55 group and despite decreases at ages under 25. At ages beyond 55, for which the numbers involved are small, the female rate fell sharply in the more developed regions and may have risen somewhat in the less developed areas, the only instance of a sex-age-specific difference between the two regional groupings in direction of trend. The seeming upward drift of the labour-force participation rate among upper-age females in low-income countries could prove to be a significant antecedent of a major development trend to come, though its meaning is obscured as yet by statistical ambiguities.

Since scale of output and levels of living in any economy depend upon the relative volumes of human and non-human factors of production, both size and growth of labour force have economic importance for reasons quite apart from their bearing on participation rates. It is worth stressing, therefore, that the labour force in the less developed regions in 1975 had become equal to the world's total labour force in 1950 and that the number of economically active persons in low-income areas increased at a rate approximately double that of the more developed regions during the intervening quarter century. Each of four large groupings of less developed areas—Latin America, Africa, East Asia and South Asia—had higher rates of growth than did Northern America, the USSR or Europe, while only the developed part of Oceania, because of high rates of immigration, deviated from this comparative pattern. The net effect of these disparities has been to raise the proportion of the world's labour force in the less developed regions from about

64 to 68 per cent, while lowering the share in the more developed regions commensurately. Barring unexpected future trends in participation rates in either group or both groups of regions, this tendency should continue and gain strength in the decades to come.

In demographic structure no less than regional composition, the world's labour force has shown marked recent transformations. The number of economically active females has risen at a rate about 50 per cent higher than the male rate, so that it constituted about 35 per cent of the total labour force in 1975, compared to 30 per cent or so at mid-century. With respect to age, the proportion of the labour force in the 25–55 interval rose substantially, mainly because of rising numbers of females, while both the young-worker and older-worker proportions declined perceptibly. The young-worker downtrend seems nearly certain to continue and might accelerate, given the rapidly changing role of women in many of the world's economies. The upper-age tendency may have a more uncertain future, not only for substantive reasons but also if statistical procedures were to change in distinguishing between the economically active and inactive parts of the older female population.

A further compositional view of the world's labour force, in terms of its distribution between agricultural and non-agricultural activities, reveals marked variations over time and enormous contrasts over space. On a world-wide scale, since 1950 the proportion of persons economically active in agriculture is estimated to have dropped by about one seventh, from nearly two thirds of the total labour force to less than half. It is doubtful that this much change (in either direction) has ever occurred before over a comparable period, if indeed it has ever taken place at all over much longer periods. In the more developed regions, the agricultural labour force declined drastically by any of several criteria: in absolute numbers by 50 per cent, quite possibly the first such quarter-century drop in history; as a fraction of the world's agricultural population, from 20 to under 10 per cent; and as a proportion of total labour force in these regions, to well under half the 1950 fraction. In starkly contrasting manner, agricultural labour force within the less developed regions rose by an unparalleled amount, about 150 million, despite rapid rates of urbanization and an unprecedented decline of its relative size, from four fifths to only five eighths of the total labour force.

These structural aspects outweigh in economic significance the fact that the world's total number of agricultural workers rose only from about 700 to 800 million. The size of this increase and its uneven distribution over time and space reflect often major variations in rates of natural increase, rates of rural-to-urban migration, levels and pace of development, international trade and, not infrequently, individual national policies.

SOME SOCIAL AND ECONOMIC CORRELATES

Education

Since universal primary education is an accepted social goal every-where, educational needs at the early school ages can be essentially defined by population size in all regions. So viewed, the trends of pri-mary-school needs by region during recent decades have been along expected lines. The global number of children between 6 and 11 years of age in 1970 was estimated at approximately 400 million. Of these, nearly three fourths were in less developed regions, and this fraction had been rising sharply. That the trends in primary educational needs within the less and more developed regions have diverged so sharply throughout the post-war period, is a direct reflection of these facts.

The extent to which primary schooling needs have been met has been only partially in accord with expectations. On the one hand, enrolment ratios of primary school-age children have been rising in all regions and have come to exceed 90 percent levels in the more devel-oped areas. On the other hand, the number of children 6 to 11 who are not at school appears to have increased, rather than decreased, in the less developed regions, where the estimated enrolment rise of three-fourths, or over 60 million, during the 1960s was well below the rise in eligible numbers.

An analogous contrast holds for the succeeding age interval of 12 to 17, which includes the years of high school education and involves greater variability of national goals. For this age group, rapid increases in both the numbers and ratios of enrolled students have taken place in the more developed regions, as could be anticipated from educational targets. However, despite a doubling of enrolment rates in the less developed regions, the increased number at school has not been suffi-cient to avoid a rise in the out-of-school number.

Calculations comparing the effects of high *versus* low enrolment ratios and high *versus* low fertility in the less developed regions by the year 2000 suggest that the influence of both differentials could be large, involving between nearly 100 million and 450 million additional stu-dents aged 6 to 11, under extreme assumptions. In the more developed regions, neither rising enrolment nor fertility variations alone would have a significant impact on primary school needs relative to present numbers.

An implication of these recent trends and future possibilities is that qualitative educational goals in the less developed regions will continue to be seriously prejudiced by limited resources as a result of the size and growth of their school-age populations, much as in the past. Pupil-teacher ratios in these areas have remained unchanged at both primary and secondary educational levels despite enormous resource inputs. At the primary grades, such ratios have been much higher, by about 50 per cent, than in the more developed regions, and attrition rates in these grades have persisted at elevated magnitudes.

In contrast to the effects of population upon primary or secondary school needs and targets, which are in good measure relatively direct, the influences of educational levels upon demographic patterns are highly uncertain and even elusive. Available studies suggest that extent of schooling is inversely related to fertility over a broad spectrum of societies, but that the threshold of significant educational effects on childbearing may be highly variable among different social systems and substantially conditioned by such background factors as urban-rural residence. Whether educational programmes explicitly focused on fertility behaviour can affect it decisively is as yet too difficult a question to assess, especially for areas with traditionally high rates of childbearing. Attempts to incorporate such programmes into organized family planning efforts or as part of formal educational curricula have not been tested sufficiently, and the results are too mixed to permit confident conclusions or forecasts.

Much research is similarly needed on the main interrelations likely to hold between education and migration. Such research, if successful, could have broad significance for agricultural, population and industrial location policies, regional and urban-rural planning, and investment decisions in the public and private sectors. Quite possibly, closer and more ramified knowledge of the reciprocal effects between educational programmes and demographic processes could lead to significant innovations and enhanced effectiveness within the educational system itself.

Labour-force Dependency

Economic support of dependents can be measured in various ways. Each method has its particular uses. The most widely utilized measure, the ratio of young plus old in a population to the number in the main economically active age group (typically the ratio of those under 15 and over 65 to persons 15–65, or some approximate variant thereof), has the advantage of being more readily available than most alternatives. It also has the useful theoretical property of showing what dependency on the labour force would be if participation rates reached the extreme level of zero before and after the main labour-force ages and a maximum of unity within such ages. In addition, it can be directly linked to the effects of fertility and mortality on age structure, as discussed earlier.

A more indicative measure of actual support patterns, since it reflects actual rather than theoretical participation rates, is the ratio of economically non-active persons to those in the labour force. Although such measures tend to be broadly linked to purely age-defined ratios, they are nevertheless sufficiently distinctive to merit separate attention. For example, because of the variable statistical treatment often accorded female, child and male upper-age farm labour, dependency ratios based on labour force tend to show less regular patterns over space and, occasionally, time than do their age-defined counterparts.

Estimates for 1950 and 1975 indicate that the global labour dependency ratio has risen by about 10 per cent, or not far from the increase of the corresponding population dependency ratio. In round terms, the number of non-active persons per 100 active persons moved up from about 125 to 140, as a result of the fact that the former group grew by about 70 per cent more in size than did the latter.

Regionally, and again as with population dependency, the main increase by far was in the less developed areas, where the labour-force measure rose from about 135 to over 150, or 15 per cent, on average. In developed regions, the over-all ratio has hardly moved at all, remaining between 115 and 120. Today, several industrially advanced regions, including Eastern Europe, the USSR and Japan, have fewer dependents than workers. In contrast, substantially more dependents than workers are found in all regional groupings of less developed populations. East Asia, as a result of marked fertility declines, shows an excess of dependents of only about 15 per cent, but in the others the excess ranges typically from over 30 to about 150 per cent.

Disaggregating the 1950–1975 increase in global labour-force dependency by sex-age composition shows that over two thirds of the rise has involved males and less than one third females. By age, most of the rise was contributed by children under 15 and appears to have involved somewhat more males than females. Beyond 15, dependency rose in the young adult and upper years among both males and females, though about twice as rapidly among the former. The largest discrepancy by far between the sexes occurred in the group between 25 and 55, the central labour-force age bracket; here, male dependency may have risen somewhat, while female dependency has decreased sharply.

About three fifths of the globally dependent population in 1975 was female and two fifths male. The decline since 1950 in the proportion of female to total dependents, from about 65 to 60 per cent, and the corresponding rise in the proportion for males, reflect the rapid expansion of the female work force simultaneously with declining labour-participation rates among younger and older males. Classified by age and sex, the world's non-active population now consists of the following: about three fifths under 15 years of age, equally divided between the sexes; another third comprised of females over 15; and the remaining tenth, males over this age. These proportions could become significantly altered over the next quarter century as a result of changing age composition, rising female labour participation and altered entry or retirement patterns among males.

Food Supply

Population during the third quarter of this century has continued to be a dominant determinant of global needs and effective demand for food. It has also been a major determinant of supply, both directly by its effects on the agricultural labour force and in less direct but significant ways through its effects on savings and investment rates, international trade, land tenure patterns and methods of food production. These factors—together with chronic causes and other irregular elements such as unfavourable weather—have often contributed to the world's long-standing mismatches between regional consumption requirements and supply capabilities.

In the less developed regions, a minimal benchmark of increasing needs is afforded by the three fourths rise in population since 1950. Even with their *per capita* food consumption held constant, thereby implying levels far below nutritional standards, an average annual growth in supply of well over 2 per cent has been required just to keep up with numbers alone. Long-run increases of this magnitude, either in output or available supply with interregional trade taken into account, would require major reorganization of methods of food production and distribution. If the large historic shortfalls of nutritional standards in the low-income regions are also taken into account, a second considerable dimension of food supply requirements becomes evident. A current third dimension of need in those areas, occasioned by several poor harvest years during the first half of the 1970s, is to replenish buffer stocks—in particular, inventories of cereals—if their chronic vulnerability to sharp short-run downturns in production—a possibility which has become especially ominous in recent years—is not to generate future disasters.

With respect to effective demand as well, population size and growth have loomed large among the factors affecting food developments in the low-income areas since the Second World War. A number of studies suggest that growth in numbers account for almost three fourths of the rise in their demand during recent periods, or for more than can be attributed, at least statistically, to income plus all other causal factors combined. The fact that the world's annual demand for cereals is expanding by two to three times the amount of such expansion only a quarter century ago can be largely traced to accelerated population growth in Africa, Asia and Latin America.

For the more developed regions, the food needs situation since the war has been of a wholly different kind. Actual consumption and nutritionally suggested standards of consumption have remained comparatively close to each other on average. Indeed, energy (calorie) intake *per capita* is one fifth too high compared to requirements in these areas, even though several tens of millions of their inhabitants are estimated to be severely malnourished. The discrepancy between these last two facts appears to be clear evidence that the main food problems in the high-income areas are of distribution rather than supply. However, higher average incomes and other economic advantages in these areas have not been the only main factors at play. Low and slowing increases in population have also been major contributing elements. As a result, the gap between growth rates of food production and those of population has remained consistently high, leading to an average annual rise in *per capita* output of well over 1.5 per cent throughout the last 25-year period.

In demand terms, demographic influences account for about half of the post-war increases in the more developed areas, according to studies, compared to the nearly three fourths contribution cited earlier for the less developed economies.

A telling indication of the burdens placed on food supply by rapid increase of population is afforded by the fact that both high-fertility and low-fertility regions had roughly comparable growth rates of food output during the 1950s and again during the 1960s. As a result, average output *per capita* grew during both decades in the two groups of areas. Despite this, the *per capita* rise in the less developed regions was only between one third and one half the rise in the developed regions during the first of these decades and less than one fifth the rise in the second. In the 1970s, a combination of several poor harvest years and a continuing rapid population increase in the low-income areas has so far resulted in generally declining *per capita* output. Only parts of Asia appear to have avoided such declines, which were especially marked in Africa and the Far East.

The recent evidence on widespread vulnerability to food shortages becomes further apparent when disaggregated by country. Among nearly 100 developing nations, almost half have experienced an average decline in food output *per capita* between about 1960 and the mid-1970s, despite substantial gains in many of the same areas during parts of this period. Undoubtedly many more than half have suffered large losses in *per capita* output since 1970.

A main uncertainty today surrounding world food and population interrelations is whether *per capita* output gains can be resumed on a self-sustaining basis in the less developed regions, or whether the declines of the early 1970s are early warning signals of forthcoming deterioration. The question would appear to involve both production and population in central ways. Thus, the 1950–1970 gains in these regions occurred despite rapid population growth, which was outweighed by production uptrends of a high order by long-run standards. Since 1970, setbacks have reversed the balance. Although output has often continued to increase at a substantial rate, it has done so erratically over time and space and at a slower pace than in preceding decades; as a result, it has become matched or out-distanced by sustained population growth in most low-income regions. Within both Latin America and large parts of Asia, whereas countries with energy intakes normally above nutritional requirements tended to improve their position after 1970, those with below-standard consumption have generally experienced deteriorating trends. The recent food setbacks in both of these regions, the only ones for which adequately current data exist, may therefore have more serious consequences for nutrition, health and possibly mortality than is suggested by the region-wide averages. In Africa, whether or not recent output declines and low levels of consumption have been similarly correlated, it has been clear that supply shortfalls have lately reached dangerous and often lethal dimensions over a large part of the northern half of the continent.

If, as estimated by the Food and Agriculture Organization of the United Nations, about one fourth of the population of the less developed areas was exposed to severe malnutrition about 1970, it follows that even the considerable gains of 1950–1970 had only overcome a fraction of their pre-war food deficiencies. It is no less clear that both the number and relative size of the severely malnourished had become substantially greater as of 1975.

Vulnerability to adverse fluctuations and trends in food production among the less developed regions during the past quarter century has been accompanied by increasing reliance on international trade to offset temporary and longer-run shortfalls. In the basic instance of grains, growth in net imports has been especially manifest in Asia and

Africa, with a similar if lesser tendency found also in Latin America. All three of these regions appear to have been net exporters of grain before the Second World War but were substantial net importers by about 1975.

An even sharper turn-about of this kind has been manifest in Eastern Europe and the USSR as a result of post-1970 developments in their agricultural sectors. However, the problem of unmet food needs in the developed regions is obviously much more a matter to be remedied through adequate trade and distribution arrangements than a matter of inadequate supply availabilities or excessive population trends.

In addition to population and average income, factors affecting national needs and demands for food include income distribution, urban-rural composition and family or household size. The causal significance of demographic processes for each of these latter determinants is not small, especially in the less developed regions, though neither the orders of magnitude nor the structural nature of the linkages has been investigated.

On the supply side, international food production and trade capabilities in the years ahead will be adversely conditioned in several respects. First, although new cultivable areas can still be added to the present world stock, it seems unlikely that increases comparable to those of the past 25 years can be achieved in the next several decades. An important special element in this connexion has been the fact that previously idle land in the United States of America had already been converted to cultivated acreage several years ago. In many low-income countries as well, such as India, extension of cultivated land will probably prove to be a less significant source of added output than has been true in prior decades. Secondly, the rising cost of petroleum and its associated balance-of-payment difficulties will impose severe constraints on the world's fertilizer-expanding and food-trading capacities, above all in the non-oil rich developing regions. Thirdly, a limiting factor which is possibly transitory but which for the present poses severe constraints on international relief capabilities, has been the drastic reduction of international grain reserves relative to consumption. Such reserves are estimated to have fallen to one-third their former size as of the mid-1970s. Unless or until they are replenished, reliance on imports to offset supply shortfalls in the near future could prove both less feasible in physical terms and more costly financially.

In this connexion, it is well to take note of the newly prominent and highly controversial possibility that climatic conditions may be taking a drastic long-run turn for the worse. Although in the absence of scientifically confirmed evidence the likelihood of such a turn cannot be judged, even a small risk in this regard could be ominous. Climatic shifts anticipated by some scientific observers could alter world-wide man-land relationships in such unpredictably disastrous ways that no knowledge of their possible demographic effects or technological remedies has been acquired, at least during the several centuries of the modern era. For these reasons alone, a degree of continuous monitoring of the question would appear appropriate on the part of analysts, planners and policy makers.

Nevertheless, it is also clear that the long-standing and all too well-known food deficiencies affecting most of the world's population will—and probably should—continue to command major attention. Furthermore, such attention should simultaneously emphasize production and population. It is true that population pressures in many less developed economies are a demonstrably major obstacle to productivity gains in their agrarian sector, even as rapidly increasing numbers make such gains ever more necessary to feed additional mouths. It is no less true that the problem of achieving a better balance between the world's food needs and supplies is very largely one of production. Although reduced population growth in the less developed areas can facilitate and add to the gains made possible through improved agrarian technology and organization, it cannot be a substitute for such progress. New land utilization patterns, improved seed varieties, favourable credit and marketing conditions, greatly expanded irrigation facilities and intensified agricultural investment, among others, are non-demographic variables whose productive potentials are still enormous and far from being realized.

5 CONCISE REPORT ON MONITORING OF POPULATION POLICIES

This report on population policies is divided into six sections: rate of natural increase, mortality, fertility, spatial distribution and internal migration of the population, international migration, and institutional arrangements for the formulation and integration of population policies in development plans. Each of these sections considers, from both a world and a regional standpoint, how governments perceive population problems and formulate policies for solving them.

All the documentation used comes from official sources: replies to the Third Inquiry among Governments, entitled "Population policies in the context of development in 1976,"[1] statements made during the regional consultations after the Bucharest Conference,[2] statements made by competent government officials in various circumstances, national development plans, and so on. All this information is assembled on a continuous basis in the population policies data bank which has been operating in the Population Division for several years.

The data presented in this report relate to 156 States Members of the United Nations or members of specialized agencies. It can therefore be said to give an almost complete picture of the world situation with regard to population policies in 1976.

The situation studied in the report is that existing in 1976, specifically as at 1 July 1976, the latest date on which replies to the Third Inquiry among Governments could be taken into account. At the end of each section there are a number of paragraphs on the most important changes which occurred during the period covered, i.e., between 1 September 1974 and 1 July 1976. For information on the preceding period, reference may be made to two other reports prepared by the

United Nations Secretariat for the World Population Conference, 1974.[3]

While the situation with regard to population policies as a whole is fairly stable, there have been changes of detail which help to render the documentation used obsolescent. The fact that the sources of information were so many and varied and that some texts or statements were at times difficult to interpret also complicated the quest for documentation. Despite all the precautions that were taken, errors may have crept in among the raw data or at the analysis stage. The Secretariat would greatly appreciate any comments that would enable improvements or corrections to be made to the information contained in this report.

In view of the limited space available for this report, the analysis was conducted at a high level of aggregation. For instance, the tables show figures only by region and by level of development. The definitions used for regional groupings correspond to the areas covered by the regional commissions. The criterion for distinguishing between developed countries and developing countries also corresponds to the one used for projections.[4]

The definition used for the study of the population policies examined in this report lays emphasis on the following points: perception of the acceptability of the relationship between demographic and nondemographic processes, identification of the appropriateness or inappropriateness of direct or indirect intervention in those processes, identification of the objectives, and identification of the means to be employed when intervention is considered appropriate. This definition thus includes policies of non-intervention.

GOVERNMENT PERCEPTIONS OF AND POLICIES RELATING TO THE RATE OF NATURAL INCREASE OF THE POPULATION

The first subject to be dealt with in this section is how governments perceive the rate of natural increase of their population. Reactions have been sorted into three categories: "higher rate desirable"; rate "satisfactory"; "lower rate desirable." Regardless of their attitude to the rate of natural increase of their population, all the governments have formulated policies, whether of non-intervention or of intervention in the level or the trend of the rate of natural increase. In the latter case, of course, the sophistication of the intervention may vary from country to country.

Policies of intervention will be considered first. These policies cover a very wide range of options, from intervention confined to demographic variables which determine the rate of natural increase—such as fertility, mortality and migration—to intervention in economic and social variables, sometimes leading to a restructuring of the society. Lastly, the use of the resources of technology is more and more frequently a feature of action programmes linked to the problems of the rate of natural increase of the population. In fact, as will be seen later, intervention is seldom confined to a single variable; governments usually opt for a combination of forms of intervention. It must also be borne in mind that there are a number of countries which take the view that the rate of increase poses no problem and that, consequently, no policy of intervention is necessary.

See below for a brief analysis of the principal changes observed between 1974 and 1976 in both perceptions and policies. First of all, Table 5.1 gives a breakdown of the perceptions of 156 governments covered by this report. Thirty-seven countries consider that a "higher rate (of natural increase) is desirable," 70 perceive the rate is "satisfactory," and 49 believe that a "lower rate is desirable." One developed country out of 42 considers a "higher rate desirable," as against 48 developing countries out of 114. In the "satisfactory" category are 25 of the 42 developed countries and 45 of the 114 developing countries. Lastly, the "higher rate desirable" category comprises 16 of the 42 developed countries and only 21 of the 114 developing countries. In terms of population, 13 per cent of the world population is resident in countries which declare a "higher rate desirable", 29 per cent in countries which feel "satisfied" and 58 per cent in countries which declare a "lower rate desirable." In the case of the developing countries, the breakdown is as follows: 3 per cent of their population is resident in countries which "desire higher rates," 16 per cent in countries "satisfied" with their rate and 81 per cent in countries which "desire lower rates."

From the regional standpoint, the perception that a "lower rate is desirable" is predominant in the ESCAP region (18 out of 30). In the ECLA region (13 out of 27) and the ECA region (17 out of 48), the proportion of countries with that perception is smaller. It will be noted, however, that in the ECLA region the number of countries in that category has shown a clear increase in the past few years. In the ECE region (1 out of 39) and the ECWA region (none), hardly any country considers a "lower rate (of natural increase) desirable." On the other hand, the category "present rate satisfactory" is predominant in the ECE region (23 out of 39). In the ECA region there is also a large group of countries which are "satisfied" with their rates (24 out of 48). Then, in descending order, come the ECLA region (10 out of 27), the ECWA region (7 out of 12) and the ESCAP region (6 out of 30). As can be seen,

TABLE 5.1: Government Perceptions of the Consequences of Current Rates of Natural Increase

A. Number of Countries, According to Categories of Perception, Membership of Regional Commissions, and Level of Development

Regions and Countries	Higher Rate Desirable	Current Rate Satisfactory	Lower Rate Desirable	Total
ECA	7	24	17	48
ECWA	5	7	—	12
ECLA	4	10	13	27
ECE	15	23	1	39
ESCAP	6	6	18	30
Developed countries	16	25	1	42
Developing countries	21	45	48	114
Total	37	70	49	156

B. Percentage of the Population, According to Categories of Perception, Membership of Regional Commissions, and Level of Development

	Higher Rate Desirable	Current Rate Satisfactory	Lower Rate Desirable	Total
ECA	6	57	36	100
ECWA	25	75	—	100
ECLA	10	53	37	100
ECE	41	55	4	100
ESCAP	1	8	91	100
Developed countries	39	61	0	100
Developing countries	3	16	81	100
Total	13	29	58	100

Source: United Nations.

the category of countries "satisfied" with their growth rate includes two groups which differ with respect to the level of development: those in the ECE region and those in the ECA region. The first group includes countries which are in general "satisfied" because their policies have been effective; the second group includes countries where the present rate, as it has evolved spontaneously, corresponds to the aspirations of the governments. The category "higher rate desirable" includes seven countries in the ECA region, five in the ECWA region, four in the ECLA region and 15 in the ECE region. There has been a marked increase in this category in the ECE region in recent years.

The consequences at the international level of the adjustments, whether successful or unsuccessful, between demographic and non-demographic processes at the national level are of great importance for the future of the international community. If it is recognized that the problem is a world-wide one and if, moreover, it is recognized that this world problem exists specifically only in the form of national population problems, it might be asked what effects the balances achieved between demographic and non-demographic processes within each country have on the world rate of increase.

On the left side of Table 5.2 we have divided the 156 countries into three categories according to their perception of their rate of natural increase: "higher rate desirable" (37), "present rate satisfactory" (70), and "lower rate desirable" (49). Next, for each country, sorted in advance into the three categories mentioned, a variant of the projection of its population between 1975 and 2000 has been assigned.[5] Several theoretical combinations were possible between the three demographic varients—high, medium, low—and the three categories of perception of the rate—"higher rate desirable," "current rate satisfactory" and "lower rate desirable." Only seven combinations have been listed— designated A, B, C, D, E, F and G. Combination A shows a perfect correlation between the assessment by the government of the present growth rate and the projection variant corresponding logically to that assessment. Thus, governments which consider a "higher rate desirable" have been assigned a high variant; those which perceive the rate to be "satisfactory" have been given a medium variant;[6] and those which consider a "lower rate desirable" have been assigned a low variant. Combination B shows a partial correlation between the demographic variants selected and the assessment by the government of the current rate of increase. Thus, governments which consider a "higher rate desirable" have been assigned a medium variant; those which consider the rate "satisfactory", a medium variant; and those which consider a "lower rate desirable" a low variant. Combination C also shows a partial correlation between the demographic variants and the assessment by the government of the rate of increase. The difference between combination C and combination B is as follows: countries which are "satisfied" with their rate have again been assigned a medium variant; on the other hand, countries which consider a "higher rate desirable" have been assigned a high variant, and those which consider a "lower rate desirable," a medium variant. Combination D shows a nearly complete lack of correlation between the perceptions of governments and the demographic variants in the two categories "higher rate desirable" and "lower rate desirable," which are determinantes. The category "higher rate desirable" has been assigned a low variant; the category "lower rate desirable" has been assigned a high variant; the "satisfactory" category has again been assigned the medium variant.

TABLE 5.2: World Population Projections from 1975 to 2000, According to Different Combinations of Variants Corresponding Completely or only in Part to Government Perceptions of Their Current Rate of Natural Increase

Combinations of Variants	Number of Countries Which Consider (variants)			Population Projection Using the Combinations of Variants Indicated			
	A Higher Rate Desirable = 37	The Current Rate Satisfactory = 70	A Lower Rate Desirable = 49	Total Population (millions) 1975ᵃ	2000	Increase (millions) 1975–2000	Indices of Increase (low variant = base 100) (millions) 1975–2000
A. *Complete correlation:* development of rates corresponds to government perceptions	High	Medium	Low	3,932	5,972	2,040	108
B. *Partial correlation:* development of rates corresponds to government perceptions for rates regarded as too high or satisfactory	Medium	Medium	Low	3,931	5,944	2,013	106
C. *Partial correlation:* development of rates corresponds to government perceptions for rates regarded as too low or satisfactory	High	Medium	Medium	3,947	6,245	2,298	122

TABLE 5.2: (Continued)

Combinations of Variants	Number of Countries Which Consider (variants)			Population Projection Using the Combinations of Variants Indicated			
	A Higher Rate Desirable = 37	The Current Rate Satisfactory = 70	A Lower Rate Desirable = 49	Total Population (millions) 1975[a]	2000	Increase (millions) 1975–2000	Indices of Increase (low variant = base 100) (millions) 1975–2000
D. *Very little correlation:* development of rates corresponds to government perceptions for rates regarded as satisfactory	Low	Medium	High	3,901	6,391	2,490	132
E. The low variant is applied systematically to all countries	Low	Low	Low	3,948	5,838	1,890	100
F. The medium variant is applied systematically to all countries	Medium	Medium	Medium	3,967	6,253	2,286	121
G. The high variant is applied systematically to all countries	High	High	High	3,980	6,637	2,657	141

[a] The size of the population in 1975 varies according to different hypotheses, as the figure in question involves a projection based on 1973.
Source: Selected World Demographic Indicators by Countries, 1950–2000 (ESA/P/WP.55).

In combination E, all countries have been given the low variant; in combination F, the medium variant, and in combination G, the high variant.

This rudimentary attempt to show the possible effects of a correlation or lack of correlation between the present views of governments regarding their rates of increase and a range of projections of demographic development more or less corresponding to their present aspirations highlights several points: (a) the effects on the volume of world population in 2000 of satisfying the aspirations of governments which consider a "higher rate desirable" or "satisfactory," compared with the effects of satisfying governments which consider a "lower rate desirable," are slight; (b) of the 49 countries which consider a "lower rate desirable," 18 are in Asia and account for the majority of the population of the region. The increase in absolute figures, between 1975 and 2000, in the countries of South Asia and of East Asia will be 1,150 million according to the *low variant* and 1,590 million according to the *high variant,* as compared with 590 million according to the *low variant* and 800 million according to the *high variant* for the countries of Latin America and Africa together.[7] Finally, it can be seen that curbing the increase in world population depends largely on achieving the low variant in Asia.

These approximate calculations furnish the only quantified evaluation of the effects of the attitudes of governments towards the rates of natural increase of their population on the possible development of world population between now and 2000. It should be noted, from a purely practical standpoint, that ultimately it is more important to help governments realize their aspirations than to try to change them. Finally, if the aspirations of governments are to be taken as the sole determinants of demographic behaviour, the results on a world scale in 2000 not only will be in conformity with the aspirations of the different countries, as indicated in Table 5.2, but also will be reflected in a volume of population only a little higher than what it would be if the low variant were applied systematically to all countries—5,972 million inhabitants as compared with 5,838 million (combinations A and E)—but considerably lower than the total for the medium variant —6,253 million compared with 5,972 million (combinations F and A) and lower still than the total for the high variant—6,637 million as compared with 5,972 million (combinations G and A). It may be thought that the differences between the calculated population totals for 2000 according to the seven assumptions in Table 5.2 are relatively unimportant in absolute terms. However, it should be noted that the period considered for the purpose of making the projections (1975–2000), that is, 25 years, is a period during which the effects of inertia, combined, for example, with the present age structure of the population of the developing countries, will be considerable. Only after 2000 will the change in trends become more noticeable. The policies applied between 1975 and 2000 will generate "interest" in terms of population growth the spectacular effects of which will not be apparent until after 2000.

Table 5.3 shows the policy options which governments most frequently choose when they perceive a problem related to their rate of natural increase. It should be noted first of all that only 24 countries out of 156, divided equally between developed and developing coun-

TABLE 5.3: Combinations of Government Policy Options for the Solution of Problems Perceived in Relation to Current Rates of Natural Increase (number of countries)

A. Combinations of Policy Options

Countries	5	4 A	4 B	4 C	3 A	3 B	3 C	3 D	2 A	2 B	2 C	1 A	1 B	1 C	0	Total
Developed countries	4	3	—	4	—	3	1	5	—	4	—	2	2	2	12	42
Developing countries	9	25	4	6	2	5	12	14	22	—	1	—	1	1	12	114
Total	13	28	4	10	2	8	13	19	22	4	1	2	3	3	24	156

B. Most Frequent Combinations of Government Policy Options

Categories of Combinations	Mortality	Fertility	Spatial Distribution	International Migration	Technology and/or Socio-economic Reform
5	x	x	x	x	x
4A	.	x	x	x	x
B	x	.	x	x	x
C	x	x	x	.	x
3A	x	.	x	.	x
B	.	x	.	x	x
C	.	x	x	.	x
D	.	.	x	x	x
2A	.	.	x	.	x
B	.	.	.	x	x
C	.	x	.	x	.
1A	.	x	.	.	.
B	.	.	x	.	.
C	.	.	.	x	.
0	.	.	.	.	.

Note: x indicates government intervention.
    . indicates no intervention.
Source: United Nations.

tries, perceive no problems related to their rates of natural increase. These countries are representative of a category (category O) of countries which considers that the rate of increase has either no effect or a favourable effect on the realization of their economic and social development objectives and therefore sees no reason for intervention.[8] Extremely varied nuances can be noted in the perceptions of 132 other countries regarding the effects of the rate of increase on development. Finally, it is only in rare cases that the rate of increase is considered to have no effect, an entirely unfavourable effect or an entirely favourable effect. In most cases, it is regarded as having both a negative and a positive effect. Government intervention may be divided into two categories: purely demographic intervention and intervention aimed at economic and social restructuring, the extent of which varies from one country to another. The number of countries having recourse to exclusively demographic options is very limited. It is covered by categories 2C, 1A, 1B and 1C in Table 5.3, or nine countries altogether. All the other countries, 123 in number, apply a combination of policy options which include intervention in the sphere of socio-economic restructuring in addition to purely demographic terms of intervention. A detailed examination of these policies of socio-economic restructuring and their relative "weight"in comparison with demographic policies will be the subject of an in-depth analysis in the second part of the report on monitoring of population trends and policies throughout the world.[9] Suffice it to observe that such policies play an increasing role in the developing countries and that some governments, notably those of the socialist countries, regard them as the main, if not the only policies for adjusting socio-demographic imbalances. A reading of the table below gives an idea of the relative weight attributed to demographic intervention and non-demographic intervention in the policies which governments apply in seeking to remedy the imbalances created by the rate of natural increase. Nineteen countries, including 13 developing countries, have policies under which the weight of non-demographic intervention predominates, although they have recourse to certain traditional forms of demographic intervention; 95 countries, including 77 developing countries, have policies under which the weight of demographic and non-demographic forms of intervention is equal; finally, only 18 countries, including 12 developing countries, have policies under which demographic intervention predominates and socio-economic intervention plays a secondary role. Only 24 countries, in which the rate of natural increase poses no problem, regard any intervention affecting demographic and non-demographic factors as inappropriate.

Countries	Intervention to influence non-demographic factors: predominates	Intervention to influence demographic and non-demographic factors: equal	Intervention to influence demographic factors: predominates	No problem related to rate of natural increase	Total
Developed countries	6	18	6	12	42
Developing countries	13	77	12	12	114
Total	19	95	18	24	156

A more detailed analysis of the policies selected in Table 5.3 with a view to modifying the rate of natural increase shows more or less frequent combinations of options. Apart from the 24 countries in which there is felt to be no problem related to the natural increase of the population, other countries more or less frequently choose certain combinations of forms of intervention. It should be pointed out that only 13 countries (category 5 in Table 5.3) use the whole range of possible options; the others use a combination of demographic and non-demographic intervention. The most frequent combination—4 A (28 countries)—consists of intervention with a regard to fertility, spatial distribution and international migration, and, at the same time, a policy of economic and social restructuring. Combination 2 A (22 countries, all developing countries) consists of intervention with regard to spatial redistribution combined with economic and social restructuring. Combination 3 D (19 countries) consists of intervention with regard to spatial distribution and international migration combined with a policy or economic and social restructuring.

Between 1974 and 1976, a number of changes have affected the perceptions of countries with regard to their rates of increase and, consequently, their policies. To take, first, the case of the developing countries, Benin and Singapore no longer state that they believe a "lower rate desirable", but consider the present rate "satisfactory." On the other hand, other countries such as Ethiopia, Honduras, Jordan, Nigeria and Surinam, while indicating that their current rate is "satisfactory", appear to recognize the existence of problems habitually associated with high rates. In a group of six countries—Ecuador, Liberia, Madagascar, Nicaragua, Senegal and Sierra Leone—there are fairly clear indications that the governments now consider a "lower rate desirable", but have taken no policy measures. In another group of developing countries, the governments have not only declared that a "lower rate of increase is desirable", but have formulated policies to reduce the rate; these countries are Grenada, Lesotho, Seychelles, Papua New Guinea and Uganda. Lastly, countries such as India and Indonesia have reinforced their policies to bring about a decline in the rate of increase. In that connexion, India has adopted more vigorous measures.

In the developed countries, rates of natural increase have declined almost everywhere. However, some countries, such as Czechoslovakia and Hungary, have changed their perception of their rate of natural increase from "higher rate desirable" to "satisfactory", no doubt as a result of the success of their family planning policies. Other countries which formerly regarded a "higher rate desirable" have reformulated their policies to check the decline in fertility. This applies to Argentina, France, the German Democratic Republic, Greece and Luxembourg. Two countries which, before 1974, had considered a "higher rate desirable" but which had not formulated policies now seem concerned to do so: these are Finland and Uruguay. Some countries which formerly did not consider a "higher rate desirable" have stated in 1976 that they now do: this applies to the Federal Republic of Germany, the Ukrainian Soviet Socialist Republic and the Union of Soviet Socialist Republics. Switzerland has for the first time shown some concern at the decline in its rate of increase.

Lastly, other developed countries such as Portugal, which previously regarded a higher rate of natural increase desirable, now consider their rate "satisfactory." Chile, which formerly considered a "lower rate desirable", now considers its rate "satisfactory." On the other hand, New Zealand, which formerly considered its rate "satisfactory," now considers a "lower rate desirable" although its rate has steadily declined.

GOVERNMENT PERCEPTIONS OF AND POLICIES RELATING TO MORTALITY

No government perceives the current levels achieved as completely satisfactory. Some, however, accept the situation, in view of the various constraints weighing on the development of mortality. The acceptability of the situation depends to a large extent, as Table 5.4 shows, on the level of mortality observed in the various countries considered. But even in those countries which have a longer expectation

TABLE 5.4: Government Perceptions of Current Levels of Average Expectation of Life at Birth and Their Acceptability in the Light of Current Economic and Social Conditions (number of countries)

Regions and Countries	Levels of Expectation of Life at Birth							
	70 Years and Over		62ª–69 Years		50–61 Years		50 Years and Under	Total
	A	Un	A	Un	A	Un	Un	Total
ECA	—	—	1	—	—	10	37	48
ECWA	—	—	4	1	2	1	4	12
ECLA	1	—	8	6	2	9	1	27
ECE	26	6	3	3	—	1	—	39
ESCAP	4	—	4	—	4	6	12	30
Developed countries	28	6	4	4	—	—	—	42
Developing countries	3	—	16	6	8	27	54	114
Total	31	6	20	10	8	27	54	156

ª An expectation of life at birth of 62 years corresponds to the world average expectation of life in 1985 mentioned in paragraph 22 of the World Population Plan of Action. The other categories in this table have been selected by reference to that figure.

Note: A = acceptable.
Un = unacceptable.
Source: United Nations.

145

of life at birth, there are still problems relating to differential mortality linked to such factors as age, sex, residence and occupation. Moreover, in some industrial countries where the levels of expectation of life at birth are among the highest in the world there has, during the past ten years, been a reversal of the movement, evident for more than a century, towards a decline in mortality, particularly among men in certain age groups.

The Third Inquiry among Governments on Population Policies in the context of Development in 1976 included a question regarding the acceptability of current mortality levels. Table 5.4 has been prepared on the basis of the replies received and information collected from other governmental sources. This table can be summarized as follows:

(a) In the developed countries (total 42), 32 consider the level acceptable and 10 consider it unacceptable;

(b) In the developing countries (total 114), 27 consider the level acceptable and 87 consider it unacceptable.

Table 5.4 shows that the degree of acceptability varies according to the level of mortality expressed by expectation of life at birth. Of 54 countries with an expectation of life at birth of 50 years, none considered that level acceptable. On the other hand, of the 37 countries with an expectation of life at birth of 70 years and over, 31 considered that level acceptable.

A regional analysis of Table 5.4 shows that it is in the ECA region that the unacceptability of the current levels of mortality is most strongly felt: in 47 out of 48 countries. The other regions of the world are less uniform in their attitude of rejection since demographic situations are more varied than in Africa. In the ECWA region, 6 out of 12 countries consider the level unacceptable; in the ESCAP region, the proportion is 18 out of 30, and in the ECE region, 10 out of 39. Of the 10 countries in the ECE region with that view, 6 have a life expectancy of over 70 years.

In Table 5.5, we have tried to estimate the situation in 1980–1985 on the basis, firstly, of the mortality projections of the Population Division[10] (medium variant) in column 2 and, secondly, of the targets announced by governments in column 3. Under the most optimistic of the forecasts, that of governments (column 3), 34 countries, representing 5.8 per cent of world population, will still have an expectation of life at birth of under 50 years in 1980–1985. Thirty-nine countries, representing 35.9 per cent of world population, will fall in the category of 50 to 62 years' expectation of life. In regional terms, the major effort will have to be made in Africa, Asia and Latin America in view of their unfavourable situation in 1975 if the world average expectation of life

TABLE 5.5: Proportion of World Population in 1985 Residing in Countries Likely to Have an Average Expectation of Life at Birth of up to 62 Years (according to United Nations projections and targets set by governments)

Level of Expectation of Life at Birth	United Nations Estimate for 1970–1975 (1)	United Nations Projections for 1980–1985 (medium variant)[a] (2)	Forecasts by Governments Which Have Set Targets (3)
Under 50 years:			
Number of countries	54	42	34
Population (in millions)	1,337	469	279
Proportion of world population (percentage)	33.7	9.7	5.8
50 to 62 years:[b]			
Number of countries	36	32	39
Population (in millions)	1,429	1,551	1,731
Proportion of world population (percentage)	36.0	32.2	35.9
Up to 62 years:			
Number of countries	90	74	73
Population (in millions)	2,766	2,020	2,010
Proportion of world population (percentage)	69.7	41.9	41.7

[a] Figures taken from "Selected World Demographic Indicators by Countries, 1950–2000" (ESA/P/WP.55).
[b] An expectation of life at birth of 62 years is the one mentioned in para. 22 of the World Population Plan of Action.
Source: United Nations.

at birth of 62 years mentioned in the World Population Plan of Action is to be attained in 1985.[11]

All governments have policies aimed at raising the level of health and lowering the death rate. However, significant differences emerge with regard to the following points in particular: (a) a restructuring of society capable of improving the level of health when the general living standards of the most disadvantaged segments of the population are improved; (b) the extension of medical technology to all segments of the population, particularly in the least accessible rural areas. It is not the intention here to discuss in detail the various possible approaches to health problems, which are within the competence of WHO; it is sufficient to point out that the governments of both developed and developing countries have quite a number of options available to them.

As regards the changes which have occurred during the period 1974–1976, a distinction will be made between the position of the developed countries and that of the developing countries. In the first group of countries, there is increasing recognition of the differential effects on mortality of the living conditions of various population groups. The adverse trend in the male death rate has already been noted. Studies have been conducted in this area, but no policy has been formulated. In the developing countries, two main trends are emerging in the perception of problems relating to mortality: a virtually universal awareness of excess mortality among very small children and of the disadvantaged position of the rural population. To deal with the first problem, more ambitious maternal and child welfare programmes have been initiated, often in connexion with birth-control programmes; to deal with the second problem, that of rural areas, small-scale health programmes involving treatment are being converted into large-scale preventive programmes, which are better suited to the living conditions of the population groups concerned.

GOVERNMENT PERCEPTIONS OF AND POLICIES RELATING TO FERTILITY

Fertility, as the demographic variable most likely to alter the trend in the rate of natural increase, has for more than 30 years received special attention from governments. It was in 1952 that the first government-support birth-control programme was launched in India. (See annex I of this report for a more detailed discussion of the development of birth-control programmes with demographic goals between 1952 and 1976.) In the debate on population growth in the third world, reduction of fertility has often been regarded as the only way to create a balance between population and the means of subsistence. The controversy quickly became even sharper as ideological arguments came to be mingled in the perhaps somewhat too technical discussion conducted until recently by economists, sociologists and demographers. Today a middle way seems to be emerging, and this has unquestionably helped to lessen not the importance of the subject but the fervour of those who have been discussing it. However, the debate has recently started up again with the emergence of a new dimension which might be characterized as individualistic in contrast to the first, global dimension. Couples, and particularly women, have insistently demanded the right and the means of freely determining their own fertility. Some governments, particularly in developed countries, have found themselves in a difficult position where the desire expressed by couples to control and, in fact, reduce their fertility was rarely in conformity with the need perceived by governments to ensure at least the replacement of the present population.

Table 5.6 presents data on the manner in which the present fertility rate is perceived. Of 156 countries, 18 (including 11 developed countries) perceive their fertility rate as "too low", 83 (including 30 developed countries) as "satisfactory", and 55 (including only 1 developed country) as "too high." Among the 83 countries which perceive their fertility rate as "satisfactory," there is wide variation in demographic conditions, as we shall see when we consider results at the regional level.

ECE includes the largest number of governments (10 out of a total of 39) which are dissatisfied because they regard their rate as "too low";

TABLE 5.6: Government Perceptions of Current Levels of Fertility (number of countries)

Regions and Countries	Rate Unsatisfactory (too low)	Rate Satisfactory	Rate Unsatisfactory (too high)	Total
ECA	5	25	18	48
ECWA	—	10	2	12
ECLA	2	9	16	27
ECE	10	28	1	39
ESCAP	1	11	18	30
Developed countries	11	30	1	42
Developing countries	7	53	54	114
Total	18	83	55	156

Source: United Nations.

next are ECA (5 out of 48) and ESCAP (1 out of 30). ECWA does not appear in this category. Most of the governments which describe themselves as "satisfied" are in ECE (28 out of 39), ECA (25 out of 48) and ECWA (10 out of 12). ECLA includes only 9 out of 27 and ESCAP 11 out of 30. Among the governments which regarded their rates as "too high," ESCAP has 18 out of a total of 30, ECLA 16 out of 27, ECA 18 out of 48, ECWA 2 out of 12, and ECE 1 out of 39. In this last category, it will be noted how large a number of countries in the ECLA region are dissatisfied because their rates are "too high." Comparison of Tables 5.6 and 5.7 shows that there is not a complete correlation between perception of a rate as unsatisfactory and the existence of a policy of government intervention. In most cases, there is a correlation, but not always; an uneven correlation appears in all three categories of perception, but particularly in the "satisfactory" category, since it includes both countries which are satisfied as a result of the success of a policy and countries which are simply satisfied with a spontaneous trend which they consider to be either favourable or neutral as regards the success of their development plans.

With regard to policies of government intervention in the matter of fertility, it is customary to make a distinction between policies whose main objective is a demographic one and those which are designed mainly to promote the well-being of the family or the individual. However, this distinction is not completely clear-cut, since a government whose policy of intervention is mainly directed towards a demographic objective will normally feel that such intervention also affects the well-being of the family and that the interests of the nation coincide with those of the individuals of whom it is composed. Conversely, it is most unlikely that a policy of intervention designed to promote the well-being of the family will have no effect on the level and trend of fertility. There are a number of subtle factors here which complicate the task of analysis, and the findings should in any case be interpreted with the utmost caution.

Table 5.7 presents a breakdown of governments whose intervention in the matter of fertility is mainly designed to affect the rate of natural increase: to raise, maintain or lower it. It should be noted, to begin with, that 82 countries have no avowed policy of intervention in that regard; 14, including 10 developed countries, have a policy aimed at increasing the fertility rate; 20, including 10 developed countries, are trying to maintain the present rate, and 40, all of them developing countries, have decided to reduce their rate. In terms of total population, this means that 3 per cent of the world's population lives in countries whose governments have policies aimed at raising the level of fertility, 10 per cent in countries whose governments are maintain-

TABLE 5.7: Government Policies Relating to Measures of Encouragement or Dissuasion with a View to Modifying Fertility (number of countries)

Regions and Countries	Measures of Encouragement or Dissuasion				
	To Increase Fertility	To Maintain Fertility	To Decrease Fertility	No Measures of Encouragement	Total
ECA	2	2	12	32	48
ECWA	—	4	—	8	12
ECLA	2	—	10	15	27
ECE	9	10	1	19	39
ESCAP	1	4	17	8	30
Developed countries	10	10	—	22	42
Developing countries	4	10	40	60	114
Total	14	20	40	82	156

Source: United Nations.

ing the present level, 56 per cent in countries where the policy is aimed at lowering the level, and 31 per cent in countries whose governments do not have a policy of intervention in the matter of fertility.

At the regional level, ESCAP has the highest proportion of countries which wish to reduce their rate (17 out of 30); then come ECLA (10 out of 27) and ECA (12 out of 48). ECWA has no countries in this category, and ECE has only one, Turkey. The countries which wish to maintain their present rate and have policies directed towards that end are concentrated mainly in ECE (10 out of 39) and ECWA (4 out of 12); then come ECA (2 out of 48) and ESCAP (4 out of 30). ECLA does not appear in this category. The group of countries whose policies are designed to increase fertility is represented chiefly in ECE, which has nine; there are two in ECA, two in ECLA, and one in ESCAP; there are very few developing countries in this group.

The question of distinguishing between fertility policies directed towards a demographic objective and policies designed to promote the well-being of the individual or the family has already been mentioned. In the latter case, government action concentrates on making modern contraceptive methods available to persons wishing to use them. In Table 5.8, it will be noted that only 15 countries in the world limit access to modern contraceptive methods. Other countries have a more or less favourable attitude to their distribution. In 23 countries, governments adopt an attitude of non-intervention; in most other cases,

TABLE 5.8: Government Policies Relating to Access to Modern Methods of Birth Control (number of countries)

Regions and Countries	Limited Access	Unlimited Access			Total
		Not Supported by Government	Indirectly Supported by Government	Directly Supported by Government	
ECA	5	12	7	24	48
ECWA	1	4	2	5	12
ECLA	2	2	2	21	27
ECE	5	3	6	25	39
ESCAP	2	2	1	25	30
Developed countries	7	2	7	26	42
Developing countries	8	21	11	74	114
Total	15	23	18	100	156

Source: United Nations.

they take direct action to help distribution. Of the 100 countries which give direct support, 26 are developed countries and 74 are developing countries. From the regional standpoint, direct government support is given in 25 out of 30 countries in the ESCAP region, 21 out of 27 in the ECLA region, 25 out of 39 in the ECE region, 5 out of 12 in the ECWA region, and 24 out of 48 in the ECA region.

If the changes which occured between 1974 and 1976 are analysed, a distinction can be made between changes relating to policies of intervention in the matter of fertility directed toward a demographic objective and changes concerning other policies. Some of the facts have been dealt with above. More especially, in fertility policies directed towards a demographic objective, the most notable fact has been the strengthening of legislation regarding sterilization and the increasing use of abortion in India. It is too soon yet to indicate how the measures will be applied and, especially, how they will be received by the population, but it is an important turning-point in the history of birth control which, in its importance and significance, reminds us of the 1948 legislation on eugenics in Japan. It will be noted, however, that abortion has made little progress as an instrument for action on the over-all fertility levels. On the contrary, in the growing liberalization of morals, a large number of countries has either made abortion completely free or made the legal and medical barriers to it considerably more flexible. In another context, it will be noted that in both developed and developing countries, an increasing effort is being made to integrate fertility policies into an over-all system of much wider measures which take account of the complexity of the processes determining fertility.

GOVERNMENT PERCEPTIONS OF AND POLICIES RELATING TO THE SPATIAL DISTRIBUTION OF THE POPULATION AND INTERNAL MIGRATION

One sphere in which governments have difficulty in accepting the population situation facing them is that of geographical distribution and internal migration. Table 5.9 shows that 78 out of 156 countries regard their situation as "largely unacceptable." Of these 78 countries, 71 are developing countries. Moreover, 59 countries regard the situation as "unacceptable to some degree." Only 19 consider the situation "acceptable." In the developing countries, there are many reasons for this attitude, including the following: one of the direct effects of demographic transition has been the creation of a surplus rural labour force which has provided an apparently inexhaustible supply of migrants for urban centres, not to mention the existence of inadequate legal, economic and social structures in rural areas; the colonial legacy has often left urban structures and regional divisions which are not very conducive to economic and social development; finally, for reasons which are

TABLE 5.9: Government Perceptions of the Degree to which the Spatial Distribution of the Population is Satisfactory (number of countries)

Regions and Countries	Degree to which Satisfactory			
	Acceptable	Unacceptable to Some Degree	Largely Unacceptable	Total
ECA	—	12	36	48
ECWA	3	8	1	12
ECLA	1	4	22	27
ECE	13	23	3	39
ESCAP	2	12	16	30
Developed countries	13	22	7	42
Developing countries	6	37	71	114
Total	19	59	78	156

Source: United Nations.

purely incidental from the point of view of optimal geographical distribution, some countries have been provided with industrial infrastructures which do not contribute to the harmonious development of their territory.

It is striking to note from Table 5.9 that 36 of the 48 countries in the ECA region, 22 of the 27 countries in the ECLA region and 16 of the 30 countries in the ESCAP region consider the spatial distribution of their population to be largely unsatisfactory. In the ECE region, only three countries are in that situation.

Policies relating to the spatial distribution of the population and internal migration concern almost all countries, including those where the current situation is regarded as acceptable. Governments are well aware that harmonious spatial distribution is the result of extremely fragile and complex balances which must be constantly restored by continuous intervention. Table 5.10 summarizes government action from two complementary approaches, a distinction being made for the convenience of the study. On the one hand, there is a choice of policies of intervention with regard to migration from rural to urban areas: policies aimed at accelerating the flow of migration, maintaining it at its present level, slowing it down or reversing it. These policies are shown in part A of Table 5.10. On the other hand, there are policies which, whether or not they are associated with such intervention, may or may not involve the remodelling of the structure of urban or rural areas, for instance by the creation of new towns. Such policies are shown in part B of Table 5.10. There again, a number of different options are possible: to change the structure of urban and rural areas, not to change it, to change the structure of rural areas only. In all, four developing countries wish both to accelerate the flow of migration and to restructure both urban and rural areas. Of the 35 countries which wish to keep migration at its current level, 29 do not wish to change the structure of urban and rural areas and 6 wish to restructure only rural areas. A majority of 100 countries wishes to slow down the flow of migration; of these, only 19 do not wish to change the structure of urban and rural areas while 81 hope to change that structure either completely or in part. If a comparison is made between developed and developing countries from the standpoint of policies designed to slow down migration, the proportion is somewhat different: 25 of the 42 developed countries and 75 of the 114 developing countries have policies aimed at slowing down migration. The most serious problems arise in the developing countries. However, it is interesting to note that the developed countries are still far from clear of all the consequences of rural migration from which some of them have been suffering for more

TABLE 5.10: Government Policies towards Spatial Distribution and Internal Migration of Population (number of countries)

Government Policies

A. Trends in Internal Migration from Rural and Small Urban Areas to Major Urban and Metropolitan Areas

B. Structure of Urban and Rural Areas

Regions and Countries	Accelerate Migration		Maintain Migration at Its Current Level		Slow Down Migration				Reverse Migration			Total
	Change in	No Change in	Change in	No Change in	Change in			No Change in	Change in			
	U, R	U, R	R	U, R	R	U	U, R	U, R	R	U	U, R	
ECA	—	7	4	7	9	—	16	—	2	—	3	48
ECWA	1	4	—	1	1	—	4	—	—	—	1	12
ECLA	1	3	—	3	5	3	12	—	—	—	—	27
ECE	1	10	—	4	—	15	4	3	—	2	—	39
ESCAP	1	5	2	4	4	—	8	—	2	1	3	30
Developed countries	—	11	—	4	—	16	5	3	—	3	—	42
Developing countries	4	18	6	15	19	2	39	—	4	—	7	114
Total	4	29	6	19	19	18	44	3	4	3	7	156

Note: U indicates urban areas; R indicates rural areas.
Source: United Nations.

155

than a century. Finally, only 17 countries have policies aimed at reversing migration.

From the regional standpoint, concentrating in this analysis on policies designed to slow down the flow of migration, it will be seen from Table 5.10 that 32 of the 48 countries in the ECA region, 6 of the 12 countries in the ECWA region, 23 of the 27 countries in the ECLA region, 23 of the 29 countries in the ECE region and only 16 of the 30 countries in the ESCAP region have such policies. Thus Africa, Latin America and Europe show, by their policies, that they are concerned to take stronger action on this phenomenon than Asia.

If an analysis is made of recent changes, it is important first of all to observe that the history of policies relating to spatial distribution is generally confused with that of planned development, and there are few countries which are not already armed with a whole range of policies for improving the distribution of their population within the space available. There has been no major change in these policies between 1974 and 1976, but a number of improvements and adjustments have been made in policies which were formulated a number of years earlier.

GOVERNMENT PERCEPTIONS OF AND POLICIES RELATING TO INTERNATIONAL MIGRATION

Government perceptions of and policies relating to international migration can be considered from two points of view: the direction of migration, and its volume. The government approach to the volume of migration is not so much demographic as subjective: do the governments of the countries concerned perceive such migration as demographically significant?

Government Perceptions of and Policies Relating to Immigration

Table 5.11 shows how governments perceive the volume of immigration into their countries. In the case of governments which regard the rate of immigration as significant, a distinction is made between those which perceive it to be "too low", those which regard it as "satisfactory" and those which see it as "too high." Only 39 countries consider immigration to be demographically significant. Of these, 8 including 2 developed countries, regard the rate as "too low," 24 including 13 developed countries, regard it as "satisfactory" and 7 including 3 developed countries, regard it as "too high." From the standpoint of

TABLE 5.11: Government Perceptions of the Demographic Significance of Immigration and the Acceptability of Current Levels (number of countries)

| | Governments Perceive Immigration to Be Demographically | | | | | |
| | Significant | | | Insignificant | | |
Regions and Countries	Unsatisfactory (too low)	Satisfactory	Unsatisfactory (too high)	More Immigration Desirable	Satisfactory	Total
ECA	3	2	2	1	40	48
ECWA	1	6	—	1	4	12
ECLA	1	1	1	—	24	27
ECE	1	13	2	—	23	39
ESCAP	2	2	2	—	24	30
Developed countries	2	13	3	—	24	42
Developing countries	6	11	4	2	91	114
Total	8	24	7	2	115	156

Source: United Nations.

government attitudes alone, 117 countries do not regard immigration as significant.

From a regional standpoint, 16 of the 39 countries in the ECE region regard the rate of immigration as significant. In the ECWA region, 7 out of 12 countries are concerned; 6 of them stating that they are "satisfied" and 1 states that it is not satisfied because the level is too low. In the other regions, only a minority express concern. In the ECE region, 13 countries state that they are "satisfied" with the level, 1 claims that it is "too low," and 2 others state that it is "too high."

According to Table 5.12, on immigration policies concerning the same countries which regard the immigration rate as demographically significant, 8 countries, including 2 developed countries, have policies which are designed to increase the rate, 17 countries, including 6 developed countries, have policies which are designed to maintain the rate at its current level, and 14 countries, including 10 developed countries, have policies aimed at curbing the rate. From a regional standpoint, the eight countries which wish to increase the rate of immigration are distributed among the membership of the five regional commissions, the membership of ECA accounting for the largest number of countries, namely, three out of the total of eight. Six developed countries in the ECE region and six others in the ECWA region have chosen the second policy option, namely the maintenance of the rate at its current level. The other countries which wish to maintain the rate of immigration at its current level are distributed among the other regional commissions. Those countries which have chosen the third policy option, that of curbing immigration, are mainly in the ECE region (9 countries out of 14).

Government Perceptions of and Policies Relating to Emigration

More governments are demographically concerned over emigration—52 countries (see Table 5.13)—than over immigration—39 countries (see Table 5.12). This situation reflects the fact that emigration, particularly from developing countries, is directed mainly to a relatively small number of developed countries and, quite recently, some developing countries. Table 5.13 includes three categories of perception concerning the rate of emigration: "too low," "satisfactory" and "too high." It will be noted that only 4 countries, including 1 developed country, find the rate "too low"; 28 including 1 developed country find it "satisfactory"; and 20 including 7 developed countries find it "too high."

TABLE 5.12: Government Policies with Regard to Immigration (number of countries)

Regions and Countries	Higher Rate	Government Policies in Favour of			Total
		Maintaining Current Rate but Subject to Strict Control	Curbing Immigration in the Future, but Maintaining the Already Established Immigrant Population	Immigration Perceived to Be Not Demographically Significant or Undesirable	
ECA	3	2	2	41	48
ECWA	1	6	—	5	12
ECLA	1	1	1	24	27
ECE	1	6	9	23	39
ESCAP	2	2	2	24	30
Developed countries	2	6	10	24	42
Developing countries	6	11	4	93	114
Total	8	17	14	117	156

Source: United Nations.

From the regional standpoint, 15 of the 19 countries concerned over emigration in the ECA region and 6 of the 15 countries in the ECLA region are "satisfied" with the level; in the other regions only a few countries are concerned (see Table 5.13).

Table 5.14 shows the policy options selected by governments with regard to emigration: policies in favour of increasing, maintaining or curbing the level of emigration. These policies concern only the 52 countries in which emigration is perceived to be significant; 9 developed countries and 43 developing countries have emigration policies. Seven developed countries out of 9 and 13 developing countries out of 43 wish to curb emigration. The policy of maintaining the level of emigration is the one selected in most cases: 28 countries, including 1 developed and 27 developing countries. Only four countries have policies of encouraging emigration.

From the regional standpoint, one country in the ECE region practices a policy of maintaining the rate of emigration and seven countries practice a policy of curbing emigration. In the ECA region, where the countries concerned over emigration are more numerous, 15 countries have policies of maintaining the level and 3 have policies of curbing emigration. In the ECLA region, nine countries have policies of curbing emigration and six have policies of maintaining the level. There are few cases in the other regions.

Between 1974 and 1976, the attitudes and policies of governments concerning international migration evolved in a fairly significant manner: this is an area where short-term events, whether political or economic, play a considerable role, sometimes concealing longer-term movements where stability is the essential feature. Various factors have affected government attitudes, sometimes in a contradictory manner. Mention might be made, in the first place, of the economic recession which has severely hit the industrial countries: the reflexes to protect the national labour force have immediately come into play at the expense of foreign immigrant labour. On the other hand, new poles of development have been created or consolidated in some developing countries, for instance the oil-producing countries in the Persian Gulf, some African countries and some Latin American countries. If an attempt is made to identify certain significant changes in the legislation of some countries which are important from the point of view of international immigration, the discussions concerning the advisability of reducing immigration to Canada, Australia and New Zealand will be noted. In the United States, few changes have been observed apart from exceptional measures in favour of refugees from Vietnam. In Europe, countries such as France and Norway have taken very restric-

TABLE 5.13: Government Perceptions of the Demographic Significance of Emigration and the Acceptability of Current Levels (number of countries)

| Regions and Countries | Governments Perceive Emigration to Be Demographically | | | | | Total |
| | Significant | | | Insignificant | | |
	Unsatisfactory (too low)	Satisfactory	Unsatisfactory (too high)	More Emigration Desirable	Satisfactory	
ECA	1	15	3	—	29	48
ECWA	—	2	1	1	8	12
ECLA	—	6	9	—	12	27
ECE	2	1	7	—	29	39
ESCAP	1	4	—	1	24	30
Developed countries	1	1	7	—	33	42
Developing countries	3	27	13	2	69	114
Total	4	28	20	2	102	156

Source: United Nations.

TABLE 5.14: Government Policies with Regard to Emigration (number of countries)

Regions and Countries	Government Policies in Favour of			Emigration Perceived to Be Not Demographically Significant or Undesirable	Total
	Higher Rate	Maintaining Current Rate	Curbing Emigration in Future		
ECA	1	15	3	29	48
ECWA	—	2	1	9	12
ECLA	—	6	9	12	27
ECE	2	1	7	29	39
ESCAP	1	4	—	25	30
Developed countries	1	1	7	33	42
Developing countries	3	27	13	71	114
Total	4	28	20	104	156

Source: United Nations.

tive measures. The only countries which are generally open, but with limited success, are Argentina and Uruguay.

Changes with regard to emigration have been a matter of concern to some countries, particularly in southern Europe, such as Greece, Spain, Italy and Malta, and northern Europe, such as Finland. Considerable efforts have been made in those countries to repatriate part of the labour force which has emigrated. There again it cannot be said that a reversal of government attitudes and policies in the countries of emigration is in progress, but it is probable that, in the medium- and long-term, some developing countries from which a large part of the labour force traditionally emigrates will either change the direction of emigration—for example, Turkey, which has signed agreements with the Libyan Arab Republic concerning the emigration of its workers— or will endeavour to limit the volume of emigration by integrating their workers into their economy while requiring from countries of immigration improved guarantees and working conditions for those of their nationals who have already emigrated.

INSTITUTIONAL ARRANGEMENTS FOR THE FORMULATION AND INTEGRATION OF POPULATION POLICIES IN DEVELOPMENT PLANS

In the developed countries, data collection and analysis does not generally give rise to the serious problems which are characteristic of the developing countries. Nevertheless, many governments of developed countries have noted that the complexity of problems relating to the interaction of demographic and socio-economic variables makes it essential not only to collect new data and establish more appropriate information systems, such as data banks, but also to strengthen existing, and establish new, multidisciplinary research institutes

In the developing countries, although the absence of certain information creates constraints at the policy-formulation level, the problems which confront governments are generally better known and the range of policy options is more limited. Nevertheless, the governments of almost all such countries attach great importance to the improvement of the still very inadequate data available to them.

The research needed to translate basic data into projections, development models, analyses measuring the effects of different policy options, and so on, is similar, but of a different degree of complexity, in the developed and the developing countries respectively. While it is true that the majority of developed countries have considerable research capacity, it is also true that some developing countries today possess not insignificant research means, as a result either of their own efforts or of multilateral or bilateral technical co-operation.

Experience clearly shows, however, that the existence of research means is not a sufficient prerequisite for the successful formulation of rational population policies and their integration in an over-all development plan. There is a need for institutional machinery that can apply the results of research to the formulation and integration of population policies. In countries which have a central planning organ, it has often been possible to establish such machinery, or to set up institutions with the specific function of conducting research related to the formulation of population policies. In countries which do not have a central planning organ, the establishment of such institutions has been less common. However, whenever the governments of such countries have perceived the significance of demographic problems, specific bodies, such as *ad hoc* committees and working groups, have been established, generally for a limited period of time and with a specific mandate.

The establishment of permanent or temporary institutions of the above-mentioned type has been more widespread in the developed than in the developing countries. Such a multiplicity of bodies in the industrial countries reflects, in part, the ability of those countries to utilize their varied resources in terms of competent staff, but it also reflects the fact that, in the developing countries, the necessary research has largely been centralized within the planning organs. Thus, it will be noted from part A of Table 5.15 that 20 out of 42 developed countries make use of research carried out by institutions having a specific function with regard to demographic research, as compared with only 17 out of 114 developing countries.

There are differences of the same type between developed and developing countries in respect of the integration of population policies in development plans. In developed countries which have a central planning organ, the formulation of policies and the preparation of plans include population policies and are entrusted either to the central planning organ or to a government institution established especially for that purpose. In developed countries which do not have a central planning organ, the institutional arrangements are often less formal: they may be of a temporary or a permanent nature. It should be noted that, in some cases, the government of those countries have complained of the limited effectiveness of temporary arrangements.

In many developing countries, the adoption of a central planning system has made it theoretically possible to integrate demographic factors in the formulation of development policies. While the institutional conditions appear to be fairly favourable, considerable improve-

TABLE 5.15: Institutions Responsible for (A) Research Directed Toward the Formulation of Population Policies and (B) the Integration of Such Policies in National Planning (number of countries)

Regions and Countries	A. Research Input from Policy-Formulating Institutions				B. Institutions Responsible for Integrating Population Policies in National Planning			
	Input from Institutions with Specific Research Functions Concerning Population Policies and from General Research Institutions	Input from General Research Institutions Only	Limited Input	Total	Central Planning Institution — Also Institutions Having Specific Functions	Central Planning Institution — Only	No Central Planning Institution — Institutions with Specific Functions	No Central Planning Institution — No Other Institution Responsible
ECA	5	19	24	48	7	41	—	—
ECWA	—	6	6	12	5	5	1	1
ECLA	6	17	4	27	8	17	1	1
ECE	19	11	9	39	9	13	5	12
ESCAP	7	15	8	30	8	18	2	2
Developed countries	20	12	10	42	10	11	8	13
Developing countries	17	56	41	114	27	83	1	3
Total	37	68	51	156	37	94	9	16

Source: United Nations.

ments must still be made with regard to the necessary techniques and procedures for identifying the policy options open to governments.

Part B of Table 5.15 shows that, out of 42 developed countries, 21 have a central planning organ, and 11 of them have entrusted the integration of their population policies to that organ. Of the 21 other developed countries, which do not have a central planning organ, 13 have no institution responsible for integrating population policies. In contrast, of the 114 developing countries, only 4 do not have a central planning organ; 83 of the remaining 110 entrust the integration of their population policies to that organ.

CONCLUSIONS AND OVERVIEW

A number of conclusions emerge from the study of the mechanisms by which government attitudes to demographic processes are formed and the mechanisms for the formulation of policies relating to the imbalance between demographic and non-demographic factors.

The changes that have recently occurred in government perceptions and policies seem less surprising if the programmes or statements of governments over the last ten years are examined more carefully. Most governments, even those which had given priority to programmes designed to modify spontaneous fertility trends, had already recognized that measures dealing only with fertility were insufficient and that global strategies were necessary to solve the problems arising from the interaction between demographic and non-demographic processes. Thus, in those countries, a very clear trend emerged in favour of integrating such programmes in development plans. Lastly, the recommendations on the need to integrate demographic processes in development contained in the World Population Plan of Action adopted at the World Population Conference at Bucharest only confirmed a need that had been felt for many years but which could not be expressed until then for lack of an appropriate international forum.

In most cases, governments do not perceive the rate of natural increase of the population to be satisfactory or unsatisfactory compared with a "theoretical value" for that rate. That "theoretical value" has no significance in itself. However, in response to pressure from that sector of international opinion which considers certain rates to be "excessive", or in response to certain attitudes which confuse population growth with the vitality of a society, the values connected with the image of a population that is "too large" or "too small" or a rate that is "too high" or "too low" help to form some government attitudes.

Fortunately, most governments perceive the implications of the complex relations between the rate of population increase and economic and social factors first and foremost as basic postulates favouring or preventing the success of their development plan. Those complex relations develop generally in a predictable manner, as a result of processes of technological innovation and the effects of economic and social restructuring observed throughout the world. However, their development may sometimes be influenced by other factors, such as the geopolitical environment, the localization of some components of the international economic system, the legacy of certain socio-cultural traditions, and so on.

One of the most striking developments in the last ten years has been the growing awareness of the complexity of the phenomena and the emergence of a very sophisticated level of perception. To take the case of the Third Inquiry among Governments on Population Policies in the context of Development in 1976, it will be noted, first, on the purely quantitative level, that 103 countries responded, compared with 74 which responded to the Second Inquiry in 1972 and 53 to the First Inquiry in 1963. Such a development certainly shows a growing interest in population problems on the part of governments. On the qualitative level, it will be noted that, although this inquiry dealt with a very difficult subject, the interaction between demographic and non-demographic variables, it produced replies not only from developed but also from developing countries. To mention Africa alone, in 1972, only 13 countries responded to the Second Inquiry; in 1976, 32 countries responded.

Thus, there is a perception of the problems and, what is more, that perception is becoming increasingly refined as it adapts to the growing complexity of the problems. With regard to intervention, the governments of developing countries, like those of developed countries, are adopting policies that are increasingly sophisticated but still insufficient to solve all the problems. As an example, mention might be made of a complex case of intervention, that of an industrialized country which is trying to check the decline in fertility while at the same time encouraging the employment of women, although it knows that the latter has a negative effect on fertility. Why should it make such an apparently contradictory choice? Because this same government, for reasons of internal or external policy, wishes to increase the national female labour force in order to reduce its dependence on what it regards as too large a foreign labour force. It would be possible to give examples of the same level of complexity in the developing countries, but their lack of human and financial resources and of institutions constitutes an additional obstacle.

Lastly, one of the new dimensions of population policies is the individual dimension. In a world where behaviour is, both in appearance and in fact, increasingly determined by systems of economic, social and political constraints imposed in the name of the general interest, there has been a growing demand for each individual and each family to be free to decide its own destiny. Thus fertility policies have very quickly responded to the need expressed by families to procreate freely without any biological or social constraint. This demand of the individual has greatly contributed to the almost world-wide dissemination of such policies in 1976. There have been frequent conflicts of interest between the individual good and the collective good. Governments have tried to resolve them in the national context in which they occurred. In that regard, history, culture and society are three interrelated factors which force governments to find original national solutions that generally exclude the application of prepared patterns of intervention.

In addition to the generalization of the awareness of the complexity of the phenomena, the elaboration of increasingly refined population policies to deal with that complexity, and the recognition of the demands of individuals, what other developments may be mentioned? On the level of the policy objectives, there has been increasing use of policies which might be described as non-demographic in their means but demographic in their ultimate purpose. An awareness of the interaction between demographic and non-demographic factors leads to the application of programmes aimed mainly at changing the general environment by ensuring the well-being of the population. Although measures designed to improve nutrition, housing and education, to provide work, to industrialize a region or to change the status of women may have no direct demographic purpose, they have an indirect effect on the demographic behaviour of individuals and therefore on the over-all demographic trends of the population. Such policies designed to promote the well-being of the population have done more than anything else to place population policies in the broader context of development, and at the same time have led to a clearer definition of their content. Things have changed considerably from the time when the term population policy was synonymous with birth-control policy. Now population policies include action with regard to the four principal demographic variables: mortality, fertility, internal migration and external migration.

To sum up, in 1976 a dual trend in the formulation of demographic policies may be observed: on the one hand, there has been a universalization of some forms of intervention which are purely demographic, such as intervention in the matter of fertility, but which have elements

that they had previously lacked; and, on the other hand, there is almost general recourse to intervention designed to act on several levels at once, such as intervention with regard to economic and social structures, which has, *inter alia,* indirect effects on population levels and trends.

NOTES

1. See "Preliminary report on the Third Inquiry among Governments on Population" (E/CN. 9/XIX/CRP. 6).

2. See "Results of the regional consultations subsequent to the World Population Conference."

3. "Population programmes and Policies" (E/CONF.60/CBP/21) and "Report on the Second Inquiry among Governments on Population and Development" (E/-CONF.60/CBP/32).

4. "Selected World Demographic Indicators by Countries 1950–2000" (ESA/P/WP.55).

5. Ibid.

6. The correlation here is approximate; it is recognized that countries which are "satisfied" with their rate of increase—whether high or low, stable, declining or rising—would choose variants which would, on balance, correspond on the whole to the medium variant of the United Nations.

7. Figures taken from "Selected World Demographic Indicators by Countries 1950–2000" (ESA/P/WP.55). Cyprus, Israel and Turkey have not been included in South Asia.

8. See "Preliminary report on the Third Inquiry among Governments on Population," op. cit.

9. "Report on monitoring of population trends and policies."

10. "Selected World Demographic Indicators by Countries 1950–2000" (ESA/P/WP.55).

11. *Report of the United Nations World Population Conference* (United Nations publication, Sales No. F. 75.XIII.3), para. 22.

6 PRIORITIES IN FUTURE ALLOCATION OF UNFPA RESOURCES

INTRODUCTION

The United Nations Fund for Population Activities has grown rapidly since its operations began in late 1969. The cumulative programme level for the period 1969–1972 was 50 million dollars. By 1977, the Fund's programme had doubled and is now operating at an annual programme level of 100 million dollars. The remarkable growth in resources available to UNFPA, however, has been more than matched by an equally rapid rise in demand for UNFPA assistance, particularly as a result of the World Population Year and the World Population Conference in 1974.

The worldwide information and communication programme undertaken in World Population Year heightened awareness among governments as well as individuals of the many facets of population, while the broad concept of population activities adopted at the World Population Conference made it possible for a large number of governments to accept the need for intensifying or initiating population projects within the context of economic and social development planning. Moreover, the World Population Plan of Action (WPPA) adopted by consensus among 135 states at the Conference established clear links between population factors and improvement of the quality of life: it also identified broad areas of activity for governments, non-governmental organizations, and organizations in the United Nations system.

Within the framework of the Plan's many guidelines and recommendations, UNFPA has reassessed its mandate according to the new perceptions of population and to changes in the international population assistance scene, in particular the increasing need for assistance. It was felt that despite the fund's neutrality on population policies and objectives, certain general principles should be evolved to serve as guidelines in the future allocation of resources and give overall direction to its assistance. With the broadening of the concept of population activities, it was also necessary to define a core programme of UNFPA assistance to provide a means of day-to-day interpretation of its mandate.

The UNFPA has developed two complementary mechanisms for setting priorities in the future allocation of its resources to countries. One of these refers to the *types of activity* to be given priority because of their importance to the promotion of national self-reliance. These activities are defined by minimum requirements or basic needs in the various population sectors. The other is the designation of a group of developing countries as *priority countries* for UNFPA population assistance by applying a set of demographic indicators for which data are generally available and which are considered indicative of a country's population problems. In this exercise also the economic conditions of countries have been taken into consideration by including per capita income as an additional qualifying factor.

Apart from activities at the country level, UNFPA supports intercountry activities. Before 1974 some 60 per cent of UNFPA resources supported intercountry activities and the remainder activities at the country level. By 1976 these proportions had been reversed to 30 per cent and 70 per cent respectively. With this change in emphasis in the UNFPA assistance programme, division of resources in the future has become an important consideration. A review of past UNFPA support to intercountry activities has been undertaken on the basis of which UNFPA will determine its priorities between country and intercountry activities and within the latter.

The following policy statements were presented by the Executive Director to the Governing Council, which discussed and endorsed them in three successive sessions, namely in June 1976 and in January and June 1977. Moreover, the general principles and criteria for establishing piorities received the endorsement of the sixty-first session of the United Nations Economic and Social Council[1] and the thirty-first session of the United Nations General Assembly in August and December 1976 respectively.[2]

AIMS AND PURPOSES OF UNFPA

In May 1973, the Economic and Social Council established the main aims and purposes of UNFPA. These aims and purposes, under which the Fund is still operating, are as follows:

(a) "To build up, on an international basis, with the assistance of the competent bodies of the United Nations system, the knowledge and the capacity to respond to national, regional, interregional and global needs in the population and family planning fields; to promote coordination in planning and programming, and to co-operate with all concerned."[3]

UNFPA and other organizations and governments have already built up considerable knowledge and capacity to respond to needs in the population and family planning fields at both national and international levels, and this continues to be an important objective for UNFPA. In the early years of the Fund, most of its resources were devoted to furthering understanding and knowledge of population matters and strengthening, on an international basis, the capacity of the United Nations Organizations to meet needs for population assistance at the regional, interregional and global levels. Recently, however, increasing demand from developing countries for direct assistance to national activities has reduced the share of UNFPA resources available for intercountry activities, particularly those provided through organizations in the United Nations system. As the largest direct—and in some areas the only major—source of international population assistance, UNFPA will continue to support activities on an international basis, but the emphasis in future will be on backstopping country-level activities and on exploring innovative approaches to population issues.

(b) "To promote awareness, both in developed and in developing countries, of the social, economic and environmental implications of national and international population problems; of the human rights aspects of family planning; and of possible strategies to deal with them, in accordance with the plans and priorities of each country."[4]

As a result of the accomplishments of the World Population Year and Conference and of other activities promoted by UNFPA, other international organizations, governments and non-governmental bodies, considerable progress has been made in the promotion of awareness of the implications of national and international population problems. Some 40 developing countries with a total of about 80 per cent of the developing world's population have as part of their overall economic and social development programmes national policies to reduce the rate of population growth. In addition, 71 developing countries have established policies in favour of disseminating information on, and distributing the means of, family planning as a basic human right and for the improvement of health, status of women, and family life. All the organizations concerned in the United Nations system and many other organizations—intergovernmental and non-governmental—have established population programmes of their own within their mandates and responsibilities.

Considerable effort, particularly in developing countries is still required to promote awareness of the many aspects of population problems. Awareness is often limited to government officials and educated groups while large segments of the population in many countries, even in those with established national population policies, still do not recognize the importance of population problems and their significance to the promotion of human well-being, the quality of life and basic human rights. This, together with limited recognition of the need for action programmes to cope with population problems, often constitutes a major handicap to delivery. Greater stress will be laid on reaching important population groups such as women, youth, local community leaders, as well as religious, political and other organized groups. Nongovernmental organizations can play an important role in this regard and UNFPA's collaboration with such bodies will continue.

(c) "To extend systematic and sustained assistance to developing countries at their request in dealing with their population problems; such assistance to be afforded in forms and by means requested by the recipient countries and best suited to meet the individual country's needs."[5]

This remains the principal objective of UNFPA and will continue to absorb the greater share of the Fund's human and financial resources. The growing demand for population assistance among developing countries, however, may make it necessary to introduce certain limitations in the stated objective. Unless the Fund's resources expand very substantially and beyond current expectations, it will not be possible to continue providing "systematic and sustained" UNFPA support to all developing countries. Assistance may in many cases have to be limited in time, and will gradually be phased out to release resources for new activities in the same country or elsewhere.

Furthermore, the concept of "population problems" as stated by the Economic and Social Council in 1973 must be clarified and its scope defined so far as UNFPA population assistance is concerned. It has always been the policy of UNFPA to respond, to the best of its ability, to the needs and priorities for population assistance as determined by the developing countries themselves. Thus, the Fund has responded not only to requests for assistance for taking population factors into account in development planning, for the collection and analysis of basic population data, and, for disseminating information on and the means of fertility regulation; support has also been extended to help solve problems of migration, distribution and structure of population and, in a few cases, insufficient rates of population growth. The broadening concept of population activities and the need to view population problems within the wider context of economic and social development, as urged by the World Population Conference and the World Population

Plan of Action, make it desirable to determine more clearly the areas of principal concern to UNFPA and to which the Fund's limited resources should be devoted.

(d) "To play a leading role in the United Nations system in promoting population programmes and to co-ordinate projects supported by the Fund."[6]

Significant progress has been made by the Fund in this regard but there is considerable need for further coordination. The Fund has recently been encouraged by several other funding organizations and governments with bilateral aid programmes to play a more vigorous role in coordinating international population assistance; the increasing difficulty felt within the international assistance community of meeting the demand with available resources makes such co-ordination more important than ever.

The Fund will redouble its efforts to

(i) develop joint or co-ordinated funding arrangements with other aid organizations;
(ii) search for strategies to solve population problems effectively in various settings; and
(iii) identify approaches to integrating population components with social and economic development programmes.

Such an expansion of the Fund's co-ordinating function will not greatly affect the allocation of resources since it can be made without substantial additional resources. This expansion is not intended to interfere in any way with the right and responsibility of recipient countries to determine the types of programmes and sources of funding they prefer.

GENERAL PRINCIPLES FOR FUTURE ALLOCATION OF RESOURCES

In making future allocations of resources, UNFPA will insofar as possible apply the following general principles:

(a) to promote population activities proposed in international strategies;
(b) to meet the needs of developing countries which have the most urgent requirements for population assistance;
(c) to respect the sovereignty of recipient countries on matters of population policies;

(d) to build up the recipient countries' self-reliance; and,

(e) to support activities of special benefit to disadvantaged population groups.

Each of these principles is discussed briefly below.

(a) A number of international strategies have been adopted which provide the framework for international co-operation and which recognize population and related matters as an integral part of socio-economic development. Such strategies include the International Development Strategy for the Second Development Decade, the United Nations Programme of Action on the Establishment of a New International Economic Order, the World Population Plan of Action, the World Plan of Action on Integration of Women in Development and the Draft Plan of Action to Combat Desertification. It is within the mandate of UNFPA to support the population elements of these instruments and to base its policy guidelines and the overall framework of its work programme on them.

The World Population Plan of Action (WPPA), which is of special importance to the work of UNFPA, emphasizes an integrated development approach to population. This plan suggests that population activities be increasingly supported as elements of activities in health, education, rural development, community development and other programmes to promote economic and social development. The greatest challenges posed by the WPPA are to determine how population and related activities can be promoted effectively as an integral part of such development programmes and how some population problems can be solved through socio-economic transformation.

The UNFPA is actively seeking ways to identify development programmes into which population activities can be integrated, particularly through increased use of its field staff and in collaboration with UNDP country programming exercises. The Fund will give increasing attention to responding to the WPPA and to the needs of developing countries in this regard by collaborating with other organizations within the United Nations system as well as with bilateral aid programmes and interested non-governmental bodies. In such collaborative efforts, UNFPA will be prepared to fund the population components while other development assistance bodies may support the non-population components of integrated programmes as required. At the same time, the Fund will encourage development assistance bodies to support development programmes which are needed for the promotion and effective implementation of population programmes and to include population components, whenever possible, in their development assistance.

(b) Recognizing that the UNFPA's main thrust will continue to be at the country level, various approaches to distributing resources among countries were considered. In June 1975, the advantages and disadvantages of UNFPA's adopting an indicative planning figure (IPF) system similar to the one applied by United Nations Development Programme were considered by the Governing Council and it was decided that the adoption of the IPF system in the field of population was not an appropriate or practical measure.

Nonetheless, it was considered necessary to concentrate the Fund's limited resources on the urgent requirements of those developing countries with the greatest need for population assistance and to promote programmes which have a measurable impact in countries with urgent needs rather than spreading the Fund's resources thinly among some 130 developing countries. As outlined below, various alternatives by which certain countries may be assigned priority in the allocation of the Fund's resources without introducing the inflexibility of an IPF system were considered. The most appropriate solution has been found to be the adoption of some population-related grouping of developing countries as priority countries for UNFPA assistance, based mainly upon a set of criteria reflecting in general terms the major problems with which the Fund has been set up to deal.

(c) From its inception, the UNFPA has fully appreciated the sovereign right of each nation to formulate, promote and implement its own population policies as recognized ,and reconfirmed by the General Assembly.[7] It is for each government to determine its population programme and approaches to meeting established policy goals. In allocating its resources, the UNFPA respects national priorities for population activities, but this does not obviate the problem of priorities for UNFPA or oblige it to play a completely passive role. In view of their past experience in dealing with population programmes, the Fund and its various executing organizations are prepared and willing, upon request, to advise governments on setting priorities in accordance with their established population objectives and on the adoption of the most effective approaches. Furthermore, the increasing demands made upon its scarce resources suggest the need as well as the opportunity for the Fund to make choices regarding the nature and size of the support to be provided. This may reflect but not necessarily be identical with national priorities in every case.

While maintaining its neutrality on matters of population objectives and policies, UNFPA provides assistance in accordance with certain basic policies and principles adopted internationally. One of these is that UNFPA supports activities designed for the voluntary participation of the population at large, especially with regard to family planning. This policy is in accordance with General Assembly resolution 2211 (XXI) which recognized "the sovereignty of nations in formulating and promoting their own population policies, with due regard to the principle that the size of the family should be the free choice of each individual family."[8]

Other guidelines may be applied in determining the Fund's own priorities, such as the principle of giving preference to activities designed to strengthen the recipient countries' self-reliance in population matters and to those which benefit disadvantaged population groups.

(d) The World Population Conference and the WPPA stressed the importance of making developing countries self-reliant as fully and rapidly as possible. Furthermore, the General Assembly has decided that the promotion of self-reliance in developing countries should be a basic purpose of technical co-operation[9] and serve as a guideline for future UNDP operations. Therefore, UNFPA support will aim particularly at building up the capacity and ability of recipient countries to respond to their own population needs. To achieve this end assistance should, as far as possible, be phased and limited to a definite period of time, especially where recipient countries have already developed basic population programmes. During the period of assistance the activity should gradually be taken over by the government or non-governmental organization concerned. In order to avoid UNFPA assistance displacing funds which would or could be committed by recipient governments or organizations—the fund's support should increasingly be devoted to programmes for which the recipient governments and organizations are committed to making their own contributions and to taking over full financial responsibility gradually.

In accordance with the principle of promoting self-reliance, high priority will be given to supporting the following activities (not listed in order of priority):

(i) Human resource development through training programmes and transfer of skills and technical know-how required in population programmes;

(ii) Institution building at the national level, particularly in the fields of population data collection and analysis, policy formulation and implementation of action programmes;

(iii) Strengthening of managerial, administrative and productive capabilities of recipient countries to enable them to execute population programmes effectively, including ensuring eventual provision of equipment and supplies locally whenever possible and to deliver services at the local level to the population at large; and

(iv) Operational research and pilot projects exploring innovative approaches to dealing with various aspects of population problems that may improve or encourage future action.

(e) In accordance with the WPPA, special attention will also be given to meeting the needs of disadvantaged population groups. This is a monumental task in view of the fact that the large majority of the population in most developing countries may be classified as belonging to such groups. This would clearly be in line with the importance given by the General Assembly to reaching the poorest and most vulnerable population sections in meeting the needs of developing countries for development assistance.[10]

The Economic and Social Council has endorsed the recommendation of the Administrative Committee on Co-ordination that alleviation of poverty, particularly in connexion with rural development, should become a major criterion influencing the design of activities and the allocation of resources of organizations in the United Nations system with the primary objective of improving the quality of life through the involvement of the rural poor in the development process.[11]

Towards this end, UNFPA will give high priority to supporting population activities for the benefit and with the participation of groups such as the poorest among rural populations, underprivileged people in urban areas, disadvantaged migratory groups and low-income families in densely populated localities. The problem of "exploding cities" is of great and growing importance in many developing countries, resulting, in many cases, in pockets of extreme poverty in inner cities. Existing organizational and institutional frameworks for reaching these sectors of the population will be fully utilized and supported. Action programmes aiming at widespread popular participation will explore all avenues for promoting community-based activities, involving particularly the underprivileged and other population groups often not greatly affected by or benefitting from development efforts.

Among disadvantaged and vulnerable groups, special attention will be given to women as an active and effective force in development in accordance with the recommendations of the World Conference of the International Women's Year. In the population field, perhaps more than in any other area of development, little can be accomplished without the active involvement and full participation of women, many of whom belong to the poorest of the poor in developing countries. They are vitally concerned as individuals, as actual or potential mothers, as homemakers and as an economically active force.

UNFPA has developed a set of guidelines for emphasizing, in its day to day operations, the inextricable link between the status and roles of women and population activities. These guidelines, which deal with programme development, project formulation, implementation and evaluation, are not meant to be used in the development of special "women's projects" but rather as directions applicable to all programmes and projects within UNFPA's mandate. They outline how issues relating to the involvement of women in development may be taken into account in population policies, research in population, data collection and analysis, information, education and service programmes.

CORE PROGRAMME OF UNFPA ASSISTANCE

In its broadest sense, "population activities" may be defined as comprising all programmes related to the determinants and consequences of population trends including economic, social, demographic, biological, geographical, environmental and political aspects. The limited financial and human resources available for international population assistance suggest that they be devoted primarily to supporting "the population aspects of development, defined as the causes, conditions and consequences of changes in fertility, mortality and mobility as they affect developmental prospects and the human welfare resulting therefrom."[12]

The primary concern of UNFPA is to support activities aimed at bringing about a fuller understanding of the population aspects of development and at influencing population factors through the formulation and implementation of policies concerning the size, growth, structure and distribution of population, to improve levels of living and quality of life.

Within this broad scope of activities a core programme of assistance has emerged for which the Fund is now a major international source of funding. The main areas of this UNFPA core programme are the following (not listed in order of priority): basic population data collection and analysis, population policy formulation and implementation including family planning and population redistribution, population education and training, and applied research. It includes communication activities in support of these programmes.

The main emphasis in the core programme is on activities directly related to and required for population policy formulation and implementation. Such activities include:

- taking censuses of population;
- registration of vital events;
- population surveys;
- research particularly on matters relevant to decision making and action programmes;
- training of personnel;
- strengthening population policy units in governments;
- meetings and seminars on the inter-relationships of population and socio-economic development;
- delivery of family planning services, including integration of family planning services with health and other social programmes;
- measures to deal with sterility and subfecundity;
- migration policy measures;
- introduction of population education into the curricula of schools and out-of-school education for various organized groups;
- activities designed to disseminate population information to target groups and the public at large.

On the other hand, programmes with the primary objective of, for example, reducing mortality, improving general health conditions, strengthening basic statistical services to improve general data collection, undertaking clinical trials of new contraceptives and providing general and professional education for health personnel, statisticians, teachers, administrators and rural extension workers should, generally speaking, be considered as falling outside the UNFPA core programme.

The Fund's present and prospective limited resources indicate that primary concern will have to be directed to supporting activities falling within the core programme. Other population activities are not necessarily considered of secondary importance for development but it does not appear to be feasible for the UNFPA to devote a substantial part of its limited resources to activities which fall outside the main objectives of the Fund and for which other sources of funding may be available.

It is neither desirable nor possible, however, to establish clear-cut borderlines for UNFPA-supportable activities. Some flexibility will be maintained to allow the Fund to support activities in areas outside the core programme—but they will be limited mainly to types of activities which are related to the formulation and implementation of activities within the core programme, for example, expansion and strengthening of maternal and child health delivery systems; adaptation of regional, rural and community development programmes to include population elements and measures to deal with spatial distribution of population, including urbanization.

The core programme and, to a limited extent, activities in related areas, indicate the types of population activities for which UNFPA support should be available in the future. The fact is, however, that the scarcity of foreseen resources will most likely make it impossible for the Fund to respond favourably to many of the requests for assistance even within these limits, thus making it necessary to be selective and to establish further priorities. In doing so the need for population assistance as well as the capacity and ability of developing countries to absorb it will be taken into account.

In order to set such priorities the following considerations will be taken into account: types of programmes needed at the national level, population problems of recipient countries, and the role of intercountry activities. The types of programmes will be considered with reference to countries' basic needs at the various stages in the evolution, formulation and implementation of national population policies. National population problems will be taken into account in designating high priority countries for UNFPA assistance. The role of intercountry activities within UNFPA's programme will be reassessed through a review of past UNFPA support to such activities in order to draw up an integrated strategy for such support in the future.

Basic Needs at Various Stages in the Evolution of National Population Policies and Programmes

There are marked differences throughout the developing world in approaches to population matters, in the degree of concern for population questions and in the level of sophistication of the measures taken to deal with population issues. This is not merely because population problems are different in the various parts of the world but also because attitudes are the outcome of a complex mix of circumstances in a continuous process ending in full "population consciousness." Various steps in the evolution of national population policies and programmes can be identified.

One or several of the following steps in the development of policies may require assistance at the country level:

    (i) promotion of awareness and understanding of population factors as related to economic and social development;

    (ii) determination of the size, growth, structure and distribution of the population;

(iii) assessment of population trends in relation to economic and social development and appreciation of the causes and consequences of their inter-relationships;

(iv) formulation of population policies based on the country's perception of population trends and their socio-economic aspects.

In implementing population policies, programmes may be required for spacing births, reducing fertility, sterility or subfecundity, raising age at marriage, influencing internal migration, redistributing population, or other types of activities.

The World Population Plan of Action provides general guidance on what is needed in various population sectors for the developing countries to become self-reliant in the development of population policies relating to population size, growth, distribution and structure. It is, of course, up to each government to decide what its policies, population objectives, targets and means of implementation are to be, but the recommendations made in the Plan of Action are meant to guide governments and international organizations.

The UNFPA will develop guidelines for providing countries with assistance in implementing programmes to meet basic needs in the fields of population, taking into account the priorities indicated by the countries themselves and their own resources as well as sources of external assistance.

Basic needs programmes will be drawn up for all interested developing countries, with a view to identifying (mainly within the UNFPA core programme) the most essential steps to be taken in, for example, census taking, vital statistics, data analysis, delivery of family planning services, communication support services, training and population education. Special attention will be given in this process to the five general principles stated above, particularly building up recipient countries' self-reliance through strengthening the human resource base, institution building and developing other capabilities to meet their needs. This task will be carried out with the participation of experts from the relevant disciplines and in consultation with the government(s) concerned.

Since this exercise would also be of use to other major organizations and governments concerned with population assistance, the study may not be limited to the UNFPA core programme in order to be of maximum usefulness. Furthermore, it may not be limited to needs in the governmental sector, but could also take into account the role and contribution of nongovernmental bodies, particularly in promoting activities at the grassroots level.

In each case, the basic needs for population assistance will be identified within the context of the country's population goals, policies and existing capacities. After discerning the population objectives of a country, and its existing policy and capacity to carry it out, a programme will be drawn up of the most essential steps to set the country on the road to self-reliance in the formulation and implementation of population policies. This programme will include components that may be supported by the UNFPA, other multilateral organizations or bilateral donors. It is, of course, up to the government to decide which donor will provide what parts of the assistance required.

In developing basic needs programmes, UNFPA is beginning with studies of interested priority countries (see below) and will eventually study all interested developing countries requesting assistance from the Fund. It is not the Fund's intention to prepare blueprints for population programmes for individual developing countries—only they can do that themselves—but to prepare the framework for international population assistance within a balanced and integrated programme, taking into account differences in population objectives, policies and approaches.

Within such a framework the role of various international, intergovernmental and non-governmental organizations and bilateral programmes as well as joint or collaborative efforts between them can be clarified and an improved division of labour developed. Such a co-ordinated approach should be of considerable benefit to recipient developing countries and will strengthen the impact of population assistance, making it more attractive to donors to continue and increase their support. The UNFPA should lead and help to co-ordinate this approach. Efforts will also be made to promote population components in related economic and social development activities, particularly through UNDP country programming.

In allocating its resources to countries, the Fund will give priority to assisting (in co-operation with other funding agencies) the establishment of basic population activities. However, the Fund will not be able to respond to all requests for assistance to such activities; further priorities must therefore be established to determine the extent to which countries should be assisted and which countries should receive assistance first.

Priorities between Countries

Allocation of UNFPA resources to countries has in the past been based largely upon the size of government requests, the types of programmes for which assistance was sought, and what internal and other external resources were available. In 1976, countries in Asia and the

Pacific received the largest share of the Fund's programme resources, just over 30 per cent; Africa received around 13 per cent, Latin America around 25 per cent, and Europe, the Mediterranean and Middle East 13 per cent, while the remainder supported interregional and global activities. Over the years the share of UNFPA programme resources allotted to Asian and Pacific countries has remained fairly constant, while moderate to sharp increases have taken place in Europe, the Mediterranean and the Middle East, Africa and Latin America. Allocations to the two last regions have increased two to threefold. 1977 allocations, however, show increases in the percentage of resources for countries in Asia and the Pacific (from 30 to 34 per cent), Europe, the Mediterranean and the Middle East (from 13 to 16 per cent respectively), and Africa (from 13 to 15 per cent) and a decrease for Latin American countries (from 25 to 18 per cent).

The large share allotted to countries in Asia and the Pacific may be explained by the fact that particularly in the early years of the Fund's existence they were, and in general terms still are, more "population conscious" and have more comprehensive action programmes than elsewhere. Population size and density of this region are also much higher than elsewhere so that more support for population activities is needed, although not necessarily in proportion to the difference.

An analysis of the Fund's 1976 allocations shows that countries in Asia and the Pacific actually received assistance at the lowest per capita level of all the regions (two US cents), Latin America had the highest per capita level (six US cents), while Africa and Europe, the Mediterranean and the Middle East were at an intermediate level (three US cents each).[13] In relation to national income, UNFPA input was largest in the African region followed by Asia and the Pacific, Latin America and Europe, the Mediterranean and the Middle East.[14]

In order to respond to the most urgent and critical needs of developing countries and to maintain the programme approach applied in the past in accordance with the general principles mentioned earlier, various approaches to setting priorities in the allocation of resources among countries have been considered.

The use of indicative figures for the allocation of resources among the major developing regions rather than for individual countries was considered, but it was found difficult to fix criteria that would take into account the specific role of the Fund. Such indicative figures would have to be established by the governing bodies of the Fund as political decisions.

The Fund explored various other possibilities for identifying a group of developing countries to be given special attention in the future allocation of resources, with the provision that assistance to other countries will continue on a more selective basis.

In the execution of the United Nations Development Programme[15] special attention is given to countries recognized as least developed countries.[16] This group includes 17 countries in Africa, eight in Asia and the Pacific, one in Latin America and three in Europe, the Mediterranean and the Middle East: total estimated population of 244 million or about 12 percent of all developing countries.[17] This concept is not considered the most appropriate for assigning high priority for UNFPA assistance; it is based primarily on economic considerations,[18] most of the countries included are comparatively small (only six of them have a total population exceeding ten million each) and many of them have population problems which are not considered more severe than those of countries not included in the group. The least developed countries urgently need assistance for their development programmes in general but may not necessarily be in urgent need of population assistance in particular.

Another group of developing countries has been designated by the General Assembly as most seriously affected countries.[19] These are developing countries suffering from serious balance-of-payments problems,[20] and benefitting from the Special Programme of Emergency Measures adopted by the Assembly. Most but not all of the least developed countries (24 of 29) as well as some 18 additional developing countries are included. Of these 25 are located in Africa, nine in Asia and the Pacific, four in Europe the Mediterranean and the Middle East and four in Latin America with an estimated 41 per cent of the population of all developing countries. Since the concept of most seriously affected countries is based largely on the existence of serious balance-of-payments problems, it is also considered unsuitable for use as a criterion for priority treatment in the allocation of population assistance. In the allocation of UNFPA resources some consideration may be given to the existence of serious foreign exchange problems, but this should only be one among several indicators of needs and it is to some extent already taken into account in a general way in the Fund's assessment of requests.

It became clear that a special system of selection of high priority countries for population assistance would have to be designed in order to take fully into account the general principle that the Fund is supposed to assist particularly countries with urgent population problems. To select high priority countries, a few demographic indicators are applied. The lack of population data in many developing countries restricts the choice of demographic indicators but estimates on population growth, fertility, infant mortality and population density on arable land are generally available. They are, in general terms, indicative of major population problems and, to some extent, of the levels of development and welfare. Various threshold levels for these demographic indicators were explored using the most recent information available. Furthermore, in order to concentrate the Fund's scarce resources in areas where they are likely to contribute most towards solving the population problems of the developing world and where assistance is most needed, consideration is also given in a general way to the economic situation of countries as indicated by the level of per capita national income.[21]

By applying the criteria of a per capita national income below $400 per annum and two or more of the following demographic criteria:

(i) annual rate of population growth of 2.75 per cent or higher;
(ii) fertility in terms of gross reproduction rate of 2.75 per cent or higher;
(iii) infant mortality of 176 infant deaths or more per 1,000 live births; and
(iv) agricultural population density on arable land of 2.2 persons or more per hectare,

the UNFPA has designated a group of 40 developing countries as priority countries for population assistance (PCPAs) out of a total of 128 developing countries.[22]

All 40 countries but one meet the criterion of fertility. In all cases the added determining demographic indicator is population growth: in seven cases infant mortality and in seven cases agricultural population density. In 14 cases, in addition to fertility, two demographic indicators prevail: population growth and density in nine cases, and population growth and infant mortality in the remainder. In the one case where fertility is below the threshold level, the criteria of infant mortality and density are met.

Of the group 17 are in Africa, 14 in Asia and the Pacific, five in Europe, the Mediterranean and the Middle East and four in Latin America (see Annex). In 1977, these countries had a total population estimated at 1.2 billion, or 53 per cent of that of all developing countries and territories,[23] and received about 45 per cent of the Fund's total resources provided at the country level. Nineteen out of 29 of the least developed countries as determined by the General Assembly and the Economic and Social Council[24] are also PCPA countries.

A ceiling of two-thirds of total programme resources available to UNFPA for population activities at the country level has been established for assistance to priority countries as a group; the level of assistance to each of these countries is to be determined largely by its basic needs in population. The ceiling is tentative until more experience is gained in determining the need and capacity of high priority countries for carrying out basic needs population programmes.

It is the Fund's intention to review and revise the PCPA group periodically. As the demographic situation in recipient countries changes, some countries will leave the group while new data may result in the addition of new countries. The present group was identified on the basis of data available in 1976 from United Nations and Food and Agriculture Organization sources.[25]

UNFPA intends to maintain some flexibility in applying the concept of priority countries. Concentration of the Fund's resources on high priority countries can be implemented only gradually because commitments have already been made for most of the resources for 1978 and, to a lesser extent, for the following years. Only as commitments expire and additional resources become available will it be possible to implement the newly established priorities effectively. Furthermore, the preparation of basic needs programmes in collaboration with the governments and the United Nations Organizations concerned will take time. Wherever UNFPA has helped countries to build up population programmes, assistance should not be reduced or terminated suddenly; but the aim should clearly be for the countries themselves eventually to take over full responsibility for the activities concerned.

It is fully recognized that since comparable official statistics are not available for all countries, the designation of countries is sometimes less than definitive. A number of countries, although strictly not within the adopted demographic and economic criteria based upon the data available in 1976, were fairly close to the threshold levels used. Fourteen of the 88 countries outside the priority list of 40 would qualify if a two per cent variance from the threshold levels were allowed. These include eight countries in Africa, two in Asia and the Pacific, two in Latin America and one in Europe, the Mediterranean and the Middle East region. In the allocation of resources among non-priority countries, it is intended to give special attention to borderline cases (for list of such countries see Annex).

It is recognized that the amount of assistance desired and needed by each developing country depends on the nature of its population problems, the degree of knowledge and recognition of its population issues, the approaches to dealing with such problems, the policies which may have been adopted and the level of sophistication of the measures planned or already taken. These factors vary considerably between regions and countries. Many countries, particularly in Asia and the Pacific, and to a growing extent also in Latin America, are advanced in the evolution of policies and programmes and, have a higher capacity to absorb population assistance. Others, particularly in Africa, where two-fifths of all the priority countries are located, are at an early stage in policy and programme evolution, concentrating to a large extent on data collection, population dynamics and training activities, and therefore often have a fairly limited need for population assistance. By determining countries' basic population needs, it is intended to respond to varying local conditions and allow for flexibility in developing UNFPA assistance. Until these programmes have been established, it is difficult to specify, either for priority countries or for borderline cases the types of population activities and the amount of assistance UNPFA will provide.

It should be pointed out that resources within the two-thirds ceiling not required for support of basic needs population programmes in high priority countries will be available for assistance in other developing countries. Support for population activities in the latter countries will have to be on a selective basis and will focus more on specific and urgent needs. Although, in principle, all developing countries and territories are entitled to support from UNFPA, those with a comparatively high per capita income may receive it on a funds-in-trust or reimbursable basis.

Allowance will be made for the possibility that one or several donors may wish to assist through UNFPA selected countries of special interest to them in their own region or to support activities which may be related to but not within UNFPA core areas of population assistance. Furthermore, multibilateral funding, funds-in-trust arrangements and other means of supplementing regular UNFPA resources will contribute to flexibility.

Priority Regarding Intercountry Activities

Many intercountry activities receiving UNFPA support, such as exchange of information and experience on population policies and action programmes, experimentation with new approaches, utilization of talent and research facilities in various countries and high level training abroad are essential to the self-reliance of individual developing countries. Furthermore, in view of their widespread ramifications, population problems and policies often have to be seen and dealt with on a broader than purely national scale.

The objectives of UNFPA support to intercountry activities are as follows:

    (i)   to create awareness of population issues;
    (ii) to develop an international capacity for supporting activities at the country level;
    (iii) to promote development of innovative concepts and approaches; and
    (iv) to provide technical backstopping for activities at the country level.

In the early years of UNFPA nearly 60 per cent of the Fund's programme resources were devoted to activities at the inter-country level. Much of this support was designed to strengthen the capacity of organizations in the United Nations system to enable them to carry out population activities, in accordance with their own mandates, mainly in the areas of training and research for the benefit of the developing countries.

In recent years, an increasingly larger proportion of the Fund's resources has been allocated to respond to the growing number and magnitude of requests from governments of developing countries for population assistance at the national or subnational levels. In 1977 support of intercountry activities had declined to about 32 per cent of allocations of total programme resources. This trend has been caused partly by a sharp increase in demand from countries for the Fund's resources and the high priority given to meeting these needs, and partly by an attempt to concentrate on activities stated above for which other sources of funding are not available.

The main types of activities UNFPA has so far been supporting and the types of activities that require continued support are briefly outlined below for each of the main programme areas of the Fund.

Basic Data Collection

Efforts to improve the quantity and quality of basic population data, which are needed for the formulation and implementation of population policies and economic and social development plans, have to be made mainly in the developing countries themselves. However, intercountry programmes can make important contributions to building up data collection systems through improving methodology and through training of personnel for population censuses, vital statistics, civil registration and population-related sample surveys.

The African Census Programme and the World Fertility Survey are two of the largest ongoing UNFPA-supported schemes at the intercountry level. They have contributed greatly to developing and strengthening the capability of developing countries in basic population data collection. In the areas of vital statistics and civil registration regional advisers provide backstopping to national counterparts and also assist by convening regional expert meetings to promote improvement of population statistics. Regional and interregional advisers have contributed substantially to the improvement of national capabilities in census and other data collection operations by helping train national cadres. As a part of continuing efforts to develop better data processing systems, computer software has been developed at the global level to expedite the processing of censuses and other population data through small computers in developing countries.

Methodological research is needed to improve the reliability of vital rates. This should include experimentation with various forms of estimation such as the use of subnational registration areas as bases for national estimates. Pilot studies are needed to improve civil registration under various conditions. The methodology must be improved for strengthening national capabilities for population surveys which would provide demographic and related socio-economic information essential for the formulation of population policies in the framework of development planning. The methodology for integrated population-related data gathering schemes should be developed through linking census programmes and population surveys with other types of data collection.

Survey design and methodology need to be developed particularly to measure the dimensions, causes and effects of international and internal migratory movements. There is also a need to develop concepts and methods to enumerate, identify and classify diverse population groups such as nomads, unemployed, underemployed, women working in their homes and self-employed.

UNFPA plans to support mainly the following activities in the field of basic data collection: Assistance in census operations should be concentrated mainly on support of training programmes. Support to the World Fertility Survey should be continued until the present programme of surveys has been completed in 1982, and further support may be limited to methodological improvements based upon the experience gained and to the funding of advisory services to countries through the United Nations. Since governments are increasingly concerned about the problems of population redistribution and in view of the serious deficiency which exists with regard to internal and international migration statistics, measures should be supported at the inter-country level to promote and improve data collection on the volume, types and motivation for migration through advisory services, preparation of manuals and training of personnel. In all areas of data collections support should be given to the dissemination of knowledge about methodological advances, to the promotion of exchange of experience between countries and to the preparation of teaching and training materials.

Population Dynamics

Intercountry activities supported by UNFPA in population dynamics have covered a broad spectrum. They included research on mortality trends; the interrelations between population growth, employment and migration; studies of population and environment in selected situations; the effects of population growth on education; and various issues concerning agriculture, food and population change. Support has also been provided for the development of demographic and economic models, notably the BACHUE model of the International Labour Organization (ILO).*

Substantial UNFPA support has been provided to the regional demographic centres for the training of personnel in developing countries in population-related research, including the processing and analysis of data. The centres have played an important role in providing basic training in demography and related subjects and in research, thus contributing significantly to building up the capability of developing countries to deal with population dynamics.

While national and sub-national planning is a process which should take place at the country level, there are a number of areas in which intercountry activities can effectively assist planning, notably the development of methodology. Countries need assistance for preparing periodic national impact reports that examine the effects of population trends on major socio-economic variables and the demographic effects of changes in the socio-economic structure. Work on national impact studies will be greatly enhanced by methodological and conceptual research on a global or regional scale so as to assist the design of such studies and to deal with difficult implementation issues such as the articulation, specification and measurement of interactions between population and socio-economic variables at both micro and macro levels.

Methodologies need to be improved for integrating population data into general and specific development planning. The application of

---

*The ILO model (named after the Colombian goddess of love, fertility, and harmony between nature and man) built in 1972 as a theoretical and learning exercise in development planning is now being used for country studies.

such improved methodologies should be promoted through training programmes and seminars for key personnel in central and sectoral planning units. However, because an integrated body of knowledge on population and development does not yet exist, training in this area has to remain experimental for some time to come. Studies are required of the organizational structures and activities of government development planning units to identify where population data can best be integrated in the planning process. Provisions should be made to give countries assistance in establishing or strengthening population units in national planning offices.

In the area of population dynamics, UNFPA plans to concentrate its support mainly on the following: Research programmes currently receiving UNFPA support should be consolidated by placing emphasis on the most urgent issues concerning population dynamics and development planning. An International Review Group on Social Science Research and Population and Development has been funded by UNFPA along with several other donors to provide an overview of what is known in this area and what are the major gaps in knowledge. After the Review Group has completed its work, a revision and consolidation of UNFPA supported research activities should be undertaken and priorities established. Until that time, recommendations are made only with regard to demographic training and modelling work.

Intercountry training courses on basic demography and population and development will no doubt be required for some time to come, and therefore continued UNFPA support to the regional demographic centres and programmes is envisaged but not necessarily at the same or a higher level as in the past, except in the Africa region where expansion of training at the inter-country level is needed.

Training at all of the regional demographic centres should be broadened and greater attention should be paid to social sciences in general and to issues of population and development planning in particular as well as to the analysis of demographic data needed for improving the formulation and implementation of population policies. Continued support should also be given for the inclusion of basic population courses and the consideration of population issues related to development in various other regional and global training programmes, such as regional development centres and statistical programmes.

Future UNFPA support to the development and use of models should be limited to the incorporation of demographic factors into broad development models and to population-focused models for national application.

Population Policies

Intercountry activities in the area of population policies include efforts to identify alternative policies for meeting various demographic goals and to promote greater understanding of the policy formulation process, particularly the role of research; studies of the impact of population policies; and assessment of the effect, if any, upon population trends of policies not specifically intended to influence population factors.

UNFPA support to intercountry activities in this area comprises workshops and seminars, mainly regional ones to familiarize policy makers with the importance of demographic variables and of population policies in development. For example, studies have been undertaken on the social welfare aspects of family planning; on social security and population factors, with emphasis on the effects of different family allowance schemes; and on the environmental and population dimensions of human settlements. Through advisory services technical support has also been given for the development and implementation of population policies in a number of countries.

A comprehensive project to develop greater understanding of cultural values as they relate to population policies and programmes has received UNFPA support. A regional population policy research project in Latin America known as the PISPAL project is also funded in part by UNFPA. A central unit formerly linked with CEDADE has been charged with planning and developing multi-disciplinary research projects on the inter-relations between socio-economic and demographic variables in the context of the formulation of population policies.

Given the importance of fertility as a population variable, considerable attention still needs to be directed to clarifying the determinants of fertility. Intercountry methodological research and comparative studies are needed to test the current research hypothesis that income distribution has significant effects on fertility, particularly as it changes over time, and how fertility is affected by the role and status of women. Further research is needed on the effects on fertility of decline in infant and child mortality, particularly in Africa. Work is also needed to determine the extent to which children in different societies are considered important for security in old age, and the extent to which they fulfil this expectation. Concern with the determinants of fertility relates both to countries which desire to decrease and to those which want to increase their populations.

Intercountry programmes are also required for monitoring and research concerning alternative population policies and their possible adaptation to differing political, social or economic settings. Countries which have undergone significant fertility declines and other important population changes have to be studied to identify the underlying policy variables. Conceptual and methodological research is needed at global and regional levels to promote studies which would yield better understanding of different cultural, religious and ethnic perceptions of population policies and programmes and of how the family and the individual are motivated with regard to fertility, migration and other demographic phenomena. Such studies could contribute considerably to improving communication with family groups and individuals for the formulation and implementation of population policies.

International and internal migration are regarded as increasingly important problems by many governments, particularly in the Middle East, Africa and Latin America. Greater attention must, therefore, be given to human resources planning as a way of giving greater rationality to the movement of persons both across and within national borders. Research is needed on resource distribution and human settlements; this should include the interrelationships between industrialization, desertification, deforestation, desalinization, and land development on the one hand, and population factors on the other. Methodological and conceptual research is also needed concerning the demographic and socio-economic impact of migration on both the departure and arrival areas, and the motivations behind the migrants' decision to move. The impact of rural and urban development policies and of programmes in the area of population dynamics should be investigated, documented and disseminated to assist countries in developing programmes most suited to their needs.

In the area of population policies, UNFPA plans to concentrate mainly on research and training activities which should be consolidated to focus on the major population issues of immediate concern to developing countries as outlined above. Conceptual and methodological research at the intercountry level should be supported to assist countries in assessing the impact of various policy packages, which should include not only population policies but also socio-economic policies not having explicit population objectives.

In terms of support to training in this area, UNFPA should focus on supporting programmes designed to create greater awareness and better understanding among researchers, policy planners and decision-makers on the role of research in population policy formulation and implementation. Courses or workshops should be supported which provide training for policy makers and planners who are in the best position to take population factors and relevant research findings into account.

Family Planning

UNFPA support of intercountry programmes in the area of family planning has made contributions in essentially three aspects: human resources development, research and delivery of services.

In human resources development, UNFPA has assisted the development of training and education programmes and materials for health workers, including medical students and traditional birth attendants, through support of teachers training, fellowships, seminars, workshops, special courses and circulation and development of teaching materials.

As regards research, support has been provided for epidemiological studies on maternal and child mortality and morbidity related to fertility trends and patterns and operational research on the high risk factors in reproduction, which will help develop more effective service strategies as well as studies on the behaviour of adolescents, abortion, sterilization, the integration of nutrition aspects and the epidemiology of infertility in some African countries.

Considerable gains have been made in the expansion of family planning services but intercountry activities continue to be urgently needed to strengthen already existing programmes, to explore alternative delivery approaches and to develop new and adapt existing contraceptive technology.

Among the needs which have to be met in the future are: the simplification of service statistics and record keeping; improvement of evaluation methods and their application; development of simplified methods of administration and financial management; improvement of supply lines; management of information systems for the training of health workers at various levels; improvement of the delivery of services to various special groups such as organized labour, migrants, youth and newly married couples.

Increasing emphasis has recently been placed on providing family planning services through community-based approaches, both inside and outside the national health system, involving existing programmes and institutions in areas such as functional education and literacy, agricultural and rural development, social security schemes and trade unions. Effective back-up support will be needed from a health system which includes community services as envisaged by the primary health care approach. Studies are needed to increase the understanding of what motivates communities to adopt family planning practices and to determine how community operated programmes can best be established.

Research to identify the most effective and acceptable community-based approaches to family planning should be encouraged, developed and analyzed through intercountry activities, and the various social, cultural, political and economic situations should be taken into account. In such studies, particular attention should be given to improving programme performance through new approaches to management, particularly at the village level. Studies are needed on how to overcome the lack of coverage and acceptability of existing family health services.

Continued attention should be given to developing effective, easily administered, inexpensive and safe methods of contraception for use in developing countries, particularly where the contraceptives delivery points are moving from clinics to community-based programmes. Clinical and epidemiological research on methods of contraception, including the development of improved or new methods, should be expanded in the developing world. Greater resources for such research should be made available and should also include the testing and adaptation of traditional as well as modern methods.

In the field of family planning, UNFPA plans to support mainly the following activities: High priority should be on operational research, so as to reinforce ongoing programmes and to advance knowledge of new approaches; coverage should thus be expanded and resources for promoting family planning used more effectively. Studies which assess the conditions for success or failure of ongoing integrated maternal and child health family planning programmes should be supported, as well as studies designed to formulate and implement community-based approaches to family planning, with built-in evaluations after a reasonable period of experimentation. Research to be supported should assist programme planners in assessing the real and perceived needs of the members of different communities, in relating family planning activities effectively to such other social programmes as education, civic involvement, family economics, food, nutrition, and employment.

As country programmes adopt and utilize improved family planning schemes and countries become self-sufficient in basic training, the regional and interregional training programmes should become more specialized in character and probably decrease in intensity, volume and cost. However, one area where action has not been commensurate with needs is health education, and considerable intercountry support of training in this area will be required.

Substantial support should also be provided for applied and operational research in family planning technology. This should include the adaptation of current methodologies, development of new contraceptives and the prevention and treatment of infertility and sterility. For this purpose, research facilities in developing countries should be strengthened particularly through grants, advisory services and through research and training at regional or global levels. The WHO Special Programme of Research, Training and Development of Human Reproduction and other appropriate international programmes should be utilized for this area of research.

Communication and Education

The success of population policies and programmes depends to a large extent upon the understanding of the relevance of population factors and related issues in decision-making at individual, family, community and national levels. The Fund has, therefore, supported intercountry programmes which promote as wide involvement of the population as possible in census taking, registration of vital events, family planning and migration schemes. Various types of intercountry support of communication and education programmes have been provided including regional advisory services, the preparation of prototype materials, sourcebooks and teaching materials, training of educators and the development of support communication strategies. Support has been provided within the context of sex education, population education, family life education, workers' and health education both formal and informal, and particular stress has been on existing institutions and channels in direct contact with the widest population groups.

Special attention should in the future be given to those intercountry activities which will help develop the appropriate modes of delivery and content for different audiences, with due account of relevant behavioural factors. The regional and interregional activities should promote training of educators, develop national training schemes for personnel in various development programmes, and establish the methodology for evaluation of population communication and education efforts.

Another need which can be met at the intercountry level is to make research findings on population communications and education more readily available and disseminated more widely for the benefit of country programmes. Through various types of intercountry activities the application of communications and education research findings should be promoted in the planning and execution of population policies and programmes.

In the area of communication and education, UNFPA plans to concentrate future support at the intercountry level mainly on efforts to promote information exchange in all types of programmes. More emphasis should be put on application of intersectoral communication and education approaches, and regional advisory services should be made available to assist in the development of specific country materials. Training for such application should also be assisted where appropriate, at the intercountry level. The development of prototype materials, sourcebooks and teacher-training handbooks should continue to receive support.

Support to intercountry clearinghouses may be continued since they complement activities at national levels by focusing principally on exchange of technical information, the transfer of skills and experiences and on new ideas and approaches. Regional activities serve as a focal point for information exchange within regions and can provide a natural mechanism for sorting out and tailoring relevant information from other countries and regions to national activities in a particular region.

SUMMARY AND CONCLUSIONS

Until recently the UNFPA was able to accommodate most requests received from the governments of developing countries. However, the recent sharp increase in the demand for assistance—to a large extent due to the Fund's success in accomplishing its main objectives—is making it increasingly necessary and indeed essential for the Fund to become more selective in granting assistance and in determining the criteria for establishing priorities.

The general principles for establishing priorities in future allocation of UNFPA resources will be: to implement relevant international strategies, to support population activities in developing countries with the greatest needs for population assistance, to respect the sovereignty of recipient countries on matters of population policies, to give special attention to disadvantaged population groups and to promote recipient countries' self-reliance.

The Fund's resources will be devoted mainly to supporting a core programme of population activities directly related to development, particularly activities required for or connected with population policy formation and implementation. However, it is clear that the Fund's resources will not be sufficient to support all technically sound requests falling within the core programme. It is desirable, then, to concentrate on supporting activities in countries which are especially in need of population assistance, taking into account *inter alia* their demographic situation, their major population problems and the progress made in dealing with them.

Certain basic needs population programmes will be developed at the country level taking into account the diversity of countries' population problems and policies, and approaches to them. Basic population programmes will be outlined for interested developing countries in which the assistance required to enable countries to implement these programmes in stages will be clearly set out. This exercise will concentrate on the core areas of UNFPA support, but may go beyond them so that its findings may be of use to other donors. This major task will be undertaken in collaboration with the governments and Organizations concerned.

Up to two-thirds of the Fund's total resources available for country programmes will be devoted to meeting basic population needs in priority countries. The remaining third will go towards meeting basic needs in other developing countries, particularly those identified as deserving special attention in the future allocation of UNFPA resources to countries. Activities in countries with a high per capita income may be supported on a funds-in-trust or on a reimbursable basis.

As regards intercountry or regional, interregional and global programmes the emphasis in the future will be on promoting and reinforcing country programmes, on developing innovative approaches applicable in developing countries and on facilitating implementation of the WPPA. The aim will be to concentrate UNFPA support on a smaller number of major programmes dealing with the most urgent problems and with the greatest multiplier effect upon activities in developing countries.

In applying priorities overall flexibility will be maintained. In many cases, UNFPA support has helped countries to gain momentum in building up population programmes and assistance will not be reduced or terminated abruptly. Allowance will also be made through earmarking arrangements for the special interest of some donors in a particular region, country, or programme area, which may or may not fall within the UNFPA core areas of assistance. Furthermore, the establishment of priorities is a long term, continuing process and should be subject to periodical review and revision.

UNFPA support to country programmes is often relatively small compared with other sources of population assistance and inputs from local governmental and nongovernmental organizations which are

usually very substantial. Yet UNFPA assistance is of great significance, particularly in generating new programmes and approaches
which have to be proved successful in order to attract regular governmental or other funds. The visibility of UNFPA assistance makes it
especially important that it be provided effectively to areas with the
greatest need.

ANNEX

Priority Countries for Population Assistance

Afghanistan
Bangladesh
Burundi
Democratic Kampuchea
Democratic Yeman
Ecuador
El Salvador
Ethiopia
Gambia
Ghana
Guinea
Honduras
India
Jordan
Kenya
Lao People's Democratic
  Republic
Liberia
Madagascar
Maldives
Mali

Mauritania
Morocco
Nepal
Niger
Pakistan
Paraguay
Philippines
Rwanda
Samoa
Senegal
Solomon Islands
Somalia
Sudan
Thailand
Tonga

Uganda
United Republic of Tanzania
Upper Volta
Vietnam
Yemen

Other Countries to Be Given Special Attention*

Benin
Central African Empire
Gilbert Islands

Nigeria
Peru
Swaziland

*Countries which would qualify as priority countries for population assistance if a 2 per
cent variance from the threshold levels were allowed.

Guatemala	Syrian Arab Republic
Indonesia	Togo
Malawi	Tuvalu
Namibia	United Republic of Cameroon

NOTES

1. Economic and Social Council resolution 2025 (LXI).
2. General Assembly resolution 31/170.
3. Resolution 1763 (LIV), operative paragraph 1.
4. Ibid.
5. Ibid.
6. Ibid.
7. General Assembly resolution 2211 (XXI) and 3344 (XXIX) adopted 17 December 1966 and 17 December 1974 respectively.
8. This principle was confirmed by the Declaration on Social Progress and Development adopted by the General Assembly (resolution 2542 (XXIV)) which declared "that parents have the exclusive right to determine freely the number and spacing of their children."
9. General Assembly resolution 3405 (XXX) of 28 November 1975.
10. General Assembly resolution op. cit.
11. Economic and Social Council Resolution 175 (LXI) of 5 August 1976.
12. UNFPA/UN Interregional Consultative Group of Experts on the World Population Plan of Action, "Final Report," (UNFPA/WPPA/20/Rev. 1), p. 17.
13. Figures are for country as well as regional activities. For country activities alone: Asia and the Pacific one US cent, Latin America four US cents, Africa three US cents and Europe, the Mediterranean and the Middle East three US cents. Support provided in 1977 at the country level indicates no change in Latin America, and slight increases in all other regions viz. in Asia and the Pacific to two US cents, in Africa to four US cents and in Europe, the Mediterranean and the Middle East also to four US cents.
14. The 1975 UNFPA contributions amounted to $179 per one million dollars national income (1971) in Africa, $145 in Asia and the Pacific, $78 in Latin America and $62 in Europe, the Mediterranean and the Middle East.
15. General Assembly resolution 3405 (XXX) of 28 November 1975.
16. General Assembly resolution 2768 (XXVI) of 18 November 1971 and Economic and Social Council resolution 1976 (LIX) of 30 July 1975.
17. Included in UNDP's second programming cycle 1977–1981.
18. The criteria applied includes per capita gross domestic products ($125 or less or $150 in some borderline cases), share of manufacturing in the gross domestic product (10 percent or less) and percentage of literates in the adult population (20 percent or less).
19. General Assembly resolution 3202 (A/RES/3202/S-VI) of 1 May 1974.
20. Following the upsurge in the prices of essential imports without corresponding increases in export earnings.
21. Application of social indicators was also explored but abandoned in view of the lack of data and the fact that several of the demographic indicators are already strongly correlated with social factors. Material provided by the ILO on estimated ranking of a

large number of countries in terms of poverty seems to indicate that all the countries selected using the criteria proposed above have half or more of their population falling below an arbitrarily set poverty line; less than one third of the developing countries which do not meet the criteria are in this position.

22. Countries and territories for which the UNDP Governing Council has established indicative planning figures for 1977–1981.

23. See Note 22.

24. General Assembly resolution 2768 (XXVI) of 18 November 1971 and Economic and Social Council resolution 1976 (LIX) of 30 July 1975.

25. United Nations, Department of Economic and Social Affairs, Statistical Office, *Statistical Yearbook 1974* (ST/ESA/STAT/SER.S/2), New York, 1975, Table 188; *Selected World Demographic Indicators* by Countries, 1950–2000 (ESA/P/WP.55), prepared by Population Division, Department of Economic and Social Affairs of the United Nations Secretariat, New York, 1975; Food and Agriculture Organization of the United Nations, Production Yearbook, 1974, Vol. 28-1, Rome, 1975, Tables 1 and 5.

7 RECENT TRENDS IN INTERNATIONAL POPULATION ASSISTANCE

The history of international population assistance is brief, but spectacular. As recently as 10 to 15 years ago, there was little consensus among governments as to the need for assistance to the Third World except in the fields of demography and statistics.* On the contrary, the forces opposing assistance to such activities as family planning and population policy on religious, cultural, or political grounds were still generally dominant. Within many developed countries the promotion of family planning was still, to a large extent, seen as the exclusive concern of voluntary endeavors, supported by private philanthropy. Today, technical cooperation and financial assistance for a wide spectrum of population activities in developing countries are fully recognized as the legitimate concern of, and high priority for, governments and the international community.

In the early 1950s, the United Nations began to assist developing countries with census-taking, training in demography, preparation of studies of the relationships between population trends and social and economic factors, as well as with some action-oriented research activities. In 1952, two nongovernmental agencies concerned with assistance

---

*A clear-cut, and generally agreed upon, definition of the term "population activities" is not available, but it is clear that it covers much more than demography or delivery of family planning services but not the entire scope of the World Population Plan of Action. Population activities covered by international assistance have been broadly classified, by the United Nations organizations concerned, into the following major subject areas: (1) basic population data; (2) population dynamics; (3) population policy formulation, implementation, and evaluation; (4) family planning; (5) biomedical research; and (6) communication and education. It includes a wide spectrum of data collection, training research, information, and operational activities in population.

to population were established—the International Planned Parenthood Federation (IPPF) and the Population Council. The Ford and Rockefeller Foundations also began to assist population-related activities. Together these four nongovernmental agencies were the main sources of assistance for population and related activities until the late 1960s, when governmental resources became available on a large scale.

The first government to give assistance for family planning to a developing country was Sweden in 1958. This was in support of an experimental program in Sri Lanka, and was followed by similar assistance to the government of Pakistan in 1961. The United Kingdom initiated its bilateral population assistance program on a modest scale in 1964. The U.S. government began to include population activities in its development assistance in 1965. In the early 1970s a number of governments followed the lead provided by Sweden, the United Kingdom, and the United States. These included Canada, Denmark, the Federal Republic of Germany, Japan, the Netherlands, and Norway.

The barriers that, to a large extent, had handicapped the United Nations system in responding directly to the needs of developing countries for assistance in the fields of population, particularly in family planning, began to lift around the mid 1960s. A consensus was reached in the General Assembly in 1966 concerning the provision of population assistance, from governments upon request, in the areas of training, research, information, and advisory services. In response, the following year, the Secretary-General established a Trust Fund for Population Activities—later renamed the United Nations Fund for Population Activities (UNFPA)—which rapidly grew into a major source of international population assistance, in terms of both financial resources and program development. In the meantime, a number of United Nations specialized agencies and UNICEF broadened their mandates to include those aspects of population and family planning falling within their areas of competence. In 1968, the World Bank* began to take into consideration the need of developing countries for assistance to family planning programs and related activites and made its first loan in this area to Jamaica in 1970.

One of the most important events in the history of international population assistance occurred in 1974 when the World Population Conference (WPC) was held in Bucharest. The World Population Plan of Action (WPPA) adopted by the conference among other things called upon developed countries as well as other countries to increase their assistance to developing countries: "In view of the magnitude of the

---

*The International Bank for Reconstruction and Development (IBRD) and the International Development Association (IDA).

problems and the consequent national requirements for funds ... considerable expansion of international assistance in the population field is required for the proper implementation of this Plan of Action."

To what extent has this call been heard? Have the main features of international population assistance changed since the Bucharest conference? What is the outlook for the future role of such assistance?

CURRENT LEVELS OF POPULATION ASSISTANCE

Total international assistance for population activities amounted to only about $2 million in 1960 and $18 million in 1965, but it increased rapidly to $125 million in 1970 and to nearly $350 million by 1977 or an estimated net amount, excluding double counting, of $345 million (see Table 7.1).*

This dramatic increase in population assistance is a clear indication of the growing commitment of governments and international organizations concerned to collaborate in, and contribute to, tackling the urgent population problems of the developing world. It is important to note, however, that the rapid growth in resources made available for international assistance has not been maintained in recent years. A peak was reached in 1974, when the annual growth in resources for population assistance reached an all-time high level of some $50 million. Because of its timing, this peak could be interpreted as a response to the spirit of the World Population Year and Conference, but is more likely a result of the devaluation of the U.S. dollar, which automatically increased the U.S. dollar equivalent of the amounts pledged by many donors in their own currency.

In the following years the average rate of growth in resources fell well below the level reached earlier in the 1970s. The annual increase was only 8–12 percent in the years 1975–77, as compared with 20 percent on the average in the years 1970–74. In view of the substantial inflationary trends worldwide and the devaluation of the U.S. dollar, the growth in international population assistance has, to a great extent if not entirely, been offset by the decline in purchasing power. Measured in constant U.S. dollar (consumer price index), the average annual increase since 1974 has been around 3 percent. Therefore, the level of resources transferred for population activities for the benefit

---

*Differences in definition of population activities and difficulties in identifying population components in multipurpose or integrated development programs make it necessary to exercise some caution in interpretation of international statistics on population assistance.

TABLE 7.1: Trends in Development and Population Assistance, 1961–77

	Total Official Development Assistance[a]	Population Assistance[b]	Population Assistance as Percentage of Total Assistance
	(in millions of U.S. dollars)		(percent)
1977	14,759	345[c]	2.3
1976	13,666	320	2.3
1975	13,588	287	2.1
1974	11,302	257	2.3
1973	9,400	182	2.0
1972	8,700	171	2.0
1971	7,700	155	2.0
1970	6,800	125	1.8
1969	6,600	86	1.3
1968	6,300	58	0.9
1967	6,600	30	0.5
1966	6,000	34	0.6
1965	5,900	18	0.3
1964	6,000	16	0.3
1963	5,800	11	0.2
1962	5,400	5	0.1
1961	5,200	6	0.1

[a] Excluding export credits, private investment, and other commercial transfers.

[b] Net totals excluding double-counting due to transfers between donors. Grants by voluntary organizations are not included for the years 1961–69. In 1970 these grants amounted to $0.9 million.

[c] Provisional.

Sources: Organization for Economic Co-operation and Development, governments, and annual reports of development assistance agencies and organizations.

of the developing countries has only increased very modestly since the World Population Year and Conference (Figure 7.1).

The magnitude of population assistance has barely kept pace with overall development assistance since the WPC (Table 7.2). In 1974, assistance in the field of population amounted to 2.3 percent of total development assistance; it declined to 2.1 percent in 1975 but increased to 2.3 percent in 1976 and in 1977 mainly due to stagnation in the overall level of official development assistance.

The main factor in the slowing down of the growth of resources for international population assistance was that the largest donor, the

United States, did not continue to make substantial increases in its population assistance as it did in the late 1960s and early 1970s, but actually reduced its annual contributions from year to year in the period 1972 through 1975. A new upward trend in the contribution of the United States, however, began in 1976, and an annual increase estimated at about 2 percent took place in 1977 and 1978. Although a number of other donor governments of developed countries at the same time showed a growing recognition of the importance of population assistance by increasing substantially their contributions, these increases were not large enough to maintain the overall growth rate of resources available for population assistance.

The dominating position of the United States in the donor community has recently been considerably reduced. Before 1974, three-quarters or more of all government resources for population assistance and well over half of all funds came from the U.S. government. In 1977, total contributions from all other governments were about equal to the

FIGURE 7.1: Total International Population Assistance, 1971–77 (excludes double counting)

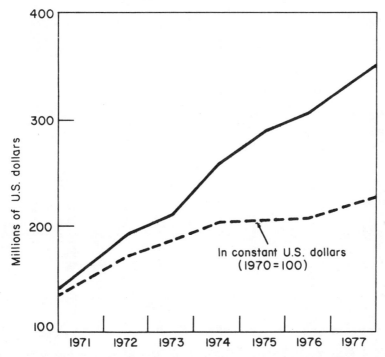

Source: United Nations.

TABLE 7.2: Population Assistance by Major Donors, 1971–77 (thousands of U.S. dollars)

	1971	1972	1973	1974	1975	1976	1977[a]
Governments							
Australia	—	357	579	639	1,587	967	1,065
Belgium	147	18	75	837	476	934	900
Canada	2,496	2,997	4,159	5,498	7,183	8,989	9,116
Denmark	1,918	2,289	2,035	4,784	3,548	4,978	6,200
Finland	507	892	1,033	2,587	2,026	1,578	1,852
Germany, Federal Republic of	1,657	2,435	4,392	5,770	13,400	8,739	8,611
Japan	2,090	2,196	2,812	5,293	7,971	12,920	15,400
Netherlands	1,106	2,232	3,718	5,785	6,695	8,954	9,649
New Zealand	—	77	40	580	880	607	573
Norway	3,870	5,539	8,600	10,800	18,500	27,400	36,363
Sweden	7,446	12,739	17,123	21,468	26,169	28,743	31,417
Switzerland	168	191	189	190	200	242	500
United Kingdom	2,311	3,257	3,861	3,032	6,450	6,983	7,168
United States	109,567	121,133	115,106	110,146	106,036	119,027	145,367
Others	1,283	1,592	1,747	2,325	3,580	11,356	12,000
Subtotal	134,566	157,944	165,469	179,734	204,701	242,417	286,181
Intergovernmental Organizations							
United Nations	6,995	5,952	8,459	20,786	24,234	28,009	27,952
UNICEF	2,382	2,371	3,711	5,753	6,725	6,611	6,700
UNFPA	8,937	19,840	34,684	57,000	71,213	75,781	78,000
ILO	165	989	2,259	3,827	4,901	6,483	6,775
PAO	607	574	1,370	1,539	2,238	—	—

UNESCO	38	28	2,554	4,130	5,337	4,042	5,034
WHO	2,823	6,374	15,991	18,932	22,979	29,324	34,679
World Bank[b]	1,600	5,700	11,200	18,600	24,900	27,000	28,200
Others	5,200	6,577	1,789	6,225	6,300	6,300	6,500
Subtotal	28,747	48,405	82,017	139,219	168,827	183,550	195,200
Nongovernmental Organizations							
Ford Foundation	15,221	14,647	12,353	13,774	10,700	10,800	8,900
IPPF	19,294	24,935	33,798	42,910	42,584	45,554	51,198
Population Council	14,084	17,360	16,128	15,582	12,076	11,000	11,338
Rockefeller Foundation	2,864	6,608	6,370	9,007	8,516	8,500	6,178
Others	3,877	4,400	7,400	6,400	6,400	6,400	7,900
Subtotal	55,340	67,950	76,049	87,673	80,276	83,000	85,514
Total	218,653	274,299	323,535	406,626	453,804	508,967	566,895
Total excluding double counting[c]							
In current US dollars	161,519	183,785	208,651	256,812	285,663	320,011	345,268
In constant US dollars (1970 = 100)	154,860	170,645	182,387	202,214	206,106	218,280	221,179

[a] Provisional.

[b] Annual estimates for the World Bank based upon its commitments according to loan or credit agreements and the planned duration of project execution.

[c] Arrived at by deducting the following from the total: governments' contributions to UNFPA; USAID contributions to IPPF, Pathfinder Fund, and the Population Council; UNFPA contributions to organizations in the United Nations System; and contributions from one foundation to another.

Note: These are actual expenditures except that some of the 1977 figures are estimates based upon allocations. All figures refer to calendar year.

Sources: Organization for Economic Co-operation and Development, governments, and annual reports of development assistance agencies and organizations. See Table I. In addition, United Nations document E/5673, "Report of the Administrative Committee on Co-ordination on Expenditure of the United Nations system in relation in programmes," and U.S. Consumer Price Index, United Nations, *Statistical Yearbook and Monthly Bulletin of Statistics.*

FIGURE 7.2: Government Donors, 1971–77

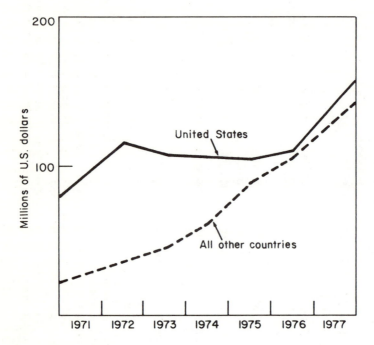

Source: United Nations.

contribution of the United States, and the latter provided about 40 percent of the total of population assistance funds (Table 7.2).

SOURCES OF POPULATION ASSISTANCE

Although over 80 governments have, at one time or another, contributed to international population assistance, the major share comes from less than a dozen countries. The largest contributor, the United States, spent about $146 million on population assistance in 1977, or 2.8 percent of its total development assistance (see Table 7.3). Around one-fifth of this amount was channeled through private and voluntary international organizations based in the United States; nearly one-quarter went to UNFPA and IPPF; about one-fifth was grants to universities and other governmental and nongovernmental institutions in the United States for research and training related to population issues of developing countries; and the remainder, over one-third, provided direct bilateral support to population and family planning projects in developing countries.

Sweden and Norway are the two largest donor governments after the United States. In 1977, the total Swedish financial contribution reached a level of over $31 million, amounting to around 4 percent of its total development assistance. Norway, which has sharply increased its population assistance since 1974 (more than tripling it), contributed over $36 million in 1977 which represented nearly 13 percent of the total Norwegian development assistance program—the highest proportion of any donor country.* Denmark and Finland also gave comparatively high priority to population assistance, with contributions in 1977 of $6 and $2 million, respectively—about 3 percent for each country, of its total assistance program. Other major contributors were Japan, with over $15 million; Canada, the Federal Republic of Germany, and

TABLE 7.3: Government Assistance for Population Activities as Percentage of Total Official Development Assistance in Major Donor Countries, 1973–76

	1973	1974	1975	1976	1977
			(percent)		
Country					
Australia	0.2	0.1	0.3	0.3	0.2
Belgium	—	0.3	0.1	0.3	0.2
Canada	1.2	0.8	0.8	1.0	0.9
Denmark	3.1	2.8	1.7	2.3	2.4
Finland	1.1	6.8	4.2	3.1	3.8
Germany, Federal Republic of	0.4	0.4	0.8	0.6	0.6
Japan	1.3	0.5	0.7	1.2	1.1
Netherlands	1.8	1.3	1.1	1.2	1.1
New Zealand	—	1.5	1.3	1.1	1.1
Norway	8.0	8.2	10.1	12.6	12.3
Sweden	4.4	5.3	4.6	4.7	4.0
Switzerland	0.3	0.3	0.2	0.2	0.4
United Kingdom	1.7	0.4	0.7	0.8	0.8
United States	3.8	3.2	2.6	2.7	3.5

Sources: Organization for Economic Co-operation and Development, governments, and annual reports of development assistance agencies and organizations.

*The Norwegian law on development assistance stipulates that 10 percent of all assistance should be for the fields of population.

the Netherlands with about $9 million each; and the United Kingdom with about $7 million. However, in all these countries, population assistance constituted merely about 1 percent of total official development assistance. A significant recent development has been the interest shown by a number of Arab governments, particularly of oil-exporting countries, in contributing to international population assistance; in 1976, these governments, which had not previously given support in this area, made contributions of about $10 million.

A number of donors provide bilateral population assistance amounting to about 28 percent of total governmental population assistance, but only in three countries is the population component of the total bilateral governmental assistance program of major significance. These three countries are Norway, Sweden, and the United States, for which the population component constituted about 4 to 5 percent of the total.

About 62 percent of total population assistance provided by governments is channeled through multilateral organizations—about 35 percent to intergovernmental bodies and 27 percent to international nongovernmental organizations. (About 11 percent of governments' population assistance is spent in institutions in the donor countries themselves.) A number of governments utilize multilateral channels for most of their support of population activities: Belgium, Canada, Denmark, the Federal Republic of Germany, Japan, New Zealand, and Norway. The Netherlands has phased out all bilateral population programs and concentrates its resources entirely on multilateral aid.

Multilateral population programs have grown markedly. Until the mid-1960s, the role of the organizations within the United Nations system was restricted, not merely by limited mandates in the population field and lack of funds, but also by the fact that few governments had yet formulated national population policies or foreign aid policies on population. About 4 percent of total government development assistance provided to multilateral programs is for population activities. Most of the resources available for population activities undertaken by the United Nations and its specialized agencies (excluding UNFPA, whose resources are entirely from voluntary government contributions) are provided by governments as voluntary extra-budgetary contributions. Only about one-sixth of the resources of these organizations is provided by assessed contributions to their regular budgets from member states.

Before the WPC, UNFPA had already emerged as the largest multilateral source of population assistance. Since 1974 the fund has continued to grow rapidly, twice as rapidly as has population assistance in general. Today, it is the largest source of direct assistance for population activities in developing countries (Figure 7.3).

FIGURE 7.3: Major Multilateral Donors, 1971–77

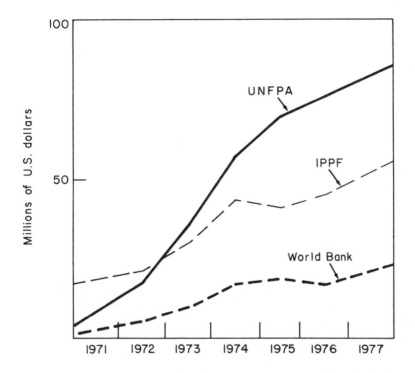

Source: United Nations.

A number of nongovernmental organizations have played an important pioneering role in the support of population activities. The four largest in this regard are the International Planned Parenthood Federation (IPPF), the Population Council, and the Ford and Rockefeller Foundations. A number of other smaller private organizations also contribute. Some of them function exclusively in the population fields; others support population activities within a broad range of purposes and programs. All these organizations provide a channel for private financial contributions, though many also draw, to some extent, on governmental or multilateral funds, and some rely on the contributions of volunteers and part-time workers.

Involvement in assistance has also spread to professional organizations in the population field, such as the International Union for the Scientific Study of Populations, the International Confederation of Midwives, and the International Association of Schools for Social Work. Other organizations are concerned primarily with assisting special target groups, mainly through education, information, and advisory services on population questions of concern to their affiliates and members.

Mass organizations, such as trade unions, cooperatives, youth and women's organizations, and other key institutional forces with international responsibilities are also beginning to support the development of population policies and programs, although the primary focus of their activities may not be population issues.

Furthermore, a number of universities and other educational institutions (most of these are in the United States but some are in Europe) conduct training programs oriented specifically toward the needs of developing countries, and support or carry out research activities relevant to selected population issues in developing countries.

TYPES AND AREAS OF ASSISTANCE

Almost all donors make their contributions to population assistance in grants, but a few governments (Canada, Denmark, Finland, the Federal Republic of Germany, and the United States) also make loans available. All the intergovernmental and nongovernmental organizations provide grants, with the exception of the World Bank, which extends only loans or credit. All donors make contributions in cash, but some also provide grants in kind, mainly equipment and contraceptive supplies (Australia, Denmark, Finland, the Federal Republic of Germany, Japan, Sweden, and the United States).

In 1975, about 48 percent of the total resources available for population assistance supported family planning programs. However, a substantial part of the resources devoted to "multisector activities" (which amounted to about 20 percent of all resources and, to some extent, a portion of the activities in the fields of communication and education) supported family planning activities directly or indirectly. Thus, the share of total resources supporting family planning was undoubtedly well over 50 percent. About 15 percent of total resources was devoted to statistical and demographic activities. A smaller share, just under 10 percent, supported biomedical research, including contraceptive development.

From a geographical point of view, the largest share of support, over 40 percent, was devoted to interregional and global activities, many of them carried out in developed countries. As for the remainder, the largest share (about 30 percent) went to the region of Asia and the Pacific, followed by Africa with 14 percent, Latin America with 10 percent, and the Mediterranean and the Middle East with 5 percent.

A comparison between the assistance provided in 1975 by the three largest donors illustrates notable differences in programatic emphasis. The United States spent over 75 percent of its resources in supporting family planning programs, while the comparable figure for Sweden was about 50 percent and for the UNFPA slightly less. On the other hand, while about 19 percent of UNFPA resources supported basic data collection, the comparable figure for the United States was only about 9 percent and for Sweden, negligible. Both the United States and the UNFPA devoted around 10 percent of their population assistance to the field of population dynamics. Biomedical research, including contraceptive development, received over 40 percent of Sweden's population assistance, about 5 percent of the United States' population assistance, and only less than 1 percent of UNFPA resources. From a geographical point of view, the United States spent around 67 percent of its resources on interregional and global projects, while for Sweden the share was just under 50 percent and for the UNFPA almost 24 percent. As for assistance to activities at the country level, all three donors spent the largest shares in Asia and the Pacific; this is particularly true of Sweden and the United States, while UNFPA had a more even distribution among regions.

THE NEED FOR INTERNATIONAL POPULATION ASSISTANCE

It is a difficult, if not an impossible, task to estimate the future needs for international population assistance. Much depends upon the criteria to be applied with regard to the types of population activities required, the extent to which support from external sources is needed, the availability of local resources, and the absorptive capacity of the developing countries.

The UNFPA has attempted to make estimates of the costs of developing comprehensive population programs to meet various targets or goals such as providing information and services on family planning for the entire population in the developing countries; conducting a complete population census in all countries at least every ten years; establishing vital statistics registration systems with a coverage of at least 90 percent; providing population education in and out of schools; training personnel required for population programmes; and supporting research required for planning and implementing effective population programs, including operational research and development of improved contraceptive techniques.

An approximate total annual cost for all relevant population activities is estimated at $1.50 per capita or $2.9 billion (1976 prices) for the developing world as a whole. The provision of family planning, maternal, and child health services according to established minimum requirements accounts for over half of this or an estimated $0.84 per capita.

Although no accurate estimates can be made of the need for population programs, and although the estimates provided here may not take fully into account certain concomitant needs in the economic and social fields, it seems fairly clear that the estimated total of about $300 million available for population assistance from international sources amounts to a small proportion, probably only about 10 percent of total estimated needs for external and internal resources for population activities.

In financial terms, international assistance defrays only a small portion of the actual costs of the population activities undertaken in the developing world. While it is recognized that such assistance cannot be, and should never be, more than a marginal addition to the development efforts of recipient countries, there is no question, however, that the role and significance of international population assistance go far beyond the often comparatively modest financial inputs. International population assistance constitutes, in many cases, an essential element in promoting national efforts and enlisting local resources. In many instances, the activities supported would probably not have taken place at all without the interest and contributions of donor governments and agencies. Very often, international assistance provides the important spark needed to overcome reluctance at the local level to expend the necessary financial, human, and material resources for worthwhile activities. Sometimes the will and the necessary local resources may be there, but crucial inputs of equipment and supplies cannot be obtained, due to foreign exchange difficulties, unless international assistance is made available. A case in point is the African Census Programme, under which a number of developing countries are for the first time involved in taking a population census.

At the same time, the role of international assistance should not be exaggerated to imply that without it there can be no major accomplishments in tackling population problems in the developing world. The People's Republic of China is an excellent example. Here the effective delivery of family planning services at all levels, measures dealing with internal population distribution problems, and contraceptive research have been undertaken successfully without any assistance from abroad. Still, the majority of developing countries need and want international assistance to expedite the process of dealing with their population problems.

One of the most significant accomplishments of population assistance is probably the contribution it has made to promoting awareness worldwide and in individual countries of population problems and issues, their implications, and the need for policies and programs to deal with them. It is not possible, in general, to demonstrate definite effects upon population trends, and in any case, results cannot be expected in the short span of a few years. Support provided for the training of personnel, for research and evaluation, for institution building, and for related education and communication activities often has important multiplier effects and long-term benefits that are difficult to measure in quantitative terms.

PRIORITIES IN FUTURE PROGRAMS

More and more attention is being devoted to setting priorities in assistance to population programs, for two main reasons. On one hand, increasing awareness of the impact of population factors on development and the adoption of population policies by more and more governments have led to rapid growth in the demand from developing countries for such assistance. On the other hand, developments at the World Population Conference have led many donors to review and reassess their development cooperation policies, with particular regard to population.

Reviews have been undertaken or are in progress in Canada, Sweden, the United Kingdom, the United States, UNFPA, the World Bank, and IPPF, often resulting in new strategies or policies for population assistance. Various concepts of setting priorities for allocation of resources have emerged or have been refined. Most donors apply more than one criterion for setting priorities. UNFPA has developed a system for setting priorities based on economic and demographic data reflecting needs.

The following résumé of criteria for setting priorities is not intended to give complete coverage for all donors but reflects mainly new strategies for population assistance resulting from recent reviews, revision, or reaffirmation of policies.

Priority Countries

Some donors intend to concentrate their resources in, or give special attention to, the needs of certain countries.

In the case of several bilateral programs, the political situation of the recipient countries or special geographical, historical, cultural, or trade considerations play an important role (Australia, Canada, Denmark, Japan, New Zealand, Sweden, the United States).

Some donors are particularly interested in assisting the poorest of the developing countries based upon criteria on estimated per capita income (UNFPA, Canada, the United Kingdom) or the extent to which they are seriously affected by balance-of-payments problems (New Zealand, the United Kingdom).

Sometimes demographic criteria are taken into account in identifying countries with the most urgent need for population programs (Canada considers birth rate, death rate, infant mortality, current and future potential population growth; the United States concentrates on countries with large populations contributing most to world population growth and where prospects for reducing fertility are best; UNFPA uses rate of population growth, fertility, infant mortality, and agricultural population density; and the World Bank takes into account population size, growth rate, population density, government's policy commitment to reduce fertility, and prospective demographic impact).

Priority Objectives

Most donors are giving increasing attention to support for population activities as an integral part of such aspects development as rural development, family health, social welfare, and participation of women in development (Finland, Federal Republic of Germany, Japan, Norway, Sweden, the United Kingdom, the United States, UNFPA, ILO, FAO, WHO, the World Bank, Ford Foundation, and the Population Council). Some support population components in such programs (UNFPA, the Population Council).

Several donors are giving priority attention to promoting activities at the local level through community or family-based programs (the United States, UNICEF, the World Bank, IPPF). Priority is given by some donors to assisting population activities for the benefit of poverty-stricken and other disadvantaged population groups (UNFPA, ILO).

Attempts are being made to determine recipient countries' basic needs in population and related fields (the United States, UNFPA, UNICEF, ILO, WHO).

Priority Areas of Assistance

Most donors of population assistance will continue giving high priority to support for family planning activities designed to attain fertility reduction, health, social welfare, or other socioeconomic development objectives. Contraceptive supplies are provided by a number of donors (Japan, Sweden, the United States, UNFPA, IPPF). Only certain donors provide financial or technical assistance for abortion and sterilization programs (Sweden, the United States (sterilization only), UNFPA, the World Bank, WHO, IPPF, and a few other nongovernmental organizations). Injectables are available only from a few donors (the United Kingdom, UNFPA, WHO, the Population Council).

Most donors are giving high priority to the training of local personnel for population programs. Many are also giving special attention to research such as in human reproduction and contraceptive development (Canada, Sweden, WHO, Ford Foundation, the Population Council, Rockefeller Foundation); to operational research (the United States, UNFPA, the World Bank); and to demographic and social science research (United Nations, UNFPA, the World Bank, Ford Foundation, the Population Council).

PROSPECTS FOR THE FUTURE

It is, of course, difficult to make any predictions of the future resource situation for international population assistance. Very much depends upon the prospects for overall development assistance. Several donors, such as Sweden and the Netherlands, have reached, or will soon reach, the overall goal for development assistance in the Second Development Decade of one percent of the gross national product, and their population assistance may not increase substantially beyond the equivalent of increases in their national income.

It seems too early to assess the impact of the WPC and the WPPA upon population assistance. Several major donors have reviewed and revised their policies mainly to broaden their approach to dealing with population issues. Many donors seem still to stress fertility control as the major objective of their population assistance, although the WPPA gives considerable emphasis to other areas as well. Problems of urbanization and spatial distribution of population, according to a United Nations inquiry, are those population problems that most governments are concerned with, but few requests are made and very limited population assistance is provided in these areas. There has not been any discernible increase in the attention given to biomedical research, including contraceptive development, despite the stress on it in the WPPA.

Donor governments and organizations have become more concerned with the views, needs, and policies of recipient countries. However, a considerable part of international population assistance is still supporting research, training, and other activities located in the donor countries themselves. Further attention should be given to building up the technological infrastructure in developing countries, in some cases on a subregional or regional basis. More use should be made of local expertise and production facilities in the recipient countries than of advisers, equipment, and supplies sent from the industrialized world. The main emphasis should be on building up the ability of developing countries to rely on themselves in coping with their population problems.

At the moment, international population assistance finds itself in a dilemma: forces are pulling in opposite directions. With the greater availability of data and trained personnel and the establishment of population policies by more and more governments, absorptive capacity for population assistance in recipient countries has substantially increased. This increase is generating a rapidly growing demand not only for population assistance itself, but also for a greater say regarding the sources and uses of such assistance. Yet, the donor community, having become more conscious, as a result of resource constraints, of the need for better coordination to maximize the effectiveness of its inputs, is involved in setting priorities to regulate the direction, areas, and modes of assistance.

It is as important to resolve this situation, perhaps on an ad hoc basis, as it is to seek financial means to minimize the gap between the demand for, and supply of, international population assistance. Apart from striving to ensure a continuous growth in the resources available for population assistance, the donor community should focus greater attention on channeling such assistance to help developing countries meet their basic needs for promoting self-reliance in the formulation as well as the implementation of population policies. It is, however, not only a matter of stepping up technical cooperation and providing financial assistance to these countries. More concerted action should also be promoted toward developing a global strategy to assist developing countries in dealing with their major population problems, rather than merely effecting a transfer of funds between donors and recipients.

ANNEX: Selected World Demographic Indicators by Region and Country or Area, 1970–75

Region and Country or Area	Population (mid-year) (thousands)		Rate of Growth, 1970–75 (percentage)	Number of Years to Double Population	Percentage of Population in 1975 Aged (years)			Crude Birth Rate 1970–75 (per 1,000)	Crude Death Rate 1970–75 (per 1,000)	Total Fertility Rate 1970–75 (per 1,000)	Life Expectancy, 1970–75 (years)	Proportion of Urban Population 1975 (percentage)	Population Density 1975[a] (persons per square kilometer)
	1975	2000			0–14	15–64	65+						
World Total	3,967,864	6,254,377	1.89	37	36.0	58.3	5.7	31.5	12.8	4,357	55.2	39.2	29
More developed regions	1,131,684	1,360,245	0.86	80	25.0	64.5	10.5	17.2	9.2	2,327	71.1	69.3	19
Less developed regions	2,836,180	4,894,133	2.31	30	40.4	55.8	3.8	37.5	14.3	5,267	52.2	27.2	38
Africa	401,314	813,681	2.64	26	44.2	52.9	2.9	46.3	19.8	6,309	45.0	24.2	13
Eastern Africa	114,498	239,861	2.74	25	45.0	52.4	2.7	48.1	20.7	6,463	43.8	12.2	18
British Indian Ocean Territory	2	2	0.00		—	—	—	—	—	—	—	—	18
Burundi	3,765	7,280	2.33	30	43.1	54.1	2.8	48.0	24.7	6,293	39.0	3.7	135
Comoros	306	475	2.50	28	43.2	53.8	3.0	46.6	21.7	6,084	42.5	9.2	141
Ethiopia	27,975	53,665	2.36	29	43.6	53.7	2.7	49.4	25.8	6,706	38.0	11.1	23
French Terr. of the Afars and the Issas	106	187	2.19	32	—	—	—	—	—	—	—	—	5
Kenya	13,251	31,020	3.28	21	46.5	50.9	2.6	48.7	16.0	6,706	50.0	11.2	23
Madagascar	8,020	17,782	2.92	24	45.3	52.1	2.6	50.2	21.1	6,706	43.5	17.7	14
Malawi	4,916	9,540	2.40	29	45.4	51.3	3.3	47.7	23.7	6,090	41.0	6.3	41
Mauritius[b]	899	1,257	1.76	39	37.2	58.7	4.1	24.4	6.8	3,258	65.5	48.1	440
Mozambique	9,239	17,649	2.30	30	43.1	54.0	2.9	43.1	20.1	5,678	43.5	6.3	12
Reunion	501	732	2.27	30	42.6	53.4	4.0	31.2	8.5	4,324	63.0	50.5	200
Rwanda	4,200	8,707	2.65	26	43.6	53.3	3.1	50.0	23.6	6,902	41.0	3.7	159
Seychelles	59	102	2.53	27	—	—	—	—	—	—	—	—	157
Somalia	3,170	6,544	2.56	27	45.0	53.0	2.0	47.2	21.7	6,096	41.0	28.1	5
Southern Rhodesia	6,276	15,147	3.35	21	47.5	50.6	1.9	47.9	14.4	6,604	51.5	19.6	16
Uganda	11,353	24,160	2.93	24	44.4	52.6	3.0	45.2	15.9	6,084	50.0	8.3	48
United Republic of Tanzania	15,438	34,045	3.02	23	46.7	50.9	2.4	50.2	20.1	6,706	44.5	6.7	16
Zambia	5,022	11,566	3.13	22	47.7	50.1	2.1	51.5	20.3	6,902	44.5	36.4	7
Middle Africa	45,310	87,732	2.27	30	42.6	54.5	2.9	44.4	21.7	5,799	41.9	23.3	7
Angola	6,353	12,462	2.27	30	42.1	55.3	2.6	47.2	24.5	6,502	38.5	18.1	5
Central African Republic	1,790	3,360	2.09	33	42.0	54.9	3.1	43.4	22.5	5,481	41.0	35.8	3
Chad	4,023	6,912	2.00	35	40.5	57.0	2.6	44.0	24.0	5,283	38.5	13.8	3
Congo	1,345	2,720	2.44	28	42.4	54.3	3.2	45.1	20.8	5,791	43.5	39.5	4

(continued)

ANNEX: (Continued)

Region and Country or Area	Population (mid-year) (thousands) 1975	Population (mid-year) (thousands) 2000	Rate of Growth, 1970–75 (percentage)	Number of Years to Double Population	Percentage of Population in 1975 Aged (years) 0–14	15–64	65+	Crude Birth Rate 1970–75 (per 1,000)	Crude Death Rate 1970–75 (per 1,000)	Total Fertility Rate 1970–75 (per 1,000)	Life Expectancy, 1970–75 (years)	Proportion of Urban Population 1975 (percentage)	Population Density 1975[a] (persons per square kilometer)
Equatorial Guinea	310	497	1.71	40	36.9	60.0	3.1	36.8	19.7	5,070	43.5	45.1	11
Gabon	526	660	1.00	69	31.8	63.8	4.5	32.2	22.2	4,056	41.0	28.2	2
Sao Tome and Principe	80	88	1.56	44	—	—	—	—	—	—	—	—	83
United Republic of Cameroon	6,398	11,583	1.84	38	40.0	56.6	3.4	40.4	22.0	5,470	41.0	23.7	13
Zaire	24,485	49,450	2.47	28	44.2	53.1	2.8	45.2	20.5	5,893	43.5	24.0	10
Northern Africa	98,185	191,824	2.74	25	44.2	52.5	3.3	43.3	15.2	6,268	52.0	39.5	12
Algeria	16,792	36,663	3.17	22	48.0	48.9	3.2	48.7	15.4	7,176	53.2	49.7	7
Egypt	37,543	64,588	2.38	29	40.7	55.9	3.4	37.8	14.0	5,210	52.4	47.5	37
Libyan Arab Republic	2,255	4,737	3.03	23	44.4	52.6	3.1	45.0	14.7	6,847	52.9	38.6	1
Morocco	17,504	35,904	2.92	24	47.0	49.3	3.7	46.2	15.7	7,053	52.9	37.8	39
Sudan	18,268	38,977	3.04	23	45.4	51.9	2.7	47.8	17.5	6,971	48.6	13.1	7
Tunisia	5,747	10,853	2.25	31	44.4	51.6	4.0	39.9	13.8	6,231	54.1	46.2	35
Western Sahara[c]	75	101	0.90	77	—	—	—	—	—	—	—	—	—
Southern Africa	27,853	56,231	2.70	26	41.1	55.0	3.9	43.0	16.2	5,596	50.8	45.8	10
Botswana	691	1,429	2.27	30	46.1	49.6	4.3	45.6	23.0	5,893	43.5	10.6	1
Lesotho	1,148	2,027	1.92	36	38.3	57.0	4.6	39.0	19.7	5,070	46.0	3.1	38
Namibia	883	1,883	2.83	24	44.4	52.6	3.0	45.0	16.7	6,084	48.7	32.4	1
South Africa	24,663	49,951	2.74	25	40.9	55.2	3.9	42.9	15.5	5,583	51.5	49.8	20
Swaziland	468	941	2.72	25	46.1	50.5	3.4	49.0	21.8	6,502	43.5	14.3	27
Western Africa	115,469	238,034	2.58	27	44.8	52.7	2.5	48.7	23.0	6,581	40.9	18.4	19
Benin	3,074	5,921	2.70	26	45.4	52.1	2.5	49.9	23.0	6,706	41.0	17.9	27
Cape Verde	295	432	1.91	36	44.0	53.7	2.3	32.8	13.7	4,056	50.0	5.8	73
Gambia	509	852	1.92	36	40.8	55.6	3.6	43.3	24.1	5,684	40.0	12.6	45
Ghana	9,873	21,164	2.70	26	47.5	49.5	3.0	48.8	21.9	6,699	43.5	33.1	41
Guinea	4,416	8,455	2.38	29	43.1	54.0	2.9	46.6	22.9	6,185	41.0	19.3	18
Guinea-Bissau	525	842	1.51	46	37.3	58.6	4.1	40.1	25.1	5,278	38.5	22.9	15
Ivory Coast	4,885	9,617	2.51	28	43.1	54.0	2.9	45.6	20.6	6,185	43.5	20.2	15
Liberia	1,708	3,219	2.29	30	41.3	55.2	3.4	43.6	20.7	5,690	43.5	15.0	15
Mali	5,697	11,257	2.42	29	44.0	53.4	2.7	50.1	25.9	6,706	38.0	13.4	5

Country													
Mauritania	1,283	2,281	1.99	35	41.9	55.0	3.1	44.8	24.9	5,893	38.5	11.0	1
Niger	4,592	9,568	2.68	26	45.6	52.1	2.3	52.2	25.5	7,105	38.5	9.3	4
Nigeria	62,925	134,924	2.67	26	45.1	52.6	2.3	49.3	22.7	6,699	41.0	18.0	68
Senegal	4,418	8,171	2.37	29	43.4	53.7	2.9	47.6	23.9	6,293	40.0	28.2	23
St. Helena[d]	5	6	0.78	88	—	—	—	—	—	—	—	—	43
Sierra Leone	2,983	5,716	2.41	29	42.7	54.2	3.1	44.7	20.7	5,875	43.5	14.9	42
Togo	2,248	4,640	2.74	25	45.6	51.8	2.6	50.6	23.3	6,706	41.0	13.4	40
Upper Volta	6,032	10,969	2.27	30	43.4	53.8	2.8	48.5	25.8	6,502	38.0	8.2	22
Latin America	324,092	619,929	2.71	26	42.0	54.1	3.8	36.9	9.2	5,265	61.4	60.2	16
Caribbean	27,116	44,504	1.93	36	40.7	54.2	5.1	32.8	9.1	4,656	63.1	48.0	114
Antigua	73	85	0.76	91	—	—	—	—	—	—	—	—	164
Bahamas	204	330	2.79	25	—	—	—	—	—	—	—	—	15
Barbados	245	285	0.50	137	33.8	57.4	8.8	21.6	8.9	3,035	69.1	44.9	569
British Virgin Islands	11	19	3.47	20	—	—	—	—	—	—	—	—	74
Cayman Islands	11	13	0.73	95	—	—	—	—	—	—	—	—	43
Cuba	9,481	15,267	2.03	34	38.0	55.8	6.2	29.1	6.6	4,034	69.8	61.4	83
Dominica	75	91	1.07	64	—	—	—	—	—	—	—	—	99
Dominican Republic	5,118	11,762	3.28	21	48.0	49.4	2.6	45.8	11.0	6,923	57.8	43.8	105
Grenada	96	106	0.42	164	—	—	—	—	—	—	—	—	279
Guadeloupe	354	493	1.55	45	40.3	54.7	5.0	29.3	6.4	4,559	69.4	49.4	199
Haiti	4,552	7,045	1.45	48	40.4	55.5	4.1	35.8	16.3	4,949	50.0	20.6	164
Jamaica	2,029	2,726	1.50	46	46.1	48.1	5.8	33.2	7.1	5,406	69.5	44.9	185
Martinique	363	485	1.44	48	40.8	53.8	5.4	29.7	6.7	4,559	69.4	62.2	330
Montserrat	13	14	0.65	106	—	—	—	—	—	—	—	—	128
Netherlands Antilles	242	389	1.71	40	—	—	—	—	—	—	—	—	252
Puerto Rico	2,902	3,723	1.13	61	33.9	59.4	6.7	22.6	6.8	2,809	72.1	65.2	326
St. Kitts-Nevis-Anguilla	66	70	0.28	250	—	—	—	—	—	—	—	—	184
St. Lucia	108	130	1.37	51	—	—	—	—	—	—	—	—	176
St. Vincent	93	109	1.22	57	—	—	—	—	—	—	—	—	240
Trinidad and Tobago	1,009	1,280	1.09	63	39.1	56.1	4.8	25.3	5.9	3,353	69.5	25.0	197
Turks and Caicos Islands	6	6	0.00		—	—	—	—	—	—	—	—	197
United States Virgin Islands	66	76	0.93	74	45.7	50.9	3.4	42.2	9.4	6,379	61.5	57.1	191
Middle America	78,652	172,670	3.21	22	—	—	—	—	—	—	—	—	32
Belize	140	234	3.11	22	—	—	—	—	—	—	—	—	6
Costa Rica	1,994	3,695	2.76	25	42.2	54.5	3.3	33.4	5.9	4,646	68.2	39.7	39

(continued)

ANNEX: (Continued)

Region and Country or Area	Population (mid-year) (thousands) 1975	Population (mid-year) (thousands) 2000	Rate of Growth, 1970–75 (percentage)	Number of Years to Double Population	Percentage of Population in 1975 Aged (years) 0–14	15–64	65+	Crude Birth Rate 1970–75 (per 1,000)	Crude Death Rate 1970–75 (per 1,000)	Total Fertility Rate 1970–75 (per 1,000)	Life Expectancy, 1970–75 (years)	Proportion of Urban Population 1975 (percentage)	Population Density 1975[a] (persons per square kilometer)
El Salvador	4,108	8,803	3.11	22	46.4	50.3	3.2	42.2	11.1	6,191	57.8	39.9	192
Guatemala	6,129	12,374	2.91	24	44.2	53.0	2.8	42.8	13.7	6,068	52.9	33.8	56
Honduras	3,037	6,881	3.48	20	46.9	50.3	2.8	49.3	14.6	7,276	53.5	35.8	27
Mexico	59,204	132,244	3.25	21	45.9	50.6	3.5	42.0	8.6	6,465	63.2	63.0	30
Nicaragua	2,318	5,154	3.26	21	48.3	49.2	2.4	48.3	13.9	6,923	52.9	47.7	18
Panama[e]	1,678	3,230	2.80	25	42.8	53.3	3.8	36.2	7.1	5,059	66.5	51.2	22
Canal Zone	43	55	1.99	35	—	—	—	—	—	—	—	—	30
Temperate South America	38,747	52,078	1.43	48*	30.4	62.3	7.3	23.3	8.9	3,150	66.5	80.7	10
Argentina	25,384	32,861	1.33	52	28.5	63.6	7.9	21.8	8.8	2,979	68.2	79.9	9
Chile	10,253	15,355	1.80	38	35.7	59.2	5.1	27.9	9.2	3,653	62.6	82.9	14
Falkland Islands (Malvinas)	2	2	0.00	—	—	—	—	—	—	—	—	—	—
Uruguay	3,108	3,861	1.01	69	28.2	62.5	9.4	20.4	9.3	2,923	69.8	80.5	14
Tropical South America	179,578	350,676	2.90	24	43.1	53.8	3.1	38.3	9.2	5,402	60.5	58.9	18
Bolivia	5,410	10,267	2.48	28	42.9	54.1	2.9	43.7	18.0	6,151	46.8	37.0	5
Brazil	109,730	212,507	2.84	24	42.0	54.8	3.2	37.1	8.8	5,150	61.4	59.3	13
Colombia	25,890	51,464	3.19	22	45.7	51.5	2.7	40.6	8.8	5,878	60.9	61.6	23
Ecuador	7,090	14,773	3.24	21	46.0	51.2	2.7	41.8	9.5	6,287	59.6	39.7	25
French Guiana	60	118	3.51	20	—	—	—	—	—	—	—	—	1
Guyana	791	1,256	2.17	32	43.7	52.7	3.6	32.4	5.9	4,524	67.9	33.3	4
Paraguay	2,647	5,274	2.80	25	45.1	51.5	3.4	39.8	8.9	6,202	61.9	37.3	7
Peru	15,326	30,561	2.91	24	44.1	53.0	2.9	41.0	11.9	5,796	55.7	58.4	12
Surinam	422	904	2.57	27	49.8	46.6	3.6	41.6	7.5	6,560	65.5	50.0	3
Venezuela	12,213	23,552	2.91	24	44.4	52.5	3.1	36.1	7.0	5,284	64.7	77.7	13
Northern America	236,841	296,199	0.90	77	25.5	64.3	10.2	16.5	9.3	2,205	71.4	76.4	11
Bermuda	56	76	1.47	47	—	—	—	—	—	—	—	—	1,062
Canada	22,801	31,613	1.26	55	27.2	64.5	8.3	18.6	7.7	2,383	72.3	78.3	2
Greenland	54	75	2.80	25	—	—	—	—	—	—	—	—	—
St. Pierre and Miquelon	5	5	0.00	—	—	—	—	—	—	—	—	—	—
United States of America	213,925	264,430	0.86	80	25.3	64.3	10.4	16.2	9.4	2,186	71.3	76.2	23

(continued)

East Asia	1,006,380	1,370,061	1.65	42	32.7	61.5	5.8	26.2	9.8	3,594	62.5	30.5	86
China	838,803	1,147,987	1.66	42	33.4	61.0	5.6	26.9	10.3	3,772	61.6	23.3	87
Japan	111,120	132,929	1.26	55	24.5	67.7	7.8	19.2	6.6	2,159	73.3	75.1	294
Other East Asia	56,456	89,145	2.15	32	38.5	57.8	3.7	30.2	8.7	4,277	61.1	48.5	32
Democratic People's Republic of Korea	15,852	27,457	2.64	26	41.6	54.9	3.5	35.7	9.4	5,192	60.6	42.5	132
Hong Kong	4,225	5,625	1.39	50	31.5	63.7	4.8	19.4	5.5	3,043	70.0	85.9	4,043
Macau	271	372	1.72	40	—	—	—	—	—	—	—	—	16,919
Mongolia	1,446	2,701	2.95	23	43.8	53.0	3.2	38.8	9.3	5,597	60.7	51.2	1
Republic of Korea	34,663	52,991	2.00	35	37.7	58.6	3.6	28.8	8.9	4,121	60.6	46.1	352
South Asia	1,249,793	2,267,266	2.53	27	43.2	53.8	3.0	41.9	16.7	5,981	48.5	22.9	79
Eastern South Asia	323,836	591,622	2.70	26	43.6	53.4	3.0	42.4	15.4	5,844	50.6	21.9	72
Brunei	147	216	1.90	36	—	—	—	—	—	—	—	—	25
Burma	31,240	54,902	2.37	29	40.9	55.5	3.6	39.4	15.8	5,546	50.0	22.2	46
Democratic Kampuchea	8,110	15,819	2.77	25	45.3	52.0	2.7	46.7	19.0	6,663	45.4	22.4	45
East Timor	672	1,145	2.13	32	42.0	55.3	2.7	44.3	23.0	6,150	40.0	11.0	45
Indonesia^f	136,044	237,507	2.60	27	43.7	53.8	2.5	42.9	16.9	5,524	47.5	19.2	71
Lao People's Democratic Republic	3,303	5,725	2.18	32	42.1	55.2	2.7	44.6	22.8	6,156	40.4	11.1	14
Malaysia	12,093	22,054	2.89	24	43.9	52.8	3.3	38.7	9.9	5,699	59.4	28.7	37
Philippines	44,437	89,707	3.34	21	45.9	51.1	3.0	43.8	10.5	6,380	58.4	35.8	148
Singapore	2,248	3,126	1.61	43	32.7	63.2	4.1	21.2	5.1	2,781	69.5	90.1	3,869
Socialist Republic of Viet Nam	43,451	75,802	2.11	33	41.1	55.2	3.8	41.5	20.5	6,150	44.6	16.9	131
Former Democratic Republic of Viet-Nam	23,789	43,141	2.35	29	41.3	54.9	3.8	41.4	17.9	6,150	48.0	14.2	150
Former Republic of South Viet-Nam	19,653	32,661	1.81	38	40.7	55.5	3.7	41.7	23.6	6,160	40.5	20.1	113
Thailand	42,093	85,618	3.27	21	45.8	51.2	2.9	43.4	10.8	6,349	58.0	16.4	82
Middle South Asia	837,799	1,501,213	2.44	28	43.0	54.1	2.9	41.7	17.0	6,027	48.0	21.1	124
Afghanistan	19,280	36,654	2.54	27	44.2	53.2	2.6	49.2	23.8	6,901	40.3	12.2	30
Bangladesh	73,746	144,347	1.71	40	46.2	51.1	2.6	49.5	28.1	7,216	35.8	8.4	517
Bhutan	1,173	2,145	2.31	30	42.1	54.8	3.1	43.6	20.5	6,150	43.6	3.4	25
India	613,217	1,059,429	2.43	28	42.1	54.9	2.9	39.9	15.7	5,740	49.5	21.4	187
Iran	32,923	66,593	2.98	23	45.7	51.0	3.3	45.3	15.6	6,868	51.0	44.1	20
Maldives	119	205	1.95	35	—	—	—	—	—	—	—	—	400
Nepal	12,572	23,196	2.25	31	42.0	54.9	3.1	42.9	20.3	6,150	43.6	4.8	89

ANNEX: (Continued)

Region and Country or Area	Population (mid-year) (thousands)		Rate of Growth, 1970–75 (percentage)	Number of Years to Double Population	Percentage of Population Aged in 1975 (years)			Crude Birth Rate 1970–75 (per 1,000)	Crude Death Rate 1970–75 (per 1,000)	Total Fertility Rate 1970–75 (per 1,000)	Life Expectancy, 1970–75 (years)	Proportion of Urban Population 1975 (percentage)	Population Density 1975[a] (persons per square kilometer)
	1975	2000			0–14	15–64	65+						
Pakistan	70,560	146,924	3.09	22	46.5	50.5	2.9	47.4	16.5	7,175	49.8	26.8	88
Sikkim	222	381	2.00	35	—	—	—	—	—	—	—	—	31
Sri Lanka	13,986	21,339	2.22	31	39.0	57.0	4.0	28.6	6.3	4,172	67.8	24.2	213
Western South Asia	88,158	174,432	2.83	24	43.1	53.0	3.9	42.8	14.3	6,319	53.8	44.0	20
Bahrain	251	536	3.08	22	—	—	—	—	—	—	—	—	403
Cyprus	673	846	1.23	56	30.2	62.0	7.8	22.2	6.8	2,802	71.4	41.9	73
Democratic Yemen	1,660	3,425	2.90	24	44.7	52.6	2.7	49.6	20.6	7,176	44.8	34.5	6
Gaza Strip[g] (Palestine[h])	594	1,348	3.40	20	—	—	—	—	—	—	—	—	1,571
Iraq	11,067	24,445	3.36	21	46.6	50.9	2.5	48.1	14.6	7,107	52.7	61.8	25
Israel	3,417	5,566	2.88	24	32.8	59.5	7.7	26.4	6.7	3,667	71.0	92.6	165
Jordan	2,688	5,889	3.29	21	46.5	50.6	2.8	47.6	14.7	7,107	53.2	56.0	28
Kuwait	1,085	3,183	7.18	—	47.2	51.4	1.4	47.1	5.3	7,211	67.2	88.4	61
Lebanon	2,869	6,118	3.00	23	43.2	52.0	4.8	39.8	9.9	6,252	63.2	59.6	276
Oman	766	1,639	3.08	22	—	—	—	—	—	—	—	—	4
Qatar	92	197	3.10	22	—	—	—	—	—	—	—	—	8
Saudi Arabia	8,966	18,600	2.94	24	44.7	52.5	2.7	49.5	20.2	7,176	45.3	20.7	4
Syrian Arab Republic	7,259	15,824	3.00	23	45.5	50.4	4.1	45.4	15.4	7,108	54.0	45.3	39
Turkey	39,882	72,588	2.48	28	41.7	53.8	4.5	39.4	12.5	5,822	56.9	42.9	51
United Arab Emirates	222	474	3.08	22	—	—	—	—	—	—	—	—	3
Yemen	6,668	13,753	2.90	24	44.7	52.6	2.7	49.6	20.6	7,176	44.8	8.8	34
Europe	473,098	539,500	0.60	115	23.9	63.8	12.3	16.1	10.1	2,295	71.2	67.6	96
Eastern Europe	106,267	121,437	0.64	109	23.1	65.4	11.5	16.6	10.2	2,214	69.7	56.1	107
Bulgaria	8,793	10,036	0.70	98	22.2	66.8	11.0	16.2	9.1	2,171	71.8	57.7	79
Czechoslovakia	14,793	16,796	0.62	111	22.7	64.7	12.6	16.9	10.7	2,157	70.4	57.9	116
German Democratic Republic[i]	17,127	17,932	0.08	864	22.3	61.1	16.6	14.0	13.2	2,111	71.1	74.8	158
Hungary	10,534	11,069	0.38	184	20.1	67.2	12.8	15.2	11.5	2,004	69.5	47.5	113
Poland	33,841	39,846	0.82	84	23.6	67.0	9.5	16.8	8.5	2,116	70.1	55.4	108
Romania	21,178	25,758	0.90	77	25.1	65.4	9.5	19.3	10.3	2,612	67.2	44.6	89

Northern Europe	81,975	91,320	0.41	168	23.8	62.8	13.5	15.8	11.2	2,338	72.5	82.6	50
Channel Islands	128	152	0.85	81	–	–	–	–	–	–	–	–	654
Denmark	5,026	5,361	0.39	177	22.3	64.3	13.4	14.0	10.1	1,907	73.9	81.9	117
Faeroe Islands	40	47	0.71	97	–	–	–	–	–	–	–	–	29
Finland	4,652	4,747	0.20	349	21.8	67.3	10.9	13.2	9.3	1,681	70.4	54.9	14
Iceland	216	278	1.15	60	29.2	61.9	8.8	19.2	7.7	2,603	73.9	86.5	2
Ireland	3,131	4,002	1.16	59	30.3	58.6	11.0	22.0	10.4	3,718	71.8	55.1	45
Isle of Man	58	68	0.77	90	–	–	–	–	–	–	–	–	99
Norway	4,007	4,483	0.66	105	24.0	62.3	13.6	16.7	10.1	2,447	74.5	45.3	12
Sweden	8,291	9,390	0.61	114	21.0	64.2	14.9	14.2	10.5	2,000	73.3	83.6	18
United Kingdom of Great Britain and Northern Ireland	56,427	62,794	0.34	204	24.0	62.3	13.6	16.1	11.7	2,409	72.3	89.1	231
Southern Europe	132,354	155,685	0.72	97	25.5	63.6	10.8	17.7	9.2	2,513	70.9	56.9	101
Andorra	23	37	3.47	20	–	–	–	–	–	–	–	–	50
Albania	2,482	4,263	2.70	26	40.8	54.9	4.3	33.4	6.5	4,882	68.6	36.6	86
Gibraltar	27	31	0.74	93	–	–	–	–	–	–	–	–	4,567
Greece	8,930	9,621	0.31	223	23.4	64.0	12.6	15.4	9.4	2,278	71.8	56.7	68
Holy See	1		0.00		–	–	–	–	–	–	–	–	2,273
Italy	55,023	60,876	0.54	129	24.0	64.3	11.8	16.0	9.8	2,277	72.0	61.4	183
Malta	329	336	0.23	295	24.6	65.4	10.0	17.5	9.0	2,077	70.8	78.6	1,042
Portugal	8,762	9,918	0.31	225	26.7	62.4	10.9	18.4	10.0	2,606	68.0	27.8	95
San Marino	20	25	1.02	68	–	–	–	–	–	–	–	–	331
Spain	35,433	44,924	0.96	72	27.0	62.3	10.7	19.5	8.3	2,885	72.1	69.4	70
Yugoslavia	21,322	25,653	0.91	76	25.7	65.7	8.6	18.2	9.2	2,359	67.6	38.5	83
Western Europe	152,503	171,058	0.58	119	23.1	63.3	13.6	14.6	11.1	2,136	72.0	77.0	153
Austria	7,538	8,118	0.24	282	23.6	61.3	15.1	14.7	12.2	2,213	71.2	52.8	90
Belgium	9,846	10,781	0.43	162	22.5	63.3	14.1	14.8	11.2	2,223	72.9	71.7	323
France	52,913	62,131	0.87	80	24.2	62.5	13.3	17.0	10.6	2,460	72.6	75.9	97
Germany, Federal Republic of[i]	61,682	66,242	0.32	215	21.8	63.9	14.3	12.0	12.1	1,824	70.6	83.3	248
Liechtenstein	22	28	1.01	68	–	–	–	–	–	–	–	–	142
Luxembourg	342	353	0.18	376	20.9	65.2	13.9	13.5	11.7	2,023	70.8	70.1	132
Monaco	24	28	0.84	82	–	–	–	–	–	–	–	–	16,242
Netherlands	13,599	16,010	0.85	81	25.8	63.6	10.7	16.8	8.7	2,281	73.8	79.3	333
Switzerland	6,535	7,366	0.84	82	22.6	65.4	12.0	14.7	10.0	1,973	72.4	57.2	158
Oceania	21,308	32,715	1.95	35	31.5	61.1	7.4	24.8	9.3	3,412	65.8	71.7	3
Australia and New Zealand	16,840	24,512	1.82	38	28.6	62.8	8.6	21.2	8.1	2,878	72.3	85.7	2
Australia	13,809	20,245	1.91	36	28.3	63.2	8.5	21.0	8.1	2,845	72.4	86.2	2
New Zealand	3,031	4,267	1.45	48	30.3	60.9	8.8	22.3	8.3	3,838	71.9	83.3	11

(continued)

ANNEX: (Continued)

Region and Country or Area	Population (mid-year) (thousands)		Rate of Growth, 1970–75 (percentage)	Number of Years to Double Population	Percentage of Population in 1975 Aged (years)			Crude Birth Rate 1970–75 (per 1,000)	Crude Death Rate 1970–75 (per 1,000)	Total Fertility Rate 1970–75 (per 1,000)	Life Expectancy, 1970–75 (years)	Proportion of Urban Population 1975 (percentage)	Population Density 1975[a] (persons per square kilometer)
	1975	2000			0–14	15–64	65+						
Melanesia	3,126	5,847	2.41	29	42.4	54.5	3.1	40.7	16.6	6,011	48.4	13.6	6
New Caledonia	125	247	2.84	24	—	—	—	—	—	—	—	—	7
New Hebrides	96	190	2.78	25	—	—	—	—	—	—	—	—	7
Norfolk Island	2	2	0.00	—	—	—	—	—	—	—	—	—	7
Papua New Guinea	2,716	5,039	2.36	29	42.0	54.8	3.2	40.6	17.1	6,013	47.7	12.8	6
Solomon Islands	187	369	2.81	25	—	—	—	—	—	—	—	—	7
Micronesia and Polynesia	1,341	2,356	2.55	27	41.4	55.8	2.8	32.9	7.4	4,591	62.8	31.8	44
Micronesia	306	556	2.70	26	41.6	55.1	3.3	35.9	9.0	5,125	61.7	33.1	77
Gilbert Islands and Tuvalu	66	123	3.38	20	—	—	—	—	—	—	—	—	75
Guam	99	184	2.34	30	—	—	—	—	—	—	—	—	180
Nauru	8	10	1.38	50	—	—	—	—	—	—	—	—	357
Niue Island	5	7	1.54	45	—	—	—	—	—	—	—	—	21
Pacific Islands	117	218	2.90	24	—	—	—	—	—	—	—	—	66
Other Micronesia[j]	10	15	1.45	48	—	—	—	—	—	—	—	—	42
Polynesia	1,036	1,800	2.50	28	41.3	56.0	2.7	32.0	7.0	4,445	63.1	31.5	39
American Samoa	32	67	3.13	22	—	—	—	—	—	—	—	—	163
Cook Islands	25	52	3.11	22	—	—	—	—	—	—	—	—	1,760
Fiji	577	847	2.08	33	37.9	59.3	2.8	25.0	4.3	3,178	70.0	38.3	32
French Polynesia	128	269	3.12	22	—	—	—	—	—	—	—	—	144
Tonga	101	212	3.12	22	—	—	—	—	—	—	—	—	144
Wallis and Futuna Islands	9	9	0.00	—	—	—	—	—	—	—	—	—	—
Western Samoa	164	345	3.13	22	—	—	—	—	—	—	—	—	58

[a] Land area of each country or area is that of 1973.
[b] Including Agalega, Rodrigues, and St. Brandon.
[c] Formerly referred to as Spanish Sahara.
[d] Including Ascension and Tristan da Cunha.
[e] Excluding Panama Canal Zone.
[f] Including West Irian.
[g] Comprising that part of Palestine under Egyptian administration following the Armistice of 1949 until June 1967, when it was occupied by Israeli military forces.
[h] Former mandated territory administered by the United Kingdom until the Armistice of 1949.
[i] Including Berlin. Designations and data for Berlin appearing on this page were supplied by the competent authorities pursuant to the relevant agreements of the Four Powers.
[j] Including Canton and Enderbury Islands, Christmas Island, Cocos (Keeling) Islands, Johnston Island, Midway Islands, Pitcairn Island, Tokelau Islands, and Wake Island.
Source: United Nations Secretariat.

ADDITIONAL READINGS

Berelson, Bernard. "The World Population Plan of Action: Where Now." *Population and Development Review* (September 1975).

Finkle, Jason L., and Barbara B. Crane. "The Politics of Bucharest: Population, Development and the New International Economic Order." *Population and Development Review* (September 1975).

Mauldin, W. Parker, et al. "The World Population Conference and the Population Tribune August 1974." *Studies in Family Planning* (December 1974).

Miro, Carmen. "The World Population Plan of Action: A Political Instrument Whose Potential Has Not Been Realized." *Population and Development Review* (December 1977).

Salas, R. M. *Population Assistance and the UNFPA—Responding to the Countries' Own Assessments of Their Needs.* New York: UNFPA, 1974.

———. *People: An International Choice.* Oxford: Pergamon, 1976.

Singh, Jyoti. "Conference Commentary." *Populi* vol. 1, no. 5 (1974).

———. "A Sense of Urgency." *Populi* vol. 4, no. 1 (1977).

Tabah, Leon. *New Emphasis on Demographic Research after Bucharest.* UNFPA/WPPA/12, September 3, 1975.

———. "The Significance of the Bucharest Conference on Population." *International Social Science Journal* 27, no. 2 (1975).

Tabbarah, Riad B. "Population Policy Issues in International Instruments: With Special Reference to the World Population Plan of Action." *Journal of International Law and Economics* (December 1974).

United Nations. *Report of the World Population Conference.* (Sales No. E 75 XIII.3).

———. *The Population Debate: Dimensions and Perspectives.* Papers of the World Population Conference, vols. I and II (Sales Nos. E/F/S.75 XIII.4 and E/F/S.75.XIII.5).

Urquidi, Victor L. "The Positive and the Negative of Bucharest." Paper submitted to UNFPA/UN Interregional Group of Experts on the World Population Plan of Action, Geneva, September 1975.

World Population Society. *Since Bucharest and the Future.* Washington, D.C., 1976.

ABOUT THE EDITOR

Jyoti Shankar Singh, who was educated at Banaras, Delhi, and London, holds degrees in political science and law. He worked with international voluntary agencies in Asia and Europe before joining the United Nations in 1972. During 1973–74 he was Assistant Executive Secretary of the World Population Year Secretariat, and is now Senior Information Officer at the United Nations Fund for Population Activities. Singh is a contributing editor of POPULI, and has written extensively on population and development issues in major journals and magazines around the world. He was at the Sixth and Seventh Special Sessions of the UN General Assembly as well as at the UN Conferences on Population (1974), Women (1975), and Human Settlements (1976).

RELATED TITLES
Published by
Praeger Special Studies

---

*Also available in paperback.